# Contents

# Preface

# *What if . . .*

*On Wednesday, February 18 1885, three weeks after the fall of Khartoum, The Times of London published the following despatch from its correspondent in Cairo, Moberley Bell:*

Aswan, Upper Egypt, February 17

'Major-General Charles George Gordon, whose successful release from the investment of Khartoum has been the subject of universal rejoicing, has requested the hospitality of the columns of *The Times* to air a number of grievances and to make serious allegations. His indictment will undoubtedly undermine the complacency of Mr Gladstone's Government and mar its enjoyment of the unwonted climate of popularity it has recently experienced in the wake of his fortuitous release.

'Following the brief messages which have come out, the Christian world has exulted at the news of Colonel Sir Charles Wilson's intrepid expedition up the Nile by steamer, his snatching to freedom of General Gordon even as Khartoum fell, and the return of the steamer party unscathed to the safety of the British forces in the Bayuda Desert. General Gordon's charges now cast a new light on this affair.

'At the General's telegraphed request, your correspondent in Cairo travelled up the River Nile to meet the hero of Khartoum at Aswan in Upper Egypt, during the latter's journey down the British headquarters at Korti. The meeting took place in the early hours of the morning on board a steam pinnace, placed at General Gordon's disposal by his friend, the Commander-in-Chief of the relief expedition, Lord Wolseley.

'General Gordon blames the British Government for abandoning the Egyptian garrisons and the people of the Sudan to the reign of terror of the Mahdiist regime. Neither will his criticisms leave the military authorities with cause for satisfaction. He has telegraphed ahead the resignation of his commissiom, so as to be free, as he puts it, "to speak freely and trenchantly about the dark deeds done in England's name".

'He nurses, in particular, a deep bitterness about his release from investment in Khartoum. "I was brought out unwillingly, illegally, and by force. The whole world knows that it was my declared intention never to be the rescued lamb, whilst the people I was sent to succour were left to their fate at the hands of the false Mahdi," the General said.

'He accused Sir Charles Wilson of bringing him away by illegal means. "It has been said that the Khedive of Egypt informed me in a message last September that my powers in Khartoum were to be severely curtailed, and that Lord Wolseley was empowered to supersede my authority. I understood no such instruction from the Khedive. Sir Charles Wilson's action in bringing me away by force was, in my opinion, a grave breach of his orders, and I shall press for censure."

'Secondly, General Gordon believes that, had Sir Charles used the forces at his disposal on board the steamers, the fall of Khartoum would have been prevented, thus paving the way for the smashing of the Mahdi by General Wolseley's main force. Referring to the wave of popular acclaim for those involved in the "rescue", he took pains to repeat a note he had made on another occasion in his Khartoum Journals: " . . . the fact is, that, if one analyses human glory, it is composed of nine-tenths twaddle, perhaps ninety-nine hundredths twaddle".

'General Gordon, in the course of two hours' conversation, dwelt on specific reasons for the failure of his mission. There is not sufficient opportunity to encompass the full detail of his charges in this brief, telegraphed report; however, your correspondent will return to them at length in a later despatch. Suffice it to say that Gordon, in spite of his frequent assertions from Khartoum that he will never again set foot in England, intends to travel to London to argue his case at the highest and most influential levels. The impression may be formed that Mr Gladstone and the Generals have retrieved from the Sudan not a "rescued lamb" but a desert wild-cat.

'The news that the British expeditionary force is to withdraw has poured fresh coals on the fire of Gordon's indignation. He declared that it was now time to smash the Mahdi. His army was a rabble and no match for Lord Wolseley's splendidly equipped and spirited forces in the desert, at present under the direct command of General Sir Redvers Buller. Of the Arabs, General Gordon said, "I think they will bolt, except for some few".'

*On the following day, Thursday, February 19 1885,* The Times *carried a brief, urgently telegraphed news item in a late special edition:*

Cairo, February 18

'There are reports from the Sudan that the British force, which successfully rescued General Gordon from Khartoum, has suffered severe losses as the result of attacks by overwhelming numbers of the enemy during a series of engagements in the Bayuda Desert. One report says that the Mahdi's forces have taken Gubat, which was the advanced base of Sir Redvers Buller's troops. Grave concern is entertained in military circles on the Nile for the safety of General Buller and his column.'

# BOOK ONE

*As it really happened*

# Chapter 1

# *Star of the Mahdi*

'It is worth while', Mr Fowle of Bickley, Kent, wrote to *The Times*, 'setting one's alarum to the hour of four in order to look for it . . . it will evidently be a grand sight for another fortnight till another moon interferes with it'. Mr White of Upper Norwood, south London, bore witness in the same columns to 'the nucleus being very bright and the tail raising at an angle of about 45 degrees, exceedingly long and very broad'. The *Pall Mall Gazette* quoted Mr Ainslie of Ealing, who had seen a brilliant apparition preceding the sun. With the authority of evidence from an observatory in Rio de Janeiro, transmitted by the Brazilian submarine telegraph, *The Times* was able to inform readers that the object of universal interest was 'probably the expected comet Pons' of 70 years earlier.

In the latter half of September and in October 1882, British newspaper readers were eager for such fresh topics to stir the imagination. A famous British victory at Tel-el-Kebir in Egypt on September 13 had sated the Victorian appetite for stories of imperial glories and put a new shine on the golden reputation of its architect, the hero-General Sir Garnet Wolseley. With textbook strategy, his troops had smashed an army of rebellious Egyptian fellaheen in a victory which quelled the revolt of Arabi Pasha, an 'upstart' Colonel.

Arabi's object had been to end the corruption of Turkish upper-class rule of Egypt — yoked under suzerainty of the Ottoman Empire — and halt European interference in the affairs of his impoverished country. But after Tel-el-Kebir, Arabi's nationalist dreams were in ruins and Wolseley's victory shored up the creaking rule of Khedive Tewfik in Cairo.

The 'specials', artists and correspondents, had enjoyed a field day depicting bluejackets bombarding heathen forts, marines succouring the innocents, and soldiers' bayonets clearing the battleground of rebels. For jingoists it was an unexpected treat from a Liberal government. William Ewart Gladstone, anguished by the dilemma on the one hand of safeguarding the Suez Canal and the interests of the British creditors, and on the other of becoming enmeshed in the affairs of Egypt, was filled with prophetic gloom.

In the newspapers the eye-witness stories of soldiers' bravery and Generals' brilliance had run to exhaustion, the Queen's delight had been recorded, and 'Our Cairo Correspondent' was being relegated to down-page obscurity. Nationalist revolution in Egypt was as dead as yesterday's news — and neither editors nor public paid more than scant attention to reports from Egypt's domain to the far south where a Sudanese religious fanatic, who called himself 'the guided one', was said to be stirring up trouble with a following of dervishes, or poor men, who dressed in patched shirts. News was what sold newspapers, and the nightly pyrotechnics of a spectacular comet, last seen when Napoleon was before Moscow, would do very nicely.

In the camp of Mohammed Ahmed, called the Mahdi, the drums fell silent when the comet appeared. Even the greatest of them all 'El Mansureh', the victorious, a vast sounding vessel of brass and elephant hide which stood before the tent of the Mahdi's highest khalifa, was stilled. Father Joseph Ohrwalder, an Austrian missionary who was a prisoner, described the scene: 'This enormous camp presented a wonderful spectacle, more especially at night, when almost every one had his own cooking fire, and the whole plain resembled a sea of fires which were lost in the distant horizon. The din and noise created by the hundreds of thousands of men, women and children can be better imagined than described. Every emir's dwelling was known by two flags which were always planted near the entrance, and beside them lay the war-drums which were beaten day and night, almost without intermission.'

Over this host, which was in fact a besieging force, and over the besieged in the city of El Obeid, there appeared out of the east before dawn the comet, blazing blue with a bright golden tail of considerable length. It was hailed by the multitude as 'Nigmet el Mahdi', the star of the guided one. A great cry went up, and the drums began to boom again, this time accompanied by the sonorous notes of the elephant-tusk horns of victory. For the sign in the heavens was regarded as auspicious: not only did it pressage a triumphant progress of the Mahdi in the new year (in a few more weeks, November 12, would be the first of Moharram, the opening month of the Muslim year 1300), but it was an augury of success in the siege of El Obeid, which had cost the Mahdi's army much blood.

On September 6 (exactly one week before Tel-el-Kebir) this Kordofan provincial capital, on trading routes 350 miles south-west of Khartoum and well defended by Egyptian troops, had been attacked by 30,000 Mahdiists, storming forward in human waves and filling the ditches ahead of them with straw bundles and their own dead in an attempt to get a foothold on the walls. The attackers were repulsed with 10,000 dead, in casualty terms their gravest reverse since the newly emerged Mahdi had begun picking off Egyptian garrisons and expeditionary forces a year earlier. Indeed, until then, Mohammed Ahmed's jehad, or holy war, had consisted of success after success, each one attracting more and more Sudanese followers to his banner.

Had it not been a struggle so deeply rooted in a religious base, the Mahdi's cause would have been severely damaged by such a reverse. But his teaching argued that death in jehad was the road into paradise; as the Prophet proved, suffering must precede victory. Nevertheless, the awful toll persuaded the Mahdi that frontal assault on a well-manned fortress was foolishness. He placed his hopes in God and starvation. Three and a half months after the sign of the comet, El Obeid capitulated.

It was both coincidental and significant that the scene of the Mahdi's greatest victory to date was roughly in the centre of the Sudan; not the Sudan that every British schoolboy was to know by heart within the space of 18 months, the portion which Churchill named 'the Sudan of the soldier', but the entire vast tract nominally under the Egyptian flag, nearly one million square miles (one third the size of the continental United States) extending from the Red Sea to the Sahara and from the lakes of Equatoria to the frontier of Egypt. Across this territory, from the lush, undulating uplands of the south to the bare deserts of the north, the flame of Mahdiism now appeared to spread unchecked. Egyptian garrisons fell one by one. Those troops who held out — there were about 40,000 in the Sudan — were in mortal danger.

Cairo ruled the Sudan from 1819, when Mohammed Ali sent an

army up the Nile, to 1883. Oppression, exploitation and corruption were the hallmarks of its dominion. Egypt made obeisance to international agreements on slavery, but a series of corrupt Governors-General in Khartoum waxed fat on the fruits of the practice: Arab traders, following a centuries-old tradition of slave gathering from the black areas of Darfur and the Abyssinian borders in the south, could pay taxes to the Egyptian pro-consuls only if trade flourished. Authority was maintained by the gun and the kurbash, the hippopotamus-hide lash.

This ramshackle empire was brought crashing by Mohammed Ahmed. He was born in the northern Sudan but moved to Abba island on the White Nile, about 200 miles south of Khartoum, where his father was a humble boat builder. The young man immersed himself in the Islamic religion and became a priest; he attracted a large following by his preaching, and in 1881 proclaimed himself, at the age of 33, the expected Mahdi, or guided one, for whom the faithful had been waiting since the prophet Mohammed left the earth.

Raouf Pasha, who was then Governor-General, summoned the troublesome fakir to Khartoum; the summons was ignored. Two hundred and fifty soldiers sent to arrest him on Abba island were set upon and most were clubbed to death. Mohammed Ahmed made a hegira, or flight, to the mountains of the south-west, where he was well received by and made many converts among the Baggara tribe of his stoutest supporter and eventual successor, Abdallahi Mohammed Turshain. The Egyptians sent troops to seize or kill the Mahdi and snuff out the incipient revolt; they were massacred. Another force was sent, and met a similar fate. The Mahdi's followers grew by tens of thousands. What had started as a small religious movement soon spread to a huge and violent rebellion. Its breeding ground was the misery the Egyptians had brought to the Sudan.

The Arabic name for the country, Bilad-al-Sudan, means the Land of the Blacks. The first Arab settlers, more than 1,000 years earlier, inter-married with, exploited and enslaved the aboriginal blacks. Egyptian invaders of the 19th century, cursed with the burden of cowardly, feckless fellaheen conscripts, 'the scum of the Nile delta', willingly recruited slave soldiers from the blacks who proved themselves the best troops in the army of occupation. In turn, the Mahdiists of the 1880s welcomed these blacks into their own ranks: conversion was quick and easy, for the blacks hated the oppressive treatment meted out by their 'Turkish' masters. Blacks formed an élite corps of the Mahdiist army, a rifle brigade known as the jehadia, armed with Remingtons provided from Cairo arsenals. In the rich vernacular of the Sudan, the Ansar, or followers, as the Mahdiists came to call themselves, referred to the blacks as 'the animals who fight, eat and drink, but never pray'. Thus, immune to Mahdiism, most of the blacks remained what they had always been, enforced mercenaries.

Of the Arabs, the nomadic, camel-owning Ababda held sway in the Nubian desert south of the Egyptian border, and historically were not averse to mercenary work themselves; for rich rewards they gave assistance to Mohammed Ali's expedition, yet retained a fierce independence. Across the Nile the Kababish straddled the caravan routes that led from the western deserts to the grasslands of northern Kordofan. Many of the excesses after the fall of Khartoum — including Gordon's killing — were attributed to the Dongolawi, neighbours of the Ababda and Kababish in Dongola province, the birthplace of Mohammed Ahmed, the Mahdi. Farther up the Nile, the Shagiyeh developed a reputation for murderous ruthlessness as bashi-bazouks, irregulars, working readily for any paymaster, and lived up to the original Turkish meaning of bashi-bazouk — 'wrong-headed'; they achieved the dubious distinction of being despised by Gordon and the Mahdi alike, though they were recruited by both. Another powerful riverine tribe was the Jaalin, whose capital was Shendy on the Nile 90 miles north of Khartoum; their domain, shared with the Shukriyeh, was the Bayuda desert where they barred the way to the Gordon relief expedition in January 1884 and suffered enormous losses. The traditional scourge of the lowland tribes were the Baggara cattle-owning Arabs of the south-west highlands, camel and horse riders termed by Sir Reginald Wingate, soldier and 'Sudanist', the 'Red Indians of the Sudan'. They were to become the cavalry spearhead of the Ansar army and a ruthless, all-powerful Praetorian Guard of their tribesman, Khalifa Abdallahi, when he succeeded to the leadership on the death of the Mahdi.

Away from the unifying influence of the Nile, in the Red Sea hills to the east, lived a people among whom the fire of Mahdiism burned as brightly as anywhere in the Sudan, the Beja tribes. Isolated from and not even sharing the same language as many of the central and western tribes (they spoke a Hamitic language), they owed their fervour to militant evangelism and the many opportunities for 'Turk killing' given to them by their remarkable leader, Osman Digna, who was the last of the Mahdiist emirs to be subdued (in 1900). Notable among them were the warlike Hadendowa, the first to meet the British in battle, the first adversaries ever to break a British square. From the warriors' custom of combing their hair upwards and outwards — after which they set it with camel urine — the British soldier gave his language the term 'fuzzy-wuzzy'.

When Allah made the Sudan, say the Arabs, he laughed. Its 'deserts of surpassing desolation' and sandstorms of 'a fiery snow, such as might fall in hell' were described by Churchill in *The River War* from first-hand knowledge. Few who fought or worked in the country had a good thing to say about it. One correspondent called it 'a man-eater — red-gorged but still insatiable'. Gordon wrote of it: 'The Sudan is a useless possession, ever was so, and ever will be so . . . No one who has ever lived in the Sudan can escape the reflection, "What a useless possession is this land". Few men can stand its fearful monotony and deadly climate.'

George Warrington Steevens, of the *Daily Mail,* spoke for the troops he marched with: 'Dust! It rose off the ground till the place was like London in a fog. On the horizon it lowered like thunder-clouds; close about you it whirled up like pepper when the lid of the caster comes off. You felt it, breathed it, smelt it, tasted it. It choked eyes and nose and ears, and you ground it between your teeth. After a few hours of it you forgot what being a man was like; you were merely clogging into a lump of the Sudan.'

By day he marched near the Nile over the dry stalks of old cotton fields where the earth crumbled in foot-deep cracks, big enough for a horse to put its foot in them. The cracks created islands which would collapse without warning, breaking a man's or a horse's leg. And the cracks were full of scorpions, which the men found when they rested. By night, men who had suffered sunstroke and heat exhaustion marching in temperatures of more than 100 degrees would shiver in the bitter cold; without warning storms would break, blowing tents away with furious dust-devils or even squalls of wind-driven rain. And yet, the Sudan held an eternal fascination for Europeans summed up in the Arab saying, 'Drink of the Nile water, and you will return to drink again'.

Churchill wrote: 'The Sudan is joined to Egypt by the Nile as a diver is connected with the surface by his air pipe. Without it there is only suffocation.' Then his imagery would change: the Nile was like a palm tree, green and fertile in the Delta where its leaves and foliage spread, its stem twisting to its roots deep in the south of the Sudan. (The terminology of Nile geography had its confusions for Victorian newspaper readers, used to thinking of north being 'up' and south 'down'. The Nile flows south to north so that lower Egypt and lower Sudan, they learned, are those parts farthest north. Khartoum, which seemed a devilish long way 'down' on their maps, was *up* river.)

The thin thread of the Nile was life and communication. In the desolate areas between Wady Halfa and Khartoum — Churchill's Sudan of the British soldier — cultivation seldom extended more than a mile on either side of the banks, and for the most part the desert encroached to within less than a hundred yards of the river. Seen by the planners of the Gordon relief expedition as a broad highway along which a number of obstacles (the cataracts) were to be found, the river was, in fact, a chain of almost continuous rough water at low time. The flood season, when navigation is made less difficult, is from June to October: the expedition's main effort was concentrated in November, December and January.

During 18 months of passionate debate and public scrutiny the names of 'squalid villages', as Churchill observed, became 'familiar to distant and enlightened peoples': Korti, Abu Klea, Kirbekan . . . all were in the heart and fighting ground of the soldier's Sudan. This cockpit extended from the southern fringe of the Nubian desert for some 300 miles south to Khartoum, the seat of power and crossroads of trade, standing on the confluence of the White Nile (which, perversely, is milky green) and the Blue Nile (which is clear dark jade). From Korti, where the British army launched a 'march of the forlorn hope' across the Bayuda desert, a river traveller bound for Khartoum must dramatically change direction, going north and north-east for many miles before resuming his southward course. For an atlas will show that the Nile, after leaving Khartoum in a northerly direction, makes a diversion. It looks on the map like a question mark. The Bayuda waste is enclosed by the curve and Khartoum forms the base of this giant question mark.

# Chapter 2

# *A small bee*

The question was, and still is: was Major-General Charles George Gordon the right man to be sent to the Sudan? It was posed in a bland paragraph of 51 words in a memorandum sent by the Foreign Secretary, Lord Granville, to the Prime Minister, Gladstone: 'Do you see any objection to using Gordon in some way? He has an immense name in Egypt — he is popular at home. He is a strong but sensible opponent of slavery. He has a small bee in his bonnet. If you do not object, I could consult Baring* by telegraph.'

It could be argued that if Gladstone had foreseen the woes that were stored up for him in Granville's suggestion he would not have replied in the way he did — assentingly. (This is to discount a more cynical view that the old political fox cared little, in the lost cause of the Sudan, whether the right man or the wrong man were chosen.) The seat of those woes was revealed in eight words of Granville's submission of late November 1883, the assertion that *'he has a small bee in his bonnet'*.

Desperate to do something to meet the challenge of rapidly deepening crisis in the Sudan, but uncertain what it should be, Britain's leaders had sought a *deus ex machina* and found it in a soldier-mystic: a fighter in China who had been a public hero — but that was nearly 20 years ago; an administrator who had scourged the slave trade and set a unique standard of probity in the Sudan — but who had since held obscure posts because the War Office could not think of anything worthwhile for him to do; a strange 'theocentric' who believed everything he did was as an

---

*Sir Evelyn Baring, later First Earl of Cromer, was British agent and Consul-General in Cairo, a link by which Whitehall managed the Egyptian finances, 'advised' Khedive Tewfik and — when it suited the British government — virtually ran the affairs of Egypt.

instrument of God; a man regarded by Gladstone's secretary to be not 'clothed in the rightest of minds'; one dubbed 'half-cracked' by Baring who said of him: 'A man who habitually consults the Prophet Isaiah when he is in difficulty is not apt to obey the orders of any one'. His casting was prompted by the suggestions of friends and admirers, who ranged from lowly unknowns to the high and mighty Wolseley, the Adjutant-General (he felt he was 'not worthy to pipe-clay Gordon's belt'). Charlie Gordon, the unwanted Major-General, was soon to emerge centre stage, as the leading actor of a long-running play in the theatre of the absurd.

The decision to consider using Gordon's services came at the end of a year of horrifying news from the Sudan. After the important city of El Obeid fell to the Mahdi on January 17 1883, adherents flocked to join the cause of the jehad. The Egyptian authorities, realising that unless resolute action were taken, the tide of religious fervour — now accompanied by a growing sense of Sudanese nationalism — would engulf Khartoum as well as the other, more isolated, garrisons. An expeditionary force was planned to take the fight deep into the Mahdi's heartland, to break his power and end Mahdiism once and for all at its new-found capital, El Obeid, more than 350 miles from Khartoum as an army marches. Abd-el-Kader, the able incumbent of the palace at Khartoum, could see the dangers of such an adventure and argued against sending a force so far into enemy territory. He was overruled and recalled to Cairo, and a civil servant, Ala-ed-Din, was made governor-general in his place. Britain played a dubious role. After Tel-el-Kebir the previous year, Gladstone was anxious to limit British responsibilities in Egypt and the Sudan and to end the occupation as soon as possible. British officers began a reorganisation of the Egyptian army, but intervention in the gradually worsening situation of the Sudan was firmly ruled out. When the idea of an expedition to El Obeid was mooted, Lord Granville refused even to allow British military advice to be given to the Egyptians. In Cairo, Baring was disgusted. He later wrote of Granville in his memoirs: 'Instead of recognising the facts of the situation, he took shelter behind an illusory abnegation of responsibility, which was a mere phantasm of the diplomatic and parliamentary mind'.

London, nevertheless, raised no objection to the appointment of a retired British officer, Colonel William Hicks — Hicks Pasha — to lead what Churchill called probably the worst army that ever marched to war: 10,000 Egyptians, Sudanese and bashi-bazouks. Early in November at a battle deep in Kordofan the Mahdi's troops annihilated the Egyptian force, the corpses being scattered in three large groups over a space of two miles. The largest heap was in a grove at Shaikan where Hicks and a group of other Europeans, including two British war correspondents, were overwhelmed by an avalanche of spearmen. The bodies of Hicks and his officers were hideously mutilated. About 100 survivors took refuge under waggons and in the bushes. They were prodded out and later dragged naked with ropes around their necks into El Obeid as part of a triumphal procession led by the Mahdi on a snow white camel. The 'Turks' had paid, soldier for soldier, the debt of the Ansar deathroll at the siege of El Obeid.

No more effective recruiting inducement was ever available for the Mahdi to use. The most significant immediate consequence of the battle was the collapse of the Egyptian administration in Darfur province and in Bahr al-Ghazal in the deep south. Ansar and potential Ansar weighed the apparent truth of the Mahdi's word in a proclamation he sent to Hicks' soldiers before the battle: 'It is not hidden from the intelligent man that the affair is in the hand of God and He is not associated therein with rifles nor cannon nor rockets, and there is no protection for any save him whom God Most High protects'. Fighters in the jehad were thus protected by God against bullets! The belief spread rapidly among the Mahdi's adherents and those shortly to be converted. When the news of Hicks' defeat and death reached Khartoum there was panic; many Europeans fled north.

The Hicks Pasha disaster eventually forced the British government to end its pose of non-intervention but not before a to-and-fro political and diplomatic game was played out by Gladstone and his ministers. At the Lord Mayor's banquet in the Guildhall, London, on November 9 — unaware that Hicks and his army had been destroyed — Gladstone had announced: 'We are about to withdraw — the order has been given — that withdrawal will include the evacuation of Cairo'. In the space of two weeks, two hammer blows fell. On the 12th news came that 500 Egyptians had been slaughtered at Suakim on the Red sea coast where Osman Digna's 'fuzzy-wuzzies' were harrying the garrison; the British Consul was among the dead. Then, on the 19th, Baring wired confirmation of reports that had been dismaying Cairo for several days — Hicks Pasha's army had been destroyed by

'300,000 rebels'.

What was the government to do? Certainly the army's evacuation of Egypt would have to be postponed. But of armed assistance farther south there was absolutely no doubt: 'Her Majesty's Government can do nothing which would throw upon them the responsibility of operations in the Sudan', the Foreign Office telegraphed to Baring. British military and diplomatic chiefs in Cairo advised London that they believed Egypt would not be able to hold the Sudan and that Khartoum should be held sufficiently long to allow the garrisons to be withdrawn; there were fears, too, for Tokar and Sinkat, near Suakim on the Red Sea.

Amid a gale of press prediction, advice and reproach, the British public indulged in a frenzy of speculation.

An engineers' Colonel, Bevan Edwards, penned a letter at his home in Folkestone. It was addressed to General Sir Andrew Clarke, RE, Inspector-General of Fortifications, and it concerned another fellow engineer who had distinguished himself against fanatical hordes in China two decades ago. 'There is one man who is competent to deal with the question', declared Edwards, ' — Charlie Gordon.' Simultaneously, Wolseley was thinking that Gordon's employment would be 'most desirable'. Sir Samuel Baker, traveller, administrator and something of an elder-statesman on Sudan affairs, was coming to the same conclusion and would soon give public vent to his thoughts.

Clarke sent on Edwards' letter to Hugh Childers, the Chancellor of the Exchequer, with the observation, 'I need not say, if England is to intervene, my advice would be to place the whole affair without reserve in Gordon's hands. If the Mahdi is a prophet, Gordon, in the Sudan, is a greater . . . I was gratified to hear Wolseley the other day speak in stronger terms of admiration and respect for Gordon than even I would do.' Childers passed the matter to Lord Granville. It was fateful coincidence that Granville received the recommendation of Gordon's services just as he was dealing with the Cairo message about the withdrawal of the garrisons. He wrote immediately to Gladstone.

# Chapter 3

# *The mystic*

Charles George Gordon was born at Woolwich in London on January 28 1833, the son of a future Lieutenant-General in the artillery, Henry William Gordon. His mother was Elizabeth, daughter of Samuel Enderby, a London merchant. He was a high-spirited, mischievous, sometimes hot-tempered boy who showed little inclination to religion or to discipline. When, at 15, he entered the Royal Military Academy as an officer-cadet he continued to display impatience with authority and rebelled against petty-fogging regulations with a violence which alarmed his superiors. He butted a cadet Corporal in the stomach, sending him head over heels down a staircase and through a glass door; he ripped off his epaulettes and flung them at the feet of his officer; his involvement in the beating of a junior with a hairbrush dashed his chances of joining the artillery, the regiment of his father and two brothers. Commissioned in the Royal Engineers, he engrossed himself with a will, and to brilliant effect, in the technical complexities of fortifications, mining, surveying and a multitude of other subjects needed to be mastered by a sapper. He was popular with fellow officers who found him generous with money, always ready to advance them 'a sub'.

Service in Britain, the Crimea and eastern European boundary commissions led to his promotion to Captain in 1859 at the age of 26. In China the following year he took part in the sacking of the Emperor's summer palace at Peking, and sent home to his family his share of loot in the shape of Chinese works of art. Now, breveted Major, he embarked on a remarkable phase of his career, one that was to make him known to the hero-seeking Victorian public. It was the making of 'Chinese Gordon'.

The task allotted to him was the suppression of the Taiping rebellion, part of a chapter in imperial history the moral

24

implications of which were uncommonly blurred, even in an era of outrageous Victorian double standards. At the root of the China war had been Britain's desire to overcome Peking's prohibition of opium imports from India, a recurring cause of conflict in the 19th century. The Taiping war lords, known as Wangs, were nominally Christian, a point at first in their favour in the eyes of the British public. But the barbarous nature of the Wangs' rebellion against the Peking overlords — beheadings, burial alive, crucifixion and torture were everyday occurences, leaving a trail of misery across the blighted land — aroused public opinion in Europe; more to the point, the excesses of the Taipings were disquieting the wealthy and influential Shanghai merchants, the channel of the opium trade. England's Victorian conscience conveniently tucked away the nasty thought that 'Christian' rebels would now have to be suppressed in their struggle against 'heathen' dominion, and war was opened on the Taipings.

Major Gordon, whose studies as an engineer had by custom included the deployment of irregular forces, was given as his instrument possibly the strangest army that was ever commanded by a British officer. It was financed by the Shanghai merchants, supported by the Chinese government and named 'The Ever Victorious Army'. Gordon's force was composed of some 4,000 Chinese, whose methods were little less barbaric than those of their adversaries. There were 150 European and American officers — 'soldiers of fortune' — of whom many were the riff-raff of regimental messes, cashiered incompetents, international adventurers and criminals; they bullied, brawled, caroused and many were habitually insubordinate. By indomitable will, Gordon united this heterogeneous force into a machine whose title of 'ever victorious' became a reality. He proved himself a master of guerrilla warfare.

Victorian writers of boys' fiction could not have dreamed up a better scenario. Aloof from his wild comrades stood this man of honour, a sparely but strongly built figure of middle height, whose piercing look and rapid glance from eyes 'like blue diamonds' instilled respect and obedience in his men. He personally led his army in the storming of fortresses, alone and exposed and carrying only a small cane; it earned him the name of 'Wand of Victory' among the Chinese. Mining earthworks, ambushing, deploying steamers to carry troops into the enemy's heartland and surprise him in the rear, by textbook tactics and unconventional genius, he led the Ever Victorious Army from success to success. There was, too, Christian charity to be noted and recorded by correspondents for adoring readers: Gordon, sweeping up and carrying to safety a naked urchin he found on the battlefield in the line of fire; Gordon feeding, caring for and employing as servants six small orphan boys.

When the 'Wand of Victory' had completed his work he wrote home to his sister, Augusta, 12 years his senior: 'In England . . . you are under twenty masters and trammelled by regulations and orders and on meagre pay . . . I could never remain in England for any length of time.' It was to be his constant affirmation that he could not stand the 'fiddle-faddle' of official life and etiquette. The seeds of a lonely exile career had been planted.

He came home to a Lieutenant-Colonelcy, the CB, and public acclaim as 'Chinese Gordon', which privately pleased him, but he studiously avoided accepting the many social invitations which followed his sudden and brief lionisation.

At this stage in his career, the mid-1860s, two circumstances are apparent to Gordon-watchers. His next appointment was the comparative obscurity of the supervision of forts being built at Gravesend in Kent, after which the War Office largely left him to his own devices: there were few jobs going in the military establishment for a master of the irregular and unconventional, who was something of a rebel. Secondly, until this time there had been no strong outward evidence of Gordon's passionate espousal of religion. In China he had prayed before and after battle, but no more fervently than any other Military Academy graduate who believed that Heaven was an extension of the British high command. He was, however, a devout Christian, like many of his soldier compatriots.

A friend of Gordon's, a woman living in Gravesend, has tried to place the timing of his religious illumination on an event in 1867 when his eye let on a sentence from *John* in the Bible: 'Whosoever shall confess that Jesus is the Son of God, God dwelleth in him and he in God'. One-ness with God was henceforth the key to his whole life, went her argument; her account is supported by words Gordon wrote about the incident years later: 'Something broke in my heart, a palpable feeling and I knew God lived in me'. In all probability, however, Gordon's mysticism had developed gradually over a long period, and rapidly since the death of his father two years earlier than the incident of the opened Bible. His belief in the feeling of the unity of self with God was to become all-consuming, an armour in which he clothed himself against the outside world, a device to rationalise what appeared to others as dismaying inconsistencies in his decisions and actions; to his most violent critics his 'God-intoxication' was seen as a defence against reason, and a cause of his downfall in Khartoum.

Letters which Gordon wrote to Augusta (they came weekly from all over the world, sometimes running to 12 pages, and she published them, heavily edited) contained numerous references to his belief that everything he did was as an instrument of God. One, from the Sudan in the 1870s, projected an interesting extension of this faith: 'I truly believe that every word I speak against anyone is mystically conveyed to that person by Satan and though that person may not know it, yet he is impelled to speak against me'. And through the letters there ran a constant theme consistent with a death wish.

From Gravesend: ' . . . we cannot wish many years will pass away before He comes to deliver us from our corruptible bodies and infirmities'. From Mauritius: 'My likings and my destiny are analogous. I do not want to hang on'; and to a friend, 'How I wish *He* would come'. From London, shortly after returning from an appointment in the Sudan: ' . . . longing with great desire for death'.

There existed in Gordon — the great paradox — an extrovert evangelist, however. At Gravesend he composed a religious leaflet which he subsequently had printed in 11 languages, including Arabic and Armenian. On daily forays around the town he thrust his leaflets into the hands of startled Gravesenders. Piers Compton, in *The Last Days of General Gordon,* has captured the maniac quality of Gordon's leaflet raids:

'He scattered them in streets, on country paths, on bulges and projections, on seats and stiles, where they were held in position by stones, and in boats. Gangs of workmen on the railway line and passengers on platforms, were surprised when a hand protruding from an open window of a passing train showered them with papers. His fellow officers watched, with considerable amusement through their telescopes, the strange peregrinations of their commander as he darted about the fields and hedgerows on his evangelising mission.

'Pedestrians going about their business would find themselves seized by the arm and questioned as to the state of their soul. They were warned to take heed lest they stumbled and while thus adjuring them the lively figure of Gordon skipped this way and that, for he always made a point of avoiding the cracks and lines on the pavement.'

Gordon was no less graphic in his own account of the distribution of his leaflets: 'What hundreds I did give away! How I used to run miles if I saw a "scuttler" watching crows in a field!'

'Scuttlers' to Gordon were boys, the target not only of his evangelising, but of his love and philanthropy. He gathered boys and young men around him, invited the destitute into his house and gave them bed and board, taught in a ragged school, and found jobs for many poor youngsters. When his protégés grew up he took an interest in their careers and families and when they went to sea he followed their progress round the world with pins on a map on his wall. He felt deeply obliged to save their priceless souls, and yet a reticence sometimes restrained him from approaching those he met in the street. After a visit to Warwick, he wrote: 'There were boys running about worth millions, and I could not have courage to speak to them'.

Rough testimonies to Gordon's work appeared here and there, so the press reported, as graffiti on the walls of Gravesend: 'CG is a jolly good feller', 'God bless the Kernal', 'Long life to our beloved teacher Gordon'. It must not be assumed, however, that Gordon pursued his religious activities at the expense of either his professional duties or personal friendships. He was a good administrator and engineer, eternally inventive, forever thinking up schemes to solve problems of the day whether they were in the Thames estuary or, later, in the headwaters of the Nile. Although he shunned the fancies of society life, he maintained a large and widely mixed circle of friends, most of whom were his fervent admirers.

As his career progressively took him more and more abroad — the River Danube Commission in 1871, the Sudan as the Khedive's Governor of the Equatorial Provinces in 1874, and again as Governor-General in 1877 — and as the truth sank home that the Army had nothing worthwhile for him to do, he began to distance himself from those who worked with him. There were long bouts of seclusion, periods of a day or more in which he shut himself away after disappointments (the first evidence of these sulking bouts had appeared in China).

At other times he exalted in the harmless joy of solitude. During his first two appointments in the Sudan his tireless work against the slave trade (which he did *not* succeed in suppressing, contrary to public belief) took him on long, solitary camel rides which he used as opportunities for introspective analysis: 'My sense of independence has gone. I own nothing and am nothing. I am a pauper and seem to have ceased to exist. A sack of rice jolting along on a camel would do as much as *I think* I do.'

Even the camels he rode provided subject matter for his inconsistencies of thought when he light-heartedly wrote in 1877: '. . . they repel all overtures and friendship and seem to be a cross-grained, ill-natured race, hating men and never looking in the least degree happy'; then, a few days later: 'It is a wonderful creature, and so comfortable with its silent cushion-like tread'; and a month later: 'The Gordons and the camels are of the same race — let them take an idea into their heads and nothing will take it out'. The last was a sentiment which would have wrung rueful agreement from Gladstone in the years ahead.

Gordon's distaste of the 'fiddle-faddle' of dinner parties was intense. After his return from the Governor-Generalship of the Sudan in 1880 he declined an invitation to dine with the Prince of Wales. A flustered equerry called on Gordon at his Chelsea lodgings.

'But you cannot refuse the Prince of Wales', said the official.

'Why not?', replied Gordom. 'I refused King John [of Abyssinia] when he invited me to go with him to his hot springs in the mountains — and he might have cut my head off for refusing. I am sure His Royal Highness will not do that.'

'Well, then, let me say you are ill.'

'But I am not ill.'

'Give me some reason then, that I can give the Prince.'

'Very well, then; tell him I always go to bed at half-past nine.'

The Prince of Wales was amused by Gordon's stubborness, and invited him to an informal, intimate lunch on the following Sunday. Gordon accepted. He was, simply, very unhappy in the social milieu, or in England for that matter, and his letters showed it. In Khartoum, on his last assignment, he wrote: 'I dwell on the joy of never seeing Great Britain again, with its horrid, wearisome dinner parties . . . I would sooner live like a dervish with the Mahdi than go out to dinner every night in London.' His words merely echoed what he had written a few years earlier in Equatoria: 'I look on the constant invitation to dinners as a

29

positive infliction'.

Virtual exile as commanding engineer officer of the Mauritius garrison in 1881, a post of dismal obscurity, was turned to spiritual profit by his discovery of what he claimed was the original site of Garden of Eden — somewhere beneath the sea off the Seychelles. His current massive obsession with the Garden of Eden must have given him a far from eclectic range of dinner-table topics, but still he had to fight an obdurate rearguard action against hostesses' invitations: 'I strike against garden parties, archery and lawn tennis meetings! I cannot go through these fearful ordeals of hours' duration.' He found solace in conversations with young subalterns in his rooms, and mixed little with officers of similar rank to his own.

The Sudan, Gordon's 'useless' Sudan, brought out the best and the worst in him. After his first sojourn there, he twice returned to 'drink of the Nile water' again. It was the time of a great and passionate European engrossment with the East, military, commercial, artistic and antiquarian. (Once, when Disraeli had thought of employing him on a mission in the Near East, a memorandum which Gordon prepared on the Eastern Question was of such unconventional nature that the Conservative Prime Minister was moved to describe it as the work of a madman.) On Gordon's first two Sudanese assignments he fell out with every member of his staffs except the faithful Romolo Gessi, an able Italian soldier and administrator. Aides who were in Gordon's good books one day were treated with contumely the next. No-one was safe from his veering changes of mood. The new Khedive Tewfik, levered in by the western powers to replace his father, Ismail, was a 'miserable creature'; and then — hey presto! — Gordon thought again about Tewfik: 'A miracle has happened. Here was a man with talent, energy and . . . honesty.'

With Baring, London's man in Cairo, Gordon embarked on a spiky relationship which inevitably led to breakdowns in human communication during the critical siege months in Khartoum. Early in this relationship, in 1877, Gordon observed: 'Baring is RA and I am RE. Baring was in the nursery when I was in the Crimea. He has a pretentious, grand, patronising way about him . . . When oil mixes with water, we will mix together.' We can be sure Gordon's reporter, the Devil, passed on the remarks to Baring.

A young Lieutenant of engineers, called Chippindall, who was with Gordon in the upper Sudan during the 1870s, went through the usual love-hate cycle, and found Gordon's behaviour intolerable — as numerous comrades did. 'He seems always to think', Chippindall wrote to a friend, 'that nobody but his blessed self can even screw a box-lid on. He is a fearful egotist.'

Charles Chaillé-Long went much further. An American, he was a 32-year-old Lieutenant-Colonel in the Egyptian army when Ismail appointed him to Gordon's staff in Equatoria in 1874 to keep an eye on khedival interests. Long, a vain, bombastic and pontifical officer, smarted under Gordon's (apparently merited) criticisms, and bided his time to avenge himself on a dead hero. History has put him down as a reckless detractor and an untrustworthy witness, but the spectre he raised has still not been satisfactorily laid: was heavy drinking the reason for Gordon's periodic bouts of seclusion and did it contribute to his veering moods and irrational judgements?

# Chapter 4

# *Scandal*

Gordon did not have much time for Charles Chaillé-Long. Having once admitted that, despite earlier shortcomings, his American aide was now 'quite *au fait* with the ins and outs of this sort of life' on the upper Nile in the mid-1870s, the Governor of Equatoria was soon forced to change his mind and put down Long as a man of procrastination and forgetfulness with whom he would never be able to get on. For his part, at various times and in various media, Long spoke of Gordon as a humbug, claimed his success in China was due to bribery, and accused him of advocating the misappropriation of ivory profits in the Sudan. In the story of Charles George Gordon, however, Charles Chaillé-Long would have lain in the obscurity his undistinguished career deserved had it not been for the massive red-herring he raised, much to the delight of the scandal-mongers and fury of the hagiographers.

Long, who profoundly believed he had not received the rewards the world owed him, published a book in Britain in 1912 entitled *My Life in Four Continents*. He was unabashed about his motives as his preface revealed: ' . . . there was not to my knowledge until recently a single word in any encyclopaedia in England which noticed my work in Africa . . . ' Long dedicated the book to Gordon's memory and then, on page 122, proceeded to lay a time-bomb under the Victorian hero. Long wrote:

'A few days after my return to Lado [in deepest south Sudan near the Congo border] the camp was attacked in force one might. I had great difficulty in repelling the savage hordes, who, with lighted torches, were endeavouring to turn us out. Gordon was in his hut and gave no sign of coming out. It was during one of the oft-recurring periods when he shut myself up and placed a hatchet and a flag at the door as a sign that he was not to be disturbed, a seclusion which lasted from three to five days. I sent an officer to warn him of our danger but receiving no reply went myself. I entered abruptly and found him seated, very calmly at a table, on which were an open Bible and a bottle of cognac and sherry. I told him of the situation, to which he made abrupt answer. "You are commander of the camp." Whereupon I hastily turned and left him, but not before I had posted an officer with a half-dozen men specially charged with Gordon's safety. The savages were finally driven away by a vigorous sortie. The next day Gordon entered my tent in the full-dress uniform of the Royal Engineers, and cleanly shaven. He came forward with a quick tripping step as was his habit, and said "Old fellow, now don't be angry with me. I was very low last night. Come and dine with me. We will have a glorious dinner." '

Long had returned to a topic he had aired some time previously, in 1884, in a book published in the United States, *The Three Prophets*. There were subtle differences, however. In the 1884 version Long found Gordon seated in seclusion with his 'ever-present Bible and Prayer Book'; no mention of cognac and sherry. The emphasis on the Bible and prayer book suited Long's 1884 work, which was based on the religious background of the said three prophets — Gordon, the Mahdi and Arabi Pasha. The only mention of drink in the earlier reference was fleeting, a reported light-hearted invitation by Gordon to join him in a brandy and soda *breakfast* the following day.

The short of it is that the incident of the attack on the camp (handled, of course, in masterly fashion by Long, according to Long) is not on record in any of Gordon's writings — which would be understandable if Gordon had spent the time in drunken oblivion. More to the point is the absence of any evidence of an attack in the copiously detailed diaries of the Austrian explorer, Ernst Marno, who was present in the camp at the time.

Long had another stab at Gordon's drinking habits. In *My Life in Four Continents* he explained how he arrived at an isolated outpost at four o'clock in the morning: 'Gordon, even at that early hour, was seated at the door of his hut cleaning an elephant gun and *smoking*. On the table near by were a bottle of quinine, a bottle of cognac, and an open Bible. "How are you, old fellow?" he cried as he espied me. "Had a tough time? How are the man eaters? Now do take some cognac and don't forget the quinine".'

Long's memoirs from four continents was no best-seller. It received scant notice (even fewer people in Britain knew of the existence of his earlier book). Then, after six years, in 1918, Long's time-bomb was detonated by one infinitely more skilled in the arts of literary terrorism and iconoclasm than he. Lytton Strachey, seeking means to topple the pedestals of *Eminent Victorians*, had found Long's testament and made it the basis of a paragraph which sought to illuminate the cause of Gordon's veering moods and wildly changing judgements:

'But the Holy Bible was not his only solace. For now, under the parching African sun, we catch glimpses, for the first time, of Gordon's hand stretching out towards stimulants of a more material quality. For months together, we are told, he would drink nothing but pure water; and then . . . water that was not so pure. In his fits of melancholy, he would shut himself up in his tent for days at a time, with a hatchet and a flag placed at the door to indicate that he was not to be disturbed for any reason whatever; until at last the cloud would lift, the signals would be removed, and the Governor would reappear, brisk and cheerful. During one of these retirements, there was a grave danger of a native attack upon the camp. Colonel Long, the Chief of Staff, ventured, after some hesitation, to ignore the flag and hatchet, and to enter the forbidden tent. He found Gordon seated at a table, upon which were an open Bible and an open bottle of brandy. Long explained the circumstances, but could obtain no answer beyond the abrupt words — "You are commander of the camp" — and was obliged to retire, nonplussed, to deal with the situation as best he could. On the following morning, Gordon, cleanly shaven, and in the full-dress uniform of the Royal Engineers, entered Long's hut with his usual tripping step, exclaiming — "Old fellow, now don't be angry with me. I was very low last night. Let's have a good breakfast — a little b. and s. Do you feel up to it?" And, with these veering moods and dangerous restoratives, there came an intensification of the queer and violent elements in the temper of the man . . . '

Lytton Strachey had patently taken what he considered to be the best bits from each of Long's books and melded them together with a reference drawn from the writings of Sir Richard Burton, the distinguished explorer. In an 1885 review of Gordon's Khartoum Journals in the magazine *Academy*, Burton had mused on Gordon's 'curious changes of policy and conduct which perplexed his friends.' After producing examples of his change of mind in matters of policy, he wrote: 'And so to minor matters; for months he would drink nothing but water, and then prefer, very decidedly, water with whisky'. The sentence gave Strachey his introduction to the passage.

The hagiographers fell on Strachey's head. Burton had only the briefest of personal acquaintance with Gordon; how could he have known his drinking habits? Long was *never* Gordon's chief-of-staff, although he claimed in his book to have been! See how Long's 'open Bible' becomes Strachey's 'open bottle'! How could Long's word be trusted when he had called Gordon a humbug, accused him of favouring peculation, charged him with taking pleasure in beating his staunchest ally, Gessi?

The Gessi episode was a classic of Long innuendo, apparently involving some unexplained letters which, somehow, would have been damaging to Gordon's reputation if published. Gordon, alleged Long, had told him: 'I cannot live peacably with anyone whom I cannot kick'. Long continued: 'Gessi paid dearly for the privilege of being his intimate by submitting to being kicked whenever his master's ill-humour required it. Gordon . . . became very angry one day, and kicked and slapped Gessi. Now . . . what had been considered a familiar, almost friendly, privilege was taken as an insupportable indignity. Gessi was furious. Chance would have it he ran into me. He recounted me the outrage with tears in his eyes. "Is it the first time, Gessi?", I asked. "No," he replied, "but it is the last!" Whereupon he drew from his pocket a package, and tapping it significantly, he added: *"I will publish them!"* "Nonsense, Gessi. You can't stuff me with such bluff. You know Gordon as well as I do. If ever there was a man incapable of an unworthy act that man is Charles George Gordon . . . You are either drunk or crazy. The letters there exist only in your imagination . . . "'

Long and history have left us in the dark about the subject matter of Gessi's 'letters'. Strachey did not touch on them, although he drew heavily on Long's interpretation of the 'hatchet-and-flag' seclusions.

Part of Strachey's crime in the eyes of the pro-Gordon lobby was his success as an author; Long's account of camp life at Lado would have been buried without Strachey's help. 'It has been necessary to deal at length with Mr. Lytton Strachey's sketch in *Eminent Victorians* because it is from this sketch that large numbers of the present generation seem to draw their impressions of Gordon's character', wrote Bernard M. Allen in *Gordon and the*

*Sudan,* published in 1931. Allen and other defenders of the Gordon hero-saint conception base the major weight of their arguments on the fact that Long was a liar with a grudge against Gordon who had publicly labelled him as 'a regular failure', 'feeble', an officer whose object was 'self-extenuation and laziness'. The alleged attack on the camp, and Gordon's abandonment of duty for drink, never took place, therefore the Strachey thesis is proved false: such was the burden of Allen's rebuttal. It was encapsulated in the following paragraph:

'But fiction, however tastily presented, is bound in the long run to give way to fact. Under the searching scrutiny of historical criticism the story about Gordon, which was published broadcast to the world in the pages of Mr Lytton Strachey's impressionist biography, proves to be a baseless fabrication; and with it his allegation of intemperance against the "Eminent Victorian" falls to the ground.' In this respect Long's intervention *was* a red-herring. Self-opinionated liars do not make the best witnesses. By linking Gordon's liking for brandy and his habit of shutting himself away for protracted periods to an incident which was apparently a figment of Long's imagination, the American destroyed his case — and demolished Strachey's, according to Gordon's defenders.

There is ample evidence, however, that Gordon did frequently lock himself away from the world; not only in devotions and struggling with the administrative problems of his duties, as Allen observed, but in bouts of depression and fits of the sulks. At a Cairo enquiry after the fall of Khartoum, evidence was heard from some who were in the city at the time that Gordon occupied part of the final fateful days in unexplained seclusion from his bewildered and desperately frightened officials. And if Strachey had looked for them he would have found in sources other than Long grounds for supposing that Gordon sometimes sought more solace in alcohol than his supporters would prefer to admit.

The defenders have eroded their own case by resort to shrill over-protestation. Lord Elton, whose *General Gordon* in 1954 followed much on the lines of Allen in this matter and included a chapter entitled 'Anatomy of a Slander', gave the impression that Gordon had been accused of being a 'dipsomaniac' and a 'drunkard'. Allen — whose devotion to the saintly myth led him to write about 'one crowded year of glorious life' followed by 'the supreme moment of a yet more glorious death' — conjured up another windmill to be tilted at: a vile allegation of 'drinking *orgies* masked under the veil of religious devotion'. Neither Long nor Strachey had gone so far.

Had Allen discovered other seditious murmurings which were unnoticed by Strachey? As a matter of fact he had, as we shall see.

Allen seems to have been the flag-bearer of curiously out-dated Victorian attitudes. In the 19th century — and, arguably, as late as the 1930s — drinking among the upper classes did not represent the crime it was manifestly made out to be among the lower echelons of society. Gordon, though not of them, suited the designs of the upper classes as a popular hero, a soldier-saint, a legend in which Christianity and imperialism were closely entwined and enshrined. In his preface to the Gordon journals, published in 1885, A. Egmont Hake touched on the core of this philosophy: 'Now I sincerely trust and believe that the Journals will be read eagerly by the working classes; they cannot occupy their leisure time better than in reading them, and, indeed, in learning much of them by heart'. It would never do for the working classes to learn that their martyred hero had feet of clay.

Each of Gordon's principal biographical champions have adduced his health to prove he could not have been a secret drinker — 'buoyant health' according to Allen; 'superb physical and mental health' from Elton. Gordon did not, in fact, enjoy unblemished health (which is admitted by Allen), although his troubles should not necessarily be ascribed to drinking. After China he suffered from a liver complaint, sometimes referred to in his letters — 'my great foe, the liver'. In 1878 when he was Governor-General in Khartoum he wrote of attacks of angina pectoris: 'It is a heart disease and makes you think you are on the brink of death. A rush of blood takes place to the head, and you think it is all over. I may say I have died suddenly over a hundred times.' A year later when he was riding camels across the south in his fight against the slave-traders, his health was making him once again wish for quick death . . . 'I do not think I can face the cross of staying here, simply on physical grounds'.

From China Gordon sent his brother, Henry, an unusually decorated cup, the loot of campaigning, with the message: 'I am afraid to say how much gin has been drunk out of it'. Later, in Shanghai, he was among a hard-drinking group of colleagues and it is known he drank brandy and gin. By second-hand a story has come down from a man named Drummond who lived in Shanghai to the effect that Gordon would visit the Drummond family 'and sit up drinking gin all night' on the veranda. The truth is, that whether or not Gordon was a heavy drinker, there were sufficient people around who *thought* he was.

A Turf Club member in Cairo who met Gordon on his last journey south remarked, 'Gordon did himself well', but the observation was based on no more than the inclusion of brandy among Gordon's travelling stores, a common enough happening in the tropics. Wilfred Scawen Blunt, a Liberal champion of the Arabs, had heard rumours of heavy drinking. A Miss Sauer, living in Cape Town, has quoted her father, who knew Gordon well, as saying: 'Gordon seemed to drink excessively but had an extraordinary ability to hold his liquor'. Sir Evelyn Baring wrote in a private letter 27 years after Gordon's death: 'There is not in reality the least doubt that he drank deeply'. Even Lord Elton has brought forward an unnamed 'distinguished man of letters' whose father believed Gordon had indulged at long intervals in bouts of secret drinking; Elton maintains, however, that he produced proof to cause his informant to retract. And there was the testimony of Joseph Reinach, the secretary of Leon Michel Gambetta, the French statesman, who became acquainted with Gordon on a voyage from Africa to Europe in 1880. They spent several days together in Naples (where Gordon stumped out of a half-naked ballet exclaiming angrily, ' . . . and you call that civilisation!'). At one o'clock in the morning Reinach found Gordon in his room in a dressing-gown, reading the Bible, on the table before him a half-empty bottle of whisky. Reinach wrote: 'He was a terrible drinker of brandy. Later, in Paris, he would often come to see me in the morning. And, before five minutes had elapsed, he would ask for brandy.' Gordon was, observed Reinach, like many heroes, 'a hero in the short term, a mystic who like the sound of his own voice and also, how should I put it? A bit of a humbug. He did not believe all he said. In the letters from him which I have kept, he quite happily treated Dizzie [Disraeli] and his friends as mountebanks. He himself was a mountebank. He greatly interested and amused me.'

Gordon's own writings produce sufficient references to the evils of alcohol to satisfy both defenders and detractors. The one could point to the evidence of a lifelong campaign against the temptations of demon drink. The other could argue overprotestation which smacked of hypocrisy. Gordon hated going to

Cairo where, he said, he drank brandy and talked too much. He undoubtedly saw in drink a weakness in his armour — 'I am always open to attack on that flank' — and he wrote to Augusta telling her that the Sacrament was 'a weapon for warfare against the flesh', and in particular for warfare against 'that immense serpent', smoking and drinking. (He was a prodigiously heavy smoker; in the Sudan he preferred fat cigarettes rolled by a servant, and two fingers raised by Gordon would be the signal to a lackey to leap forward, place a new cigarette in them and light it.)

The 'temperate Gordon' lobby blames Charles Chaillé-Long and his 1912 book, *My Life in Four Continents*, for the roots of what it sees as calumnies. Strachey's 'feline' account fails to stand up, it argues, because it was based on this tendentious version. Allen summoned two witnesses to conclude his defence of Gordon, the temperate drinker. They are Lord Esher and the daughter of a clergyman friend of Gordon. Lord Esher, at whose house Gordon was a frequent visitor, wrote: 'Many lies have been told about him. Even his moral character has not been spared. It has been said that he failed to do his duty, and he been called an inebriate. These accusations are absurdly false.'

Allen's second of these witnesses, the daughter of the Rev R.H. Barnes, was on a visit to Burma where she met Lord Kitchener. As Allen put it — 'Troubled by the rumours that she had heard in India about Gordon drinking, she turned to Lord Kitchener and asked him if there was any truth in them. A flush came to Kitchener's cheek and his eye flashed as he replied with unwonted animation: "They say it of Gordon; they have said it of me. Well, I am in a position to know the facts, and you may take it from me that the whole thing is a *damned lie*."'

Lord Esher's rebuttal of 'false accusations' was made in 1908. Lord Kitchener's condemnation of a 'damned lie' was delivered in 1903. But Long did not write the offending paragraph in his memoirs until 1912. Before then, 'rumours' must have been very persistent for them to have spread so far and wide. Believers in no smoke without fire could reasonably point out that a smouldering bonfire existed some considerable time before Long struck a tiny match in 1912 and Strachey fanned the flames into a forest fire in 1918.

Gordon did not marry and there is no evidence that he had a relationship with any women that was not platonic. Throughout his career he eschewed dinners and parties or any other social occasions which would bring him into contact with young women. In the mess he preferred, in mature life, the company of young men to those of his own age. Nor is there any evidence that he was homosexual. He was in favour of the institution of marriage: 'A man who is not married cannot know his faults' . . . 'To marry is the best thing a man should do, and it is one which I recommend to all my friends'. But he also believed that 'I could make no woman happy'. To his sister, Augusta, who played a dominant role in his early life, he wrote: 'Cursed is the man who makes flesh his aim', and once confessed to his friend, the Rev Barnes: 'I wished I was a eunuch at 14'.

Much that was Gordon remains mystery and paradox. Churchill wrote of him: 'It was a pity that one, thus gloriously free from the ordinary restraining influences of human society, should have found in his own character so little mental ballast. His moods were capricious and uncertain, his passions violent, his impulses sudden and inconsistent. The mortal enemy of the morning had become a trusted ally before the night. The friend he loved today he loathed to-morrow. Scheme after scheme formed in his fertile brain, and jostled confusingly together. All in succession were pressed with enthusiasm. All at times were rejected with disdain . . . His virtues are famous among men; his daring and resources might turn the tide of war; his energy would have animated a whole people; his achievements are upon record; but it must also be set down that few more uncertain and impracticable forces than Gordon have ever been introduced into administration and diplomacy.'

Contradictions abound on every page of Gordon's life. There is Gordon the violent, ordering summary executions, or going into a blazing temper and beating his servants: 'In matters like my head camelman giving me a stumbling camel or placing my camel-saddle badly, etc, etc, I use my whip'. One day a servant brought him a bad egg for breakfast and Gordon, in a towering rage, jabbed a fork into the man's wrist. And Gordon the gentle, personally undressing, bathing and putting to bed a filthy, exhausted urchin he found in the cold; or digressing in his Journal, during black days in Khartoum: 'A mouse has taken Stewart's place at table; she (judging from her swelled-out appearance) comes up and eats out of my plate without fear'. Amid many a bitter and reproachful telegram, there was also humour in his official despatches: 'Anyhow, it matters little — a few years hence a piece of ground six feet by two will contain all that remains of ambassadors, ministers and your obedient humble servant, C.G. Gordon'.

On a rare — and the last — British official assignment abroad before he received the government's summons to go to the Sudan in 1884, Gordon, now a Major-General, expressed these sentiments from South Africa: 'Egypt moves me no more. I would not go back even if I could . . . It is odd how little I think of Egypt or the Sudan; it is all now passed from me.' Not for the first time, Gordon would take a direction different from that plotted in his schemes.

# Chapter 5

# *A dangerous vagueness*

On the first day of 1884 a letter appeared in *The Times* giving public airing to Sir Samuel Baker's belief that Britain should send Gordon to the Sudan. Baker also wrote to Gordon, who replied: 'I will not go to the Sudan, for I feel it is too late'. In the meantime, since Gladstone had nodded at the idea of possibly using Gordon, the telegraph wires between the Foreign Office and Baring, the British agent in Cairo, had been busy. Baring's response was unfavourable; he personally distrusted Gordon and thought that Khedive Tewfik, with whom Gordon had parted on poor terms, would be averse to the idea of accepting him back.

Gordon had been many months isolated from the whirl of British foreign affairs, exploring Palestine's holy sites. He was in Brussels on the day Baker's letter appeared in the *The Times*, pursuing a fresh avenue in his career. His new employer was to be King Leopold of Belgium who wanted him to lead an anti-slavery expedition in the Congo. Gordon had come to the weary conclusion that the Army did not want him, and he did not want the Army, a view summed up in a letter to his family: 'Having the views I have I could nor curb myself sufficiently ever to remain in H.M. Service'. Now, he was determined to turn his back on England and go to the Congo, even if it meant resigning his commission and forfeiting his pension rights as a Major-General (Leopold promised to find £7,000 to make up these losses).

Four days after Baker's letter, *The Times* in a leading article headed 'Gordon and the Congo', lamented the loss of one of the 'brightest ornaments' in the British Army to a foreign power. The leader stirred other newspapers to comment, and the public joined the 'Send Gordon' campaign for the first time, for it had known nothing of the exchanges at high levels. The campaign gathered such momentum, both in the public domain and Whitehall councils, that within an amazingly short period of time — by the 18th of the month — Gordon had left London in a train on the way to his destiny in Khartoum. In the meantime, however, he dramatically joined the public debate by giving an explosive interview to a journalist. The views he expressed were at such variance with the government's commitment to withdrawal that it is a matter of utter astonishment that Gladstone and his ministers did not exclude the name of Gordon entirely from their thoughts.

The journalist was W.T. Stead, a God-fearing Nonconformist and a pioneer of the personal interview, newly appointed editor of the *Pall Mall Gazette*. Gordon, who returned to Britain in the first week of January, had at first refused a request to give his views on the Sudan. But Stead persisted and was invited to the home of Gordon's sister in Southampton. There he found Gordon in the company of an old friend, Captain Brocklehurst, of the Horse Guards. Gordon was seated on a couch covered by a leopard skin. Stead was impressed by a 'a child-like simplicity of speech and manners' and vouched that 'notwithstanding his fifty years, his face is almost boyish in its youthfulness, his step is as light and his movements as lithe as the leopard'. And, let those who doubted Gordon's fitness for high office take note: 'Although he is still excitable and vehement, those who know him best say that he has under much firmer control those volcanic fires which blazed out with fiercest fury in his younger days . . . '. Stead henceforth was a devoted slave of Gordon's.

Gordon showed reluctance to talk about the Sudan at first. Then the flood gates broke. His views poured out for more than two hours, as Stead remarked, 'with vehemence'. Yes, Darfur and Kordofan in the south-west must be abandoned (the Mahdi already held these areas) but the rest of the Sudan must be held: 'In self-defence the policy of evacuation cannot possibly be justified'. Whatever was decided about evacuation, 'you cannot evacuate, because your army cannot be moved. You must either surrender absolutely to the Mahdi, or defend Khartoum at all hazards. The latter is the only course which ought to be entertained.' There would be no serious difficulty about it — 'The Mahdi's forces will fall to pieces of themselves'. The Turks were the cause of all the trouble with their plunder and oppression; the Mahdi was merely a puppet of the slave-traders, with no real religious support.

There was one subject, said Gordon, about which he could not

43

imagine anyone could differ: 'That is the impolicy of announcing our intention to evacuate Khartoum. Even if we were bound to do so we should have said nothing about it. The moment it is known that we have given up the game every man will go over to the Mahdi. All men worship the rising sun. The difficulties of evacuation will be enormously increased, if, indeed, the withdrawal of our garrison is not rendered impossible.'

Stead hurried back to London with his scoop. On the following day, January 9, the interview was published, filling a page and running over into the next. It thrust into second place such matters as a review of the iron and steel trades 'by a North Country Ironmaster', the composition of Nubar Pasha's new ministry in Cairo, a brutal assault by a policeman, and news of 'Mr. Willings' choir'. Having written nine columns on the interview, the indefatigable Stead penned a trenchant leading article which he placed on the front page under the headlines. 'Chinese Gordon for the Sudan'. Following Gordon's revelations, argued Stead, the government must change its policy. 'General Gordon not only impeaches directly the policy of evacuating the Sudan, but he absolutely denies the possibility unless we are willing to admit that when we say evacuation we mean massacre.' There was only one answer: 'We cannot send a regiment to Khartoum, but we can send a man who on more than one occasion has proved himself more valuable in similar circumstances than an entire army. Why not send Chinese Gordon with full powers to Khartoum, to assume absolute control of the territory, to treat with the Mahdi, to relieve the garrisons, and to do what he can to save what can be saved from the wreck in the Sudan?'

The interview was reprinted in many papers throughout the land, including *The Times*. Stead's advocacy of Gordon had its origins in one religious zealot's regard for another, but it was now taken up by newspapers of all shades; Gordon was the man for Khartoum, they agreed, but most were notably imprecise about what he should be employed to do.

On January 11 another telegram arrived at the Foreign Office from Baring turning down a fresh offer to send Gordon.

No-one in any official capacity had yet asked Gordon's views on being sent. But a seed was growing in his mind. On the afternoon of January 12, Gordon, Sir Samuel Baker and the Rev R.H. Barnes, vicar of Heavitree, Exeter, were in a carriage driving near Newton Abbot. Barnes describes what happened: 'Sir Samuel

Baker pressed on Gordon the expediency of his going again to the Sudan as Governor-General, if Her Majesty's Government should require it. Gordon was silent, but his eyes flashed, and an eager expression passed over his face . . . Late at night, when he had retired, he came to my room and said in a soft voice, "You saw me to-day?" "You mean in the carriage?" "Yes; you saw *me* — that was myself — the self I want to get rid of".'

Lord Wolseley, Gordon's old friend, made the next move. Garnet Joseph Wolseley, four months younger, had fought along-side Gordon in the trenches of the Crimea where a common bond of religion drew them together. Like Gordon, Wolseley was a fatalist through his religious beliefs. Each sought heroes, as Victorians did, and found one in the other. While Gordon had been largely forgotten by the British public after his triumphs in China, however, Wolseley had enjoyed steadily mounting popular esteem. He served with distinction in the Indian Mutiny, China (where he was present, with Gordon, at the disgraceful sack and burning of the Summer Palace in Peking in 1860), Ashanti, the Canadian Red River campaign and the Zulu War. His was the victory over Arabi Pasha's rebels at Tel-el-Kebir in 1882. He had been called 'England's only General'. George Grossmith had made himself up as Wolseley to sing 'I am the very model of a modern Major-General' in *Pirates of Penzance*. After Wolseley's knighthood, to say 'All Sir Garnet' was popularly to say 'All correct'. Gordon was one of the few men he knew, said Wolseley, 'who came up to my estimate of the Christian hero'; he referred to him as 'God's friend'. Every night Gordon prayed for two men — one was Wolseley and the other was Brocklehurst.

Wolseley, the Adjutant-General, had been trying to sort out the question of Gordon's pension rights should he have to resign from the Army. He asked Gordon to come to see him at the War Office on January 15, ostensibly to talk about that matter. The real purpose of the meeting was to test Gordon's reaction following a small but significant shift in government thinking. The new plan was for Abd-el-Kader, the Egyptian war minister (the opponent to the Hicks expedition scheme), to be sent to Khartoum to oversee evacuation, and for Gordon to use his influence on the tribes near Suakim to safeguard the escape route.

Wolseley greeted his old friend with the news that there was no longer opposition to his serving King Leopold, and no need for him to resign his commission. But now Britain needed his services. Would Gordon be prepared 'to go to Suakim to enquire into the conditions of affairs in the Sudan?' There was no discussion about Gordon's recently published views on evacuation of the Sudan, so opposed to the government's. Gordon gave his answer quickly, apparently unconcerned by his dramatic change of course; God was working out the pattern and Gordon was following it. Yes, said Gordon, he would go. Asked by Wolseley to draw up suggestion for carrying out the proposed mission, Gordon duly wrote down some notes that night. One of the points he made was: 'I understand H.M.G. only wish me to report and are in no way bound by me'. *Report,* not *act:* the mandate was clear to both Wolseley and Gordon.

Baring was telegraphed on the night of the 15th, being told that the suggestion was that Gordon would go straight to Suakim without passing through Cairo 'on the understanding that the only object of his mission is to report on the military situation in the Sudan'. Gladstone agreed with this telegram, but growled a note of caution to Granville: ' . . . must we not be very careful in any instructions we give, that he does not shift the centre of gravity as to political and military responsibility for that country?' (the Sudan). Fixed firmly in Gladstone's mind however was that Gordon's role would be *advisory* and not *executive.*

Events had been moving swiftly in Cairo. To Baring's surprise and dismay Abd-el-Kader refused to go to Khartoum. Having previously turned down the offer of an officer from London, Baring now telegraphed a request on behalf of the Egyptian government for 'a qualified British officer to go to Khartoum with full powers civil and military to conduct the retreat'; he should be sent 'at once'. Baring's telegram was despatched before he had received London's message of the 15th about the proposal to send Gordon to Suakim. The crossing of the telegrams caused confusion in Baring's mind. London had offered him an officer in an advisory capacity. He had asked for a man *with full powers to conduct a retreat.* Without more ado, Gordon was on his way within two days.

That Baring was convinced he was getting an *executive* officer is clear from yet another telegram he sent during the interim period. In it he agreed Gordon would be the best man 'if he will pledge himself to carry out the policy of withdrawal from the Sudan as soon as possible'.

Gordon skipped across to Brussels and told a disappointed

Leopold that the Congo venture would have to be postponed, then back to London in answer to a summons from Wolseley to meet him and some of the Cabinet at the War Office on the afternoon of Sunday, January 18. There were four ministers present, most of the Cabinet being out of town for the weekend: Lord Granville, Foreign Secretary; Lord Hartington, War Minister; Sir Charles Dilke, President of the Local Government Board; and Lord Northbrooke, First Lord of the Admiralty, who was Baring's first cousin. There is no detailed official report of the meeting. In a letter to the Rev Barnes, however, Gordon wrote: 'Ministers said they were determined to evacuate and would I go and superintend it? I said "Yes".'

To his sister, Gordon wrote: 'Wolseley . . . said "H.M.G. want you to understand this Government are determined to evacuate the Sudan . . . Will you go and do it?" I said "Yes" . . . I went in and saw them. They said "Did Wolseley tell you our ideas?" I said "Yes; he said you will not guarantee future government of the Sudan and you wish me to go and evacuate it?" They said "Yes", and it was over . . . '

There was no doubt whatever that Gordon now believed he was to act in an *executive capacity* — to evacuate the country. Ministers' impressions of what was agreed at the meeting, however, varied in important particulars. The confusion created in Cairo by the crossing of telegrams was now compounded by the gang of four's differing versions. The official instructions given to Gordon before his departure were taken from a sheet of paper on which Granville wrote: 'To proceed to Suakim to report on the military situation in the Sudan and on the measures to be taken for the security of the Egyptian garrison . . . He will consider the best mode of evacuating the interior . . . and will perform such other duties as may be entrusted to him by the Egyptian government through Sir Evelyn Baring.'

Northbrooke wrote to Baring a letter in which there was a paragraph following closely to Granville's text. It included the last sentence about 'other duties'. Here was a dangerous vagueness, opening up vast possibilities — a loophole through which Gordon's 'small bee' might fly out of his bonnet and multiply. It was also a cynical device to shift the onus of executive action on to the Egyptian government. Dilke recorded that Gordon had been merely asked to 'collect information and report'. So firmly was he convinced that Gordon's duties were limited to reporting that later he became a leader of those accusing him of disobedience.

Hartington, who had a lackadaisical streak, planted a seed of confusion that was to grow and grow in the months ahead. He had undertaken to report to Gladstone, who was at his country retreat. He left Gladstone with the firm impression that Gordon had been instructed only to 'report' — adding that Gordon might recommend he be appointed Governor-General — and made no mention of the last sentence of the instructions, the possibility of 'other duties'. Nor did he inform his Prime Minister of Baring's request for an officer 'with full powers'. Although Gladstone subsequently assented to *executive* action in the Sudan, he could never shake from his mind the idea that Gordon had wilfully disobeyed instructions.

Did anyone at all the course of the meeting in the War Office raise the question of the *Pall Mall Gazette* interview, the absurdity of sending as an instrument of government policy a man who had flaunted views diametrically opposed to that policy in a leading London newspaper only nine days previously? There is no record of any reference by ministers to Gordon's apparent dichotomy of thought. From Gordon's point of view, if he was to go to the Sudan on whatever mission, then it was part of God's ordained plan. And the suspicion remains that he was seeking fulfilment of his death wish.

When — the ministers had asked Gordon — could he go? 'Tonight', said Gordon. And so it was. What about clothes?, he was asked. 'I'll go as I am'. What about money? He had none, and said he had borrowed cash from the King of the Belgians to pay his hotel bill in Brussels. While Gordon dined with Brocklehurst at Knightsbridge barracks, Wolseley toured several clubs and collected £300 in gold sovereigns. At Charing Cross station a nephew dashed up at the last minute carrying Gordon's General's uniform in a metal case. Wolseley carried a hand bag with a few items of kit. Granville bought the ticket. The Duke of Cambridge, the Army's Commander-in-Chief, held open the carriage door. Wolseley gave the gold sovereigns, not to Gordon, but to his only travelling companion, Colonel Donald Stewart. Stewart had been chosen to accompany Gordon to add mental ballast and in case Baring thought him a better choice to be sent to Khartoum; the officer had spent several months in the Sudan. 'They sent Stewart with me to be my wet-nurse'. Gordon remarked later. At 8 pm the boat train pulled out of the station for the continent.

# Chapter 6

## *Blunder at Berber*

Gordon sent a telegram to Barnes before leaving Britain: 'I go to Sudan tonight. If He goes with me, all will be well.' On the train through France he drafted several proclamations he proposed making to the tribes, one announcing his appointment as Governor-General, another his plans to give areas independence under the old ancestral sultans. As the railway miles fell behind so did any vestiges of thought that he was going simply to report. His executive function, only implicit in the instructions, began to develop in detail. He scribbled his plans and views on reams of paper for Baring, and sent back copies to a bemused Cabinet in London.

While he was travelling, his destination was changed at Baring's suggestion. Prospects were looking brighter in the Suakim area in the east, where a force of gendarmerie and black troops was being deployed by Valentine Baker, a former British officer and brother of Sir Samuel; it would be better now if Gordon came to Cairo first.

Cairo? The London newspapers, exulting in his appointment, were quick to project his journey to Khartoum. Khartoum? 'While I was at the War Office I heard nothing of his going to Khartoum, or anywhere else except to Suakim', fumed Dilke. If Gordon were carried off 'we shall have to send a terrible force after him'. Granville felt a gnawing responsibility. 'We were proud of ourselves yesterday. Are you sure that we did not commit a gigantic folly?', he asked Hartington. What did Baring think about this mountain of paper thoughts? Baring telegraphed his approval. An uneasy Cabinet nodded consent.

Gordon was in Cairo by the 24th. The next morning, before General Sir Gerald Graham had risen, Gordon was hammering at his door and calling out the name of his old Royal Engineers' comrade. For an hour he poured out a torrent of proposals and views — no religious element in the rebellion — the Mahdi was a figurehead — wouldn't fight on the plains . . . Graham was filled with foreboding. 'I don't like his programme', he wrote in his diary. Some long time afterwards he summed up Gordon's mission: 'He was appointed the Moses of a new Exodus, *but with the Red Sea closed against him*'.

A meeting with Khedive Tewfik went better than Gordon or Baring could have hoped. The Khedive gave him two firmans, or edicts, leaving it to his discretion to decide the appropriateness of the moment to reveal them. One would tell the people he had been appointed Governor-General of the Sudan. The other would reveal that he was going to evacuate the country, withdraw the troops and 'take the necessary steps for establishing an organised government': in effect, Egypt was abandoning the Sudan. In the comings and goings of the past week the choice of Khartoum as Gordon's destination had passed through the stages of rumour and assumption, and was now established fact.

Two to three days in Cairo were crammed with a round of meetings; Gordon chain-smoked his way through discussions that went on all night and into the dawn; his energy amazed everyone who met him. One meeting laid the foundations of what was to be one of the most acrimonious of many quarrels with the British government, the beginning of an affair which exemplified Gordon's inconsistency of thought.

The affair concerned Zebehr Pasha, a man of considerable standing and influence in the khedival establishments in Cairo, but whose greatest renown had been as 'king of the slave-traders'. Zebehr Rahma Mansur, a Jaalin Arab, had first crossed paths with Gordon when the latter was Governor of the Equatorial Provinces from 1874 to 1876. A brilliant businessman and an accomplished soldier, Zebehr rationalised the slave trade and put it on a proper commercial footing. The khedival authorities, paying court to the international anti-slavery cause on the one hand and profiting by the trade on the other, came to terms with him because of his power and influence. He was the virtual ruler of Bahr al-Ghazal in the south, and with a private army conquered Darfur, ostensibly on behalf of the Cairo government. He remained a threat to Egyptian authority, however, and in the mid-1870s he was lured to Cairo — and kept there. He was given the exalted rank of Pasha.

Zebehr nurtured a fierce hatred of Gordon who as Governor-

General in 1879, had ordered Romolo Gessi to execute Zebehr's 22-year-old son, Suliman, for rebellion. Zebehr, then in Cairo, was also sentenced to death for inciting Suliman to revolt; the sentence was set aside but the slave-trader blamed Gordon for allegedly forging the evidence. In 1884 Gordon had made plain his views about Zebehr. On his way to Egypt he had suggested his old adversary should be exiled in Cyprus where he could not communicate with the Mahdi. When there was a suggestion that Zebehr should lead Valentine Baker's black troops, Gordon declared himself set against it. Zebehr would swiftly go over to the Mahdi and become his commander-in-chief, he told Stead in the famous interview.

On January 25 a sudden change came over Gordon. He met Zebehr by accident at the house of an Egyptian statesman. It was the briefest of meetings, but Gordon was seized by a mystic feeling that the cruel slave trader of yesterday could be the saviour of the Sudan. Zebehr should go with him to Khartoum to be the rallying figure for tribes to defeat the Mahdi. A further meeting was arranged the following day. Zebehr refused to shake hands with Gordon. A bitter argument ensued over the evidence on which Zebehr Pasha was sentenced to death. One version of the meeting claims Zebehr remained implacable in his hatred of Gordon, another is that he was reconciled to being the Englishman's servant in the Sudan. Friends of Gordon feared Zebehr would plot his murder.

Whether or not Zebehr was converted, Gordon now burned with an unquenchable zeal to have him by his side at Khartoum. Among the group of senior British and Egyptians at the meeting there was a balance against the idea which persuaded Baring not to sanction Zebehr's employment. 'I have no confidence in opinions based on mystic feelings', he later wrote. Gordon held tenaciously to his obsession and for nearly two months scorched the wires between Khartoum and Cairo, Cairo and London, with bitter telegrams arguing his case. Baring later came to support Gordon in this, believing that Zebehr might be of value in the progressively worsening crisis.

Before London delivered a final, categorical veto in March, however, Gordon's insistence stirred up a hurricane of protest in Britain, alienating him from friends in the Anti-Slavery Society, appalling liberals and mystifying his admirers. John Morley, a Liberal MP, raged against the idea of employing the bloodthirsty talents of 'an unscrupulous and tyrannical slave-driver'. To allay fears that a Zebehr in the south would be fox in a chicken farm, Gordon devised safegaurds to prohibit him entering the slave catchment areas of Equatoria and Bahr. One of his brief notions was to make him supreme in Khartoum when his, Gordon's, work was finished. In Britain a hero-worshiping public experienced the first tremors of disillusionment.

Accompanied by Stewart and his friend, Graham, Gordon left Cairo by train on January 26. It was exactly one year by date to his death. Gordon used the rail journey to Assiut to formulate more schemes on paper and in discussion with his two companions: matters of import and others comparatively trivial. What headgear should he wear as Governor-General? A sun helmet thought Stewart. A fez though Graham. Gordon agreed with Graham. A fez it would be. And there was an interlude of high farce, but one which left Gordon deeply irritated for it meant that another of his schemes had been derailed.

In support of the policy of re-establishing the ancestral rulers in the wake of Egyptian withdrawal, Gordon had picked out a young man living in Cairo exile, Abd-al Chakour, a relation of the former Sultan of Darfur, to be the new potentate of that province. One account has it that his father had been killed by Zebehr. Aside from the reality of Darfur's recent fate — it had come firmly under the rebels' control and had a fierce and powerfully-backed Mahdiist on the 'throne' — Gordon reserved high hopes for his Cairo-domiciled protégé and took him along with him on his journey south. The choice was an unmitigated disaster.

At Cairo railway station the party was held up while the sultan fussed about with his immense piles of baggage and 23 wives; two of his brothers, travelling with them, brought a further 25 wives. The train was delayed while an extra carriage was put on. At Assiut, where Gordon's party embarked on a Nile steamer, the sultan emerged to view in an elaborate gala uniform, the absurdity of which was heightened by the sash of a recently conferred order constantly slipping off his shoulder. 'Followed by his retinue of dirty, ill-favoured women and ruffianly-looking men, he pushed by us like an ill-bred savage, without taking any notice of the plainly dressed Governor-General, and proceeded to take possession of the saloon of the steamer', noted Graham.

Gordon ordered him out of the saloon — and out of his uniform. That, he explained, should be saved for when he regained his throne. The sultan demanded that Gordon should provide food for his retinue and himself. Gordon told him bluntly that he had a £2,000 pension and that he should feed himself. The sultan retired and reappeared, according to Graham, 'in a dirty grey overcoat, with a crestfallen look on his heavy black face'. Henceforth, he began to drink heavily; a trail of empty gin bottles bobbed in the wake of the steamer. Gordon's temper snapped. He ordered the short-lived pretender off the boat at Aswan. Abd-al Chakour travelled independently as far south as Dongola, where he spent several months in disconsolate drinking before giving up all hope of his throne and returning to the fleshpots of Cairo.

Gordon's mind was leaping a hundred ways at once. He dashed off a telegram to the people of Khartoum: 'Don't be panic-stricken. You are men, not women. I am coming.' He refused to be drawn by Graham on his views of 'no withdrawal' expressed in the *Pall Mall Gazette* interview. He drew out a plan of campaign which appeared to push peaceful measures aside and began with smashing the Hadendowa who were blocking Suakim. Graham tried to dissuade him from sending it to Cairo. 'Speech is silver; silence is golden', opined Stewart — and received a curt rebuke from the irritated Gordon.

It was clear that Gordon was projecting the course of his mission, not only beyond reporting, advising and evacuating, but into those dangerous areas shunned by his critics in the Cabinet. In a hotel at Luxor he told a traveller, Professor A.H. Sayce, that under pressure from Granville he had undertaken the task of withdrawing the garrisons by peaceful means if possible; if not, he expected the 'support of troops'. Two weeks later at Berber, Giuseppe Cuzzi (an Italian adventurer who subsequently survived 14 years as a prisoner of the Mahdi and Khalifa), received the impression that Gordon believed he would be backed in the last resort by British military power.

Graham listened with patience to Gordon's schemes, trying his best to temper his friend's enthusiasm for some of the more outlandish ones. Now he would write to King Leopold offering Belgium the Equatorial and Bahr al Ghazal regions, thus ensuring their protection against the slavers. The strange idea would arise again in communications from Khartoum with Cairo. Next, he would propose Leopold incorporate the whole of the Sudan in the planned new Congo State, the King paying £100,000 for it and appointing Gordon to run it. A small voice from Graham asked:

'The question is: If the King of the Belgians agrees, will the British Government raise any objection?'

Graham was concerned that Gordon was surrounding himself by a dangerous complacency in deluding himself that the Mahdi's cause had little or no religious support. Osman Digna's Hadendowa were disaffected, said Gordon, because they had been short-changed on payment when they acted as transport drivers during the preparations of gathering camels for the Hicks expedition. Their unrest could be put down to the simple matter of resentment at being paid one dollar a camel instead of six dollars! A letter was written to the Mahdi. Gordon would have preferred to go to see him. He had aired the idea to a fellow passenger on the ship from Europe to Egypt; when Baring heard of the proposal, he forbade the visit. Later, when Gordon learned that Mohammed Ahmed was the nephew of a poor Dongolawi called Abd-el-Kader, who used to act as a guide to him on his camel rides through the desert, he was more than ever convinced that the so-called Mahdi had no great influence; in Gordon's book, if a camel man erred he must be whipped. And Gordon telegraphed to the British authorities his scorn of the Mahdi and his conviction that the risings were local troubles. His underestimation of his enemy led him to send the Mahdi the derisory offer of the sultanate of Kordofan (an area where the Mahdi's power was supreme after the Hicks disaster), accompanied by a red robe of honour and a tarbush. The Mahdi sent back a contemptuous answer and, with it, a simple, patched jibbeh, the symbol of piety and poverty which his Ansar wore with pride.

Drafting his thoughts on to paper occupied a large part of Gordon's time. He consumed a vast amount of paper in writing letters to friends, family, employers and subordinates. His Khartoum journals were meant to be read by the authorities and, expressly, to be published. Graham could see no harm in a British officer informing his superiors, day by day, hour by hour, what he was thinking and doing. Gordon 'thought on paper'. A telegram of the morning would be swept aside by one in the evening, proposing an entirely different course of action to that put forward a few hours earlier.

Although, when compared, some telegrams from the Sudan appeared to be contradictory, Gordon's deluge of wired words achieved an insidious effect: sometimes conditioned the minds of the recipients in Cairo and London to dumb acceptance of what he was proposing. Thus, on February 12, while Gordon was still on his way to Khartoum, Gladstone went as far as telling the House of Commons that Gordon had been sent 'for the dual purpose of evacuating the country by extricating the garrisons and reconstituting it by giving back to those sultans their ancestral powers'. At the back of the prime minister's mind there was still a hard nugget of thought labelled 'reporting and advisory capacity', to be retrieved and thrown into the debate when things went wrong. For the time being, the vague instructions about 'other duties' and Gordon's prodigious paper-work had created a *fait accompli* in the Sudan. And in the manner of his working, observed Graham, Gordon was not in the least afraid of seeming to be inconsistent.

Graham's steamer voyage with Gordon and Stewart ended at Korosko, 700 miles south of Cairo. Gordon's last words to his friend were 'God bless you'. On February 1, in a desolate valley rimmed by black volcanic crags, Graham watched them set forth on a 250-mile camel ride across the Nubian desert to Abu Hamed, which lies at the top of the huge question mark formed by the Nile. They were escorted by a small group of Arabs bearing cross-hilted swords and shields of rhinocerous hide. Stewart carried a revolver. Gordon, unarmed, sported a white umbrella given to him by Graham.

Nearly a week later, Gordon was at Abu Hamed where he told the people he was not going to wage war on the Mahdi; he was, however, going to amnesty all offences, cut taxes by half and remit all arrears; in future the Sudan would be ruled with kindness and justice. The people took the vague promises equably, if with a large pinch of salt. Five days farther up the Nile at Berber, the vital link between Khartoum and Nile passage downriver to Egypt, and between Khartoum and the caravan routes to the coast at Suakim, Stewart was roused at five o'clock on the morning of February 12. Gordon, who had been up all night pondering deeply, told him he had 'come to the decision of opening the Pandora-box'. At eight o'clock the mudir, or local governor, Hussein Pasha Khalifa, and a leading judge were summoned and shown a number of proclamations, which were later read to a larger group of notables.

There was the news about amnesties and taxes to which the village of Abu Hamed had been made privy. In addition, however, Gordon announced the right of the people to keep the slaves in their service without any interference from the government or anybody else. An Anglo-Egyptian convention of 1877 made slave-holding punishable by death, but Gordon explained that the provisions would no longer apply as the Sudan would be independent of Egypt. (Gordon had no alternative to making this declaration: he recognised the reality of the situation. But the news was greeted in Britain as condonation of the slave trade. It was as though Gordon, the scourge of the slavers, had joined the evil trade, first by demanding the services of Zebehr, and secondly by his proclamation on slave-holding. The liberals of Britain cried out in shame.)

The most explosive content of his 'Pandora-box' was to come — the Khedive's 'secret' firman. He told the notables, who knew nothing of such proposals, that the Khedive intended to withdraw all Egyptian officials and troops and leave the Sudan to run its own affairs. *The Sudan was to be abandoned.*

By revealing his hand so early in the game he gave, as the Mahdi's prisoner Father Ohrwalder said, 'a death blow to himself and his mission'. It was the death warrant also for thousands of people. Gordon had second thoughts the next day in discussions with Stewart, but explained away his action by arguing that the Sudanese had to be spurred — shocked — into action to run their own affairs. Had he forgotten his own words to Stead: 'All men worship the rising sun'? The Mahdi's sun would rise with a vengeance now.

It was significant that of all those notables at Berber who first heard Gordon's proclamation of abandonment, not one remained faithful to the government cause. Berber fell within three months, and with it Khartoum's rescue route was closed. The defenders, knowing they would be left to the Mahdi's vengeance, despaired of success. Hussein Khalifa later told the Austrian Rudolph Slatin in the Mahdi's lines that the incident sealed Gordon's doom; they knew that any assistance given to him 'meant the annihilation of themselves and the enslavement of their families'. Why, asked Slatin, should they commit this self-sacrifice?

In spite of some misgivings, more than shared by Stewart, Gordon repeated the proclamation of few days later at Metemmeh, farther up the Nile (at Khartoum the proclamation was not repeated, but by then it was too late, and the news had spread along the Nile valley). Around Metemmeh the wild Jaalin tribe was wavering. The news helped to throw them into the

Mahdi's arms. The town's emir, Ali Wad Said, later told Ohrwalder: 'How could I have remained loyal to a government which I knew intended to leave me in the lurch afterwards? I would only have been paving the way for the Mahdi's vengeance.'

Gordon sailed south in the steamer *Tewfikieh*, troubled by doubts but believing in his influence on the people of the Sudan, and not comprehending fully the consequences of his folly.

# Chapter 7

# *Generals on trial*

While Gordon progressed by camel and steamer to Khartoum, a British military diversion was beginning in the eastern Sudan on the Red Sea coast. 'A pointless concession to ill-constructed public opinion', was how it was described by Charles Royle, a contemporary historian and barrister who made scathing criticisms of British politicians and Generals in *The Egyptian Campaigns,* published in 1886.

General Valentine Baker's deployment at Suakim of 3,000 Egyptian gendarmes and black Sudanese under the Khedival flag had been uncommonly well attended by the London press corps. For one thing, it offered the most likely opportunity of war in the 'Sudan question' which for the past few months had been mostly jaw-jaw. Moreover, Valentine, Samuel's brother, was a figure of some spicy notoriety to the British public. Less than a decade earlier he had been sentenced to a year in prison and cashiered from the British Army after he, a promising Colonel of 48, had been found guilty of indecent assault in a railway carriage. His victim was a Miss Dickinson, aged 22, a woman of respectable background who accused him of unwelcome advances in a Liphook to Waterloo train on a hot afternoon of June. His British Army career in ruins, on leaving goal he fought the Russians on behalf of the Turks and was later seconded to service in Egypt.

Baker's attempt to relieve the outposts of Sinkat and Tokar ended in débâcle. His gendarmes and blacks were routed, with 2,000 dead, by the forces of Osman Digna. Blow by blow, the defeat was described by the reporters who filled columns of print with stories of the terrible suffering in the besieged garrisons. The Cabinet in London succumbed to public opinion. Conveniently shelving its policy of 'no intervention in the Sudan', by somehow pretending the eastern Sudan was 'different', it sanctioned a

British military expedition to crush the rebellion of Osman Digna.

'Celebrated and perhaps immortal' was how Winston Churchill described Osman Digna. He goes down in history as one of the Mahdi's most astute Generals. But had it not been for the British his career might have run in an entirely different direction. The son of a Kurdish-descended father and a Hadendowa mother, Osman Digna was in his early forties when he first fought the British in February 1884. He had grown up in a wealthy commercial family at the Sudanese port of Suakim where outgoing trade was based on copper, ivory, hides — and slaves. In 1877 Osman and his brother Ahmed were caught redhanded by a British man o'war: they were carrying slaves. They were imprisoned by the Egyptians and the family fortunes fell to ruin. Thereafter Osman nursed a fierce grudge against the 'Turks' and the British. Osman espoused the Mahdi's cause and was created an emir in 1883. He had enormous success in rousing the 'fuzzy-wuzzy' Hadendowa and other Beja tribes and it was to his credit that the rebellion was as violent in this isolated region as anywhere in the Sudan. He cherished strong hopes of succeeding Mohammed Ahmed as the leader of the movement and was enraged when Khalifa Abdallahi was chosen. Militarily, his art was that of the surprise attack, the sudden devastating onslaught after which his warriors would vanish in a wilderness of thorny mimosa and tortuous ravines. He was called Osman 'the slippery eel' by Wingate and was popularly known as 'Osman the Ugly' in the British press.

Osman Digna, short, wiry, beak-nosed and dark-skinned, was the adversary through two campaigns in successive years of Gerald Graham, a genial blond giant of 6 feet 6 inches, said by Wolseley to have 'the heart of a lion and the modesty of a young girl'. Graham was the son of a Cumberland doctor; he married a parson's widow and they had six children. His regiment was the Royal Engineers. He had been a comrade of Gordon at the Royal Military Academy, in the Crimea (where Graham won the Victoria Cross) and in China. At the age of 53, a Major-General, Sir Gerald Graham was chosen from the British officers in Cairo to lead the Suakim expedition of February 1884. Just over a year later he was again at Suakim at the head of a British force when, after the failure of the Gordon relief expedition, a dismayed and vilified government in London agreed to another brief and ill-considered intervention in the eastern Sudan.

Misjudgement was the staple ingredient of the Gordon affair. It was not, however, confined to the politicians, the military planners and Gordon. The fatuities of commanders in the field played their part. In the Sudan campaigns of the mid-1880s there were times when British forces reached the very edge of disaster. The prospect of British military catastrophe is believable if only because the unimaginable became commonplace in the fiascos of 1884-85. Certain judgements and deeds of Sir Gerald Graham and one other, Sir John McNeill, in the eastern Sudan, warrant a detailed digression in the telling of this story.

The main events of the brief campaign of 1884 were the British victories of El Teb (the site of Baker's defeat) on February 29, and Tamai on March 13, both in the Suakim hinterland. Both resulted in huge slaughter of the enemy. Neither succeeded in quelling the rebellion nor disheartening Osman Digna. The victories were greeted with rejoicing in Britain, tempered by liberal dismay at the horrific toll of rebel dead. An unfortunate incident in the first battle and its immediate aftermath, however, almost led to tactical disaster in the second engagement.

The 42nd, known as the Black Watch or The Royal Highlanders, a regiment with battle honours going back more than a century, were in the front line at El Teb. Graham said after the battle: 'The Royal Highlanders were somewhat out of hand . . . formed in an irregular manner'. At the crux of the fight they had spoiled his scheme for a unified, sweeping, forward surge when the order to charge was given. The reason was that the Black Watch were unable to charge. They had come up against a hedgehog of rifle pits, earthworks and fortified huts in the village of El Teb. The emplacements were filled with Hadendowa warriors, savagely determined to fight to the death. Each pit and trench had to be taken in turn. And still the wounded rose behind the highlanders, stabbing with spears and hacking with swords. Inevitably any warrior who still lived, even though wounded, was finished off by Black Watch bayonet or bullets. It was slow, brutal business, and much of the slaughter that horrified liberals at home and brought criticisms down on Graham's head, happened here where the fight was fiercest.

When, just over a week later, the regiment was paraded before the battle of Tamai, Graham addressed them. To the amazement of officers and men he declared that he could not say he was altogether pleased with their performance at El Teb. They had not broken into a double when among the rifle pits and he was disturbed by the rate their ammunition was fired off. To show that he had not lost confidence in them, however, he was going to place the regiment in the front in the coming operation. The dressing-down, with its implied slur on their honour, wrankled with the 42nd whose motto is 'No-one provokes me with impunity'. There was, said one officer, 'ill feeling bordering almost on insub-ordination'.

For the attack at Tamai, Graham deployed his troops in two squares, advancing in echelon. The Black Watch formed the left front face of the leading square, commanded by General Sir John Davis. They moved across a sloping plateau, seamed by dry water-courses, towards a deep ravine which was about 100 yards wide and filled with tumbled boulders. About 5,000 of Osman Digna's men could be seen on the other side of the ravine. The Navy's Gardner and Gatling guns were trundled out in front of the corners of the slow-moving square and the whole mass of troops was almost on to the ravine when the highlanders heard a bellowed order from Graham — who had taken command of the square from Davis: 'Forty-second! Charge!' There was, as officers of the regiment later pointed out with bitterness, nothing to charge at: Graham had committed a classic tactical mistake. But the 'Forty-twas' cheered and broke into a run. Alongside them on their right, the 65th Regiment had heard no order to charge. They hesitated, then tried to catch up with the Black Watch line. The front of the square was coming loose as the highlanders surged forward and the line infantry trailed to the right and behind them in fragments.

Thirty yards from the ravine the charging highlanders halted and a ceasefire was ordered. Most ignored it for now there appeared from deep in the ravine a horde of spearmen, unseen before, who overwhelmed the Gardners and smashed through the disordered front of the square, hurling the 65th back on to the Marines behind them. In bloody hand-to-hand fighting the British soldiers saved their shattered square and rescued the guns. The second square, under General Sir Redvers Buller, moved up in support and Graham had his victory.

Graham said afterward — against the evidence of those present — that he had no recollection of having ordered a charge. In his despatch, he wrote of the incident: 'For this disorder I am to some extent responsible as the charge took place under my own eyes and with my approval'. There was, perhaps, a further allegation of misjudgement to be laid on him. Reporters said that he had fore-knowledge that Osman Digna would use the ravine to conceal masses of men. A native spy, who was paid £100 for his services, told the British that the ravine was an ambush danger and that it should be taken from the flank after it had first been swept by artillery fire. Graham disregarded the advice.

The Black Watch felt they had been needlessly exposed. Criti-cised for not charging at El Teb, they felt that at Tamai they were given a chance to retrieve their reputation by being given a place of honour in the front. They obeyed the order to charge knowing it was foolish — 'but we were on our mettle', said officers. Their anger was not assuaged by a phrase in Graham's orders of the day: 'There was only one critical moment when discipline was for-gotten . . . '.

Graham's folly in ordering part of the square to charge — it was like lifting the lid off a box — drew attention to the drawbacks inherent in the traditional British infantry fighting formation. A square is useless if it rushes in fragments; its unity is all. Furthermore, critics questioned the efficacy of the fighting square in the Sudan. Its principal purpose in battle was to repel attacks by cavalry. The Sudan was to prove its vulnerability to onslaught by waves of fanatical opponents, and Osman Digna taught his fellow emirs a clever tactic of attacking at the corners where the square's massed firepower was least effective.

Continental newspapers, feeding on the eye-witness reports of British correspondents at the battle, used the incident of the broken square to dwell on 'the decadence of the British Army'. Graham was far from nonplussed by the criticisms. He returned home to be fêted, was promoted Lieutenant-General, dined with the Queen, and at the Royal School of Military Engineering (com-manded by Gordon's brother, Henry) he was carried by the officers shoulder-high around the mess while the band played *See the Conquering Hero Comes.*

The government withdrew its army from the eastern Sudan, refusing to allow an attempt to reach Berber in succour of Gordon. Suakim remained a garrisoned enclave of Egyptian authority, hemmed in by Osman Digna. Within less than a year,

---

* Baring wrote to the Queen's private secretary on March 21, 1885: 'Graham should not have been sent to command at Suakim. He is a fine fellow but no general.'

however, Graham was back at Suakim, much to the dismay of his critics★, this time at the head of an army of 12,000 British and Indian troops. In the aftermath of Gordon's death, Wolseley was led to believe — for a brief, intoxicating period — that he was going to be allowed to launch the reconquest of Khartoum. Part of the plan involved building a railway from Suakim to Berber.

For the moment, therefore, the narrative must leap ahead of Gordon's doings to these heady days of March 1885 to pursue the theme of military incompetence. Under scrutiny are the deeds of General McNeill.

The first business of the young officer in his profession of soldiering, is to try to get himself killed, Lord Wolseley stated in an opinion delivered late in life. No-one could argue that Sir John Carstairs McNeill, distinguished in the Indian Mutiny, decorated with the Victoria Cross for bravery against the Maoris, was not a disciple of this dictum of his friend and superior. Major-General McNeill was a stolid Hebridean whose life had been the Army, ungifted by imagination and a confirmed bachelor. Whatever intellectual qualities he lacked, however, there was no reason why his career record of dash and courage under fire should not lead, were he to survive, to honours in retirement. In the meantime, his military association with big Gerald Graham, under whom he commanded an infantry brigade in the eastern Sudan, was chemistry for potential disaster. On the evidence of history, at Tofrek on Sunday March 22 1885, John Carstairs McNeill at the age of 54 was still trying very hard to get killed.

As work progressed on the railway it was necessary to build posts to protect the line. With this intention, Graham despatched a force under McNeill from Suakim towards the old battleground of Tamai. McNeill marched out in two squares into scrub country that was the domain of Osman Digna's tribesmen; large numbers had been sighted on the hills that morning. McNeill had an Indian infantry brigade, 650 Berkshires, 500 Marines, 100 Engineers, a squadron each of 5th Lancers and 20th Hussars, and four naval Gardner guns. As usual in the Sudan, the British had not gathered enough transport camels, so those available had to shuttle to and fro with armed escorts.

The plan was to establish a forward post about eight miles from Suakim. The Indian brigade was then to return to base, leaving a battalion in a half-way post. The dense bush forced McNeill to alter his plans. The mass of baggage animals enclosed in the moving Indian square was constantly getting into disorder owing to the high prickly bushes. With such slow progress, it was apparent to McNeill that if the force advanced eight miles there would not remain enough daylight to allow the Indians to return and build the intermediate defensive post. He therefore stopped after six miles near a place called Tofrek. Here there were to be three thorn-bush zeribas closely grouped in echelon so that each could give supporting fire to the others — a classic defensive formation adopted by British troops in the Sudan.

It was, critics said afterwards, sheer lunacy on McNeill's part not to have recognised the danger of the thick bush, six to eight feet in height. Nevertheless, he placed pickets of lancers, in groups of four, only 1,000 yards out from his force, put the remainder on open ground 500 yards nearer still, and kept his hussars patrolling between the encampment and Suakim, the side least likely to be attacked. Four-man groups of infantry were positioned 80 to 120 yards in front of the Indian lines, a distance a Hadendowa athlete can cover, thorn bushes notwithstanding, in less than ten seconds, as many were shortly to demonstrate.

While parties of Berkshires, Engineers and Madras sappers chopped brushwood for the zeribas and cooking fires, and built barriers of sandbags and thorn, others were fed and watered. The Marines were eating and their arms were piled. Around this domestic scene McNeill rode on an approving tour of inspection, accompanied by his aide, Lieutenant the Honourable Alan Charteris of the Coldstream Guards. The comparatively few British troops standing to arms seems, in retrospect, the result of a remarkably relaxed attitude considering the morning's sighting of the enemy. It was 2:30 in the afternoon.

Shouts and shots from the lancer pickets gave the briefest warning of trouble. The yellow mimosa scrub sprouted a crop of fluttering white that grew within seconds to a mass of onrushing, shrieking figures who, it seemed to the astonished and unarmed woodcutters, kept pace, stabbing and hacking, with the horses themselves as the cavalry galloped for the safety of the nearest zeriba. Fifty Engineers, sent into the bush to collect their tools before returning to Suakim, raced back to where they had stacked their rifles. A few found weapons. Some turned and fended off the attacking tribesmen with billhooks and hatchets; men of the Berkshires, caught equally unprepared, had snatched up any rifles they could find, their own or those of the Engineers.

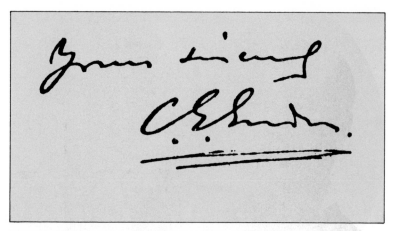

Gordon's signature.

**Previous page** *Charles George Gordon in the uniform of Governor of the Equatorial Provinces in 1874, a watercolour by Richard Simkin* (Christie's).

*Mohammed Ahmed, the Mahdi.*

66

**Above left** *General Lord Wolseley, commander of the Gordon relief expedition.*

**Above right** *Colonel Sir Charles Wilson, blamed for wasting three vital days.*

**Below left** *Colonel Frederick Gustavus Burnaby, killed at Abu Klea; a contemporary portrait miniature* (Phillips, the international fine art auctioneers).

**Below right** *Osman Digna, probably the greatest of the Mahdiist fighting emirs, pictured after his capture in 1900 at the age of 60.*

*Melton Prior (left) and Harry Pearse, war correspondents who accompanied the Camel Corps in the Bayuda desert* (National Army Museum).

**Left** *Khedive Tewfik of Egypt, festooned with international decorations in a cartoon by Spy, Sir Leslie Matthew Ward* (Forbes Magazine, New York).

In the immediate onset half the Gardners were silent. At the southern redoubt where there was yet only a shallow row of sandbags, sailors were still bolting together two of the guns which were carried in pieces on four camels. Despite its tendency to jam, the Gardner was a devastating weapon against a massed attack when the cranking handle was operated cooly and skilfully. One revolution of the crank fired five rounds. Used by the Navy as a quick-firing answer to the growing threat of swift, small torpedo boats, Gardners were trundled ashore to augment land forces' firepower, but many a senior Army commander, steeped in infantry lore, accepted them on sufferance, regarding them as the Navy's toys.

A phalanx of spearmen and swordsmen hit the unfinished zeriba and engulfed the unprepared Gardners, killing and wounding several sailors. As the attackers smashed into the square they were met by a curtain of fire from some of the Berkshires. But a crisis of nightmare proportions was developing at the central and 'soft' zeriba. Outside the unfinished thorn fence, lines of Indian infantry stood their ground against attacks from the front and their own comrades' fire from behind. Trouble came, however, from the camels they were protecting. The mass of terrified animals, 2,000 of them, surged forward, a stampede of roaring camels, kicking mules and panic-stricken handlers, headlong into the zeriba.

Under cover of the chaos, Hadendowa poured into the zeriba, gliding under the camels' bellies, hamstringing animals and maiming men with their long two-edged swords. Camels and natives inside the thorn fence joined the general rush out through an open side. Defenders' fire mowed down camels by the score and exacted terrible toll of the crazed transport natives. The uncontrolled herd of animals and men careered on and into the northern zeriba. To plug the gap, the Marines had to slaughter the camels; their corpses and loads lying in stinking bile and blood provided a barricade.

McNeill, true to form, got close to being killed in the general melee. His horse shied as he was about to jump it into a zeriba. His aide, Charteris, rushed to his help, turning aside one gun pointed at the General and cutting down another assailant with his sabre.

The action, which came to be known as the engagement of McNeill's Zeriba, was at an end after 20 minutes. McNeill lost nearly 500 dead, missing and wounded, 15 per cent of his force.

More than 900 camels were killed. Graham reported 1,000 enemy corpses on the field.

Lord Charles Beresford, a naval officer on Sudan service, visited the battleground with Wolseley more than a month after the action. He wrote: 'A dusky cloud of kites and vultures hovered sluggishly and unafraid among a wilderness of discoloured mounds. The sand was heaped so scantily on the dead, that lipless skulls, and mutilated shanks, and clenched hands, were dreadfully displayed. The bodies of the camels were clustered upon by the birds of prey . . . in the dust and glare of the sunlight the hot air carried a dreadful waft of corruption.'

The odours were beginning to reach London. Despite a covering of complacency and understatement which Graham gave to his official despatch on Monday, March 23, some disturbing facts were emerging, as noisome and persistent as the bones of McNeill's dead by the roadside at Tofrek, and to the critics of Graham and McNeill they spelled incompetent generalship. Graham had reported: 'McNeill did everything possible under the circumstances . . . although the enemy gained a temporary success by surprise, they have received a severe lesson . . . '

Newspaper correspondents orchestrated the first notes of criticism. Their questioning approach was taken up by Charles Royle: 'It has been said that General McNeill has denied that what occurred was a surprise . . . But that the attack, when it came, found the British force in a state of unpreparedness, is a proposition which can scarcely be contested.' The thick bush should have suggested to McNeill the necessity for the utmost caution. There should have been a proper system of cavalry scouts and outposts. Instead the lancers were little more than a half mile out from the zeribas, the hussars were virtually unused, most of the British infantry had their arms stacked, a good part of the Indians were forming up for the return march, and the whole was encumbered with a mass of camels marshalled beyond the protection of the zeribas, which formed a ready-made, living battering ram waiting to be used by an opportunist enemy.

By omission, Graham brushed aside most of these considerations when he wrote an extended account of the action. In it he betrayed the foggy thinking that typified senior military attitudes towards the opponent throughout the Sudan campaigns of the 1880s. A compound of complacency, misleading intelligence, arrogance and contempt consistently resulted in the under-estimation of Mahdiist capabilities. 'Although our sacrifice has been severe', Graham wrote, 'I am convinced that the complete repulse and heavy loss which the enemy has sustained . . . will prove to have produced an impression which will definitely facilitate my future operations.'

Osman Digna could be excused for seeing the affair of McNeill's Zeriba in a different light. He had out-generalled and inflicted heavy casualities on a force equipped with weapons far superior to his own, including machine-guns. Whether or not the results had 'produced an impression' on him, whether or not he had 'received a severe lesson', within a week he was attacking a column of Guards and Marines out in the open and was boldly harrassing the perimeters of Graham's army four miles from Suakim.

In Britain the engagement at Tofrek was refought in Parliament, press and military mess. In the official history of the Corps of Royal Engineers, a regiment which suffered heavily in the action and, ironically, Graham's own, Major-General Whitworth Porter was to call the day's doings 'this disastrous affair'.

Such errant military voices were rare, however. McNeill, admittedly, was retired from service very swiftly, but he was strongly supported by his friend Graham, and enjoyed the patronage of his sovereign who employed him as an equerry. To the Queen's private secretary, McNeill wrote: 'I believe myself that I have had the fight of the season'. Graham, decorated with the Grand Cross of St Michael and St George after the Suakim campaign, was sustained in his approval of McNeill by Wolseley. In the *London Gazette* in August 1885 Graham fiercely deprecated the sharp criticisms of his infantry brigade commander. Piece by piece, by argument, excuse and omission, the Generals restored the integrity of McNeill's Zeriba.

# Chapter 8

# 'Indelible disgrace'

On the morning of Monday, February 18 1884, Gordon stepped ashore at the landing stage in front of the Governor's Palace at Khartoum to an exuberant reception. The crowd surged forward to kiss his hands and feet. The actor in Gordon rose to the occasion. He had a huge bonfire lit in front of the palace, in which he burned whips and other instruments of punishment — the symbols of misrule; records of outstanding tax debts were thrown on the flames; prisoners were set free from their cells. In a speech he declared: 'I come without soldiers but with God on my side'.

Without soldiers? On hearing the news two important religious and tribal leaders in the vicinity of Khartoum went over to the Mahdiist cause.

Ohrwalder, summing up with the hindsight of years, believed the people of Khartoum thought Gordon was the precursor of a British expedition. In the week of his arrival the city was excited by news of troops going to Suakim. Had the people not believed the English were coming they would have fled, wrote Ohrwalder. His indictment goes further: had Gordon not been sent then undoubtedly the evacuation originally ordered could have been carried out without difficulty. 'Those who escaped the massacre in Khartoum have often told me that they were perfectly ready to leave, and it was only Gordon's arrival that kept them back.' The imputation is harsh but clear: Gordon's coming contributed to the massacre that followed.

Gordon sent a blithe message down to Cairo by letter: Khartoum was as safe as Cairo or Kensington Park. In the end, he held, Britain would shoulder the responsibility for the security of the garrisons. He could not know, and subsequently was never told, of a declaration made in Parliament by Lord Hartington on behalf of the government on February 19, the day after Gordon's triumphant entry into Khartoum: 'I contend that we are not responsible for the rescue or relief of the garrisons either in the western or the southern or the eastern Sudan.'

The telegrams flowed down the line to Cairo, so many that Baring sometimes held them up in batches before passing Gordon's views on to London. Some arrived at the Foreign Office out of sequence, which, coupled with Gordon's natural inconsistencies and habit of 'thinking on paper', compounded the confusions and doubts in ministers' minds. In one of his Journal entries Gordon reflected: 'I wonder what the telegrams about the Sudan have cost Her Majesty's Government?'. At the same time he wrote: 'I own to having been very insubordinate to Her Majesty's Government and its officers, but it is my nature, and I cannot help it . . . I know if *I* was chief I could never employ *myself*, for I am incorrigible. To men like Dilke, who weigh every word, I must be *perfect poison.'*

Some of the telegrams concerned the arrangements to send down women, children and officials; one mentioned 1,800 troops who would need quartering arrangements made at Korosko. But Gordon was under pressure now from those around him to retain the soldiers in Khartoum; the city's difficulties were growing, sheikhs in the neighbourhood were defecting, the Mahdi was hemming in the outposts on the Blue Nile, the proclamation of abandonment was having its effect on the riverine tribes below Khartoum. To Gordon it was becoming clear that defence would have to take priority over evacuation.

In truth, Gordon's influence over the Sudanese, even at its height, was less than he or the British public realised. Indeed, as far as many of the Nile valley tribes were concerned, there could not have been a worse choice than Gordon to send on a mission of evacuation which demanded peaceful response and co-operation along the route to safety. Among the riverine people there were old scores to settle with Gordon.

Towards the end of the 1870s when Gordon, as Governor-General, was fighting to suppress the rebellion of Zebehr's son, Suliman, he ordered ruthless measures aimed not only at the dissidents but at the heart of the slave trade. The target was a host of itinerant soldier-traders known as 'jallaba' who came principally from the river tribes of the Jaalin, Dongolawi and Shagiyeh. Their business in Kordofan and Darfur was the supply of arms and ammunition to Suliman in exchange for slaves. Finding it impossible to check them because of their large numbers and the vastness of the territory in which they operated, Gordon ordered the 'jallaba' to evacuate all districts south of a certain line. When they ignored the order, Gordon instructed the sheikhs of the indigenous nomad tribes, camel and horse-riding warriors, to expel them under pain of harsh punishment. The nomads, in spite of their commercial interests, seized with delight the opportunity to attack, plunder and slaughter the 'jallaba', whom they detested and despised as exploiting leeches from the river lowlands. The Jaalin traders, in particular, were mercilessly hunted down as if by official warrant. Among their warlike kinsfolk on the river a deep legacy of hatred was stored up for Gordon, especially among the prosperous middle-class and sheikhs who exerted influence below Khartoum.

To Gordon, the continuing absence of government consent to his request for Zebehr's assistance must have seemed blindly unreasonable, knowing as he did that the old slave-trader commanded respect among his own Jaalin. He kept up the telegraphic pressure about Zebehr, but now he was preoccupied with an upsurge of Mahdiist activity as the rebels' resolution stiffened following news of General Graham's appearance in the eastern Sudan. Principally, Gordon's counter-measures consisted of an armed steamer expedition up the White Nile, under a white flag, in which not a shot was fired. Nevertheless, the telegram barrage with which it coincided on one day — Tuesday, February 26 — had momentous consequences in Britain.

The first telegram of the morning from Gordon told Baring he was now 'sending out forces to show our force'; it added that 400 sick soldiers would go downriver that day and widows and orphans on the next day. London did not receive from Baring the last piece of information — nor did Baring transmit a further message about the commencement of 'paper warfare by emissaries' into the Mahdi's country. London did receive, however, yet another telegraphed message from Gordon, saying: 'Expedition starts at once to attack rebels in the vicinity . . . '.

There was more to come. Gordon cheerfully telegraphed the gist of a proclamation in Arabic which he issued on that day. It included the phrase that 'the troops of the British Government are now on their way and in few days will be at Khartoum'. Bluff? A misunderstanding in translation (one of Gordon's failings was his lack of command of Arabic)? Wishful thinking about Graham who was only 250 miles away from Berber? Whatever the reason for the statement it caused Dilke to fume about 'this amazing lie'.

It was in the course of preparing and despatching these various messages that Gordon received a shattering blow in a telegram from Granville: ' . . . the public opinion of this country would not tolerate the appointment of Zebehr Pasha'. It prompted from him the most potentially explosive telegram of the day. His staccato, telegraphic response did not try to hide the disappointment and anger he felt: 'That settles the question for me . . . If Egypt is to be quiet, Mahdi must be smashed up. Mahdi is most unpopular, and with care and time could be smashed . . . If you decide on smashing Mahdi, then send up another £100,000 and send up 200 Indian troops to Wady Halfa . . . I repeat that evacuation is possible, but you will feel the effect in Egypt, and will be forced to enter into a far more serious affair in order to guard Egypt. At present it would be comparatively easy to destroy Mahdi.'

The phrases *'to attack rebels'* and *'Mahdi must be smashed up'* fell like a bombshell on the Cabinet — 'Gordon frightened us out of our senses', observed Dilke. And later in his memoirs he wrote: 'Gordon, having heard that Zebehr was refused, telegraphed his policy of smashing up the Mahdi . . . We were dealing with a wild man under the influence of that climate of Central Africa which acts upon the sanest man like strong drink.' Apparently lost on Dilke was an irony that should have been obvious. In the week of Gordon's bombshell a British army was endeavouring precisely to smash up the Mahdi at El Teb.

The sheer volume of telegraphic verbiage from Gordon on that day meant that some of his more pacific statements and intentions were overlooked. But at the same time, the tremors of alarms he caused also set loose the first thoughts of a relief expedition, for the British public was becoming increasingly aware of the ring closing around him. On March 11 Gordon wrote to his sister informing her that 'the tribes have risen' between the capital and Berber. On the same day London sent its final, categorical No on the subject of Zebehr. Twenty-four hours later Arabs at Halfaya, on the Nile a dozen miles from Khartoum, cut the telegraph wire; all messages henceforth would have to be smuggled by camel riders or travel by armed steamer.

One message to Gordon failed to get down the line before it was cut: it was London's refusal to send Graham's troops from Suakim to Berber. 'Gordon is in danger. You are bound to save him',

Queen Victoria telegraphed Hartington. 'Surely Indian troops might go from Aden. They could bear the climate. You have incurred fearful responsibility.' Hartington replied that the sending of Indian troops was not possible, Khartoum had provisions for six months and could not be taken frontally; any troops would be better sent in the autumn.

In Cairo, Baring was told that the government left entirely to Gordon the discretion to remain in Khartoum 'if he thinks necessary, or to retire by the southern or any route which may be available'. Baring despatched the cold words to Gordon by messenger, but only after pondering over them for some time (Gordon never received the message). In indignation the government's representative in Cairo lectured London: ' . . . it appears to me that it is our bounden duty, both as a matter of humanity and policy, not to abandon him'. The Queen read the telegram and declared: 'If not for humanity's sake, for the honour of the Government and the nation, he must not be abandoned'. Gladstone dug in his heels, belittled the dangers surrounding Gordon, and faced Cabinet pressures both for and against a military expedition.

In the second week of March one message got through to Khartoum. It was to tell Gordon of the government's intention not to send troops. He wrote to Baring explaining that if he could not hold out and suppress the rebellion he would retire to Equatoria 'and leave you the indelible disgrace of abandoning the garrisons . . . '. Strong words. And wild schemes. He informed Baring that he had asked Sir Samuel Baker to appeal to British and American millionaires to raise a £300,000 fund to provide 3,000 Turkish soldiers for the Sudan. He drafted further requests to the Pope and the European powers to send Turks. In April Frank Le Poer Power, a 26-year-old Irishman who was acting British Consul in Khartoum and a *Times* correspondent, sent out a despatch which said that the city was 'the centre of an enormous rebel camp'. Earlier despatches from Power had engendered apprehension in the British public and wrath in Gladstone. The Prime Minister indulged in a war of semantics; Gordon was not 'surrounded' but 'hemmed in'; there was 'no military or other danger threatening Khartoum', he told the Commons. John Morley's view was that 'people were tired of Gordon'.

Then, on May 1, Gordon's thrust about 'indelible disgrace' struck home. The message in which the phrase was contained was published in a government Blue Book which revealed recent correspondence in the affair. Meetings demanding a relief expedition were held up and down the land. Society woman vied with each other to see who could raise the most for a Gordon Rescue Fund. Gladstone was hissed when he went to a health exhibition at South Kensington.

Within two weeks the old fox was fighting back against a vote of censure in Parliament: an expedition would involve 'a war of conquest against a people struggling, and rightly struggling, to be free.' Gordon in Khartoum was struggling with the problems of feeding the city, strengthening its defences and dealing with fresh defections, new encroachments. On May 26 Berber fell in a welter of bloodshed. Gordon's river lifeline was blocked. In the censure debate on May 14, however, Hartington had held out a gleam of hope of a relief expedition at an unspecified date. Perhaps in the autumn, MPs believed. The fall of Berber heightened the speculation, and increased the pressure on Gladstone.

The months of June and July brought a lull in political and parliamentary activity, however. Little was heard from Gordon. But on July 30 he sent off a messenger with a letter to Baring saying: 'You ask me "to state cause and intention of staying in Khartoum, knowing government means to abandon Sudan", and in reply I say "I stay at Khartoum because Arabs have shut us up and will not let us out".' A day later Hartington moved into unwonted action. The normally easy-going leader of the Whig faction in the Liberal Party was threatening his resignation. Gladstone could not risk his government toppling. He agreed personally to propose a parliamentary grant of money — £300,000 — for a relief expedition. He did so on August 5. Gladstone half-heartedly hinted that this was only a contingency, but the expedition plans, with Wolseley directing them, had a momentum of their own (Hartington later wrily told Dilke that by September 1 he had already spent £750,000 of the £300,000). The Gordon relief expedition was a reality.

In the months ahead Gordon's role become lonelier. On September 8 he sent Stewart and Power down the river with a group of people who wanted to leave the city. They sailed in the steamer *Abbas* safely past Mahdiist Berber, but the ship struck a rock not two days' voyage from Dongola. All aboard were murdered. Inexplicably, Gordon had sent with Stewart his official ciphers by which coded messages were translated. He hinted in his journals that he wanted to prevent them ending in the Mahdi's hands if Khartoum fell (he knew nothing of the relief expedition when the *Abbas* sailed). Without the ciphers he was unable to read any coded communications which he received. The suspicion remains that Gordon, waiting for the end, wished to shut his ears to voices from the outside world. His bitterness was apparent. In his last letter to his friend, Sir Charles Watson he wrote: 'I will accept *nothing whatsoever* from Gladstone's government . . . I will never set foot in England again, but will (*D.V.*, if I get out) go to Brussels and to Congo).'

An interlude of high farce, never far behind the tragedy of the Gordon affair, now intrudes into the swift-moving events. The scene changes from beleaguered Khartoum in the blistering, oppressive heat of a September morning to breakfast in the Scottish baronial elegance of the dining room at Brechin Castle in cool and verdent Angus. The Prime Minister, a guest of the Earl of Dalhousie during a triumphant tour of Scotland, is reading the morning's copy of the *Dundee Advertiser*, the local Liberal newspaper, and draws much satisfaction from column after column of prose describing the enthusiastic reception he received on the previous day. Suddenly, all is changed as he turns to a column of news from Khartoum.

A fellow guest, a Mr G.W. Smalley, has left us an eye-witness account: 'As he read his face hardened and whitened, his eyes burned as I have seen them once or twice in the House of Commons when he was angered — burned with a deep fire as if they would have consumed the paper on which Gordon's message was printed . . . Then he rose and left the room and was seen no more that morning.'

What Gladstone had read was a garbled Dundee version of a garbled Cairo version of a message from Gordon. It told of a plan to send a steamer to burn Berber. Gordon appeared also to be asking for *200,000* Turkish troops. Gordon's original request, it will be recalled, was for £300,000 to pay for 3,000 Turks; he had apparently scaled this down to £200,000 for 2,000 Turks. The cost of the contingent had been confused with its numbers. Gladstone obviously shared the alarm of the *Dundee Advertiser's* good Liberal editor who saw Gordon 'careering up and down the Nile, crying for the blood of the Mahdi, and burning towns and slaying rebels to his heart's content'.

Gladstone lost no time in contacting Granville, who told Baring that Gordon was to be placed under Wolseley's orders and reduced from Governor-General to Governor of Khartoum. The Khedive's version — in Arabic — of these instructions reached Khartoum more than two months later. In the translation Gordon missed the meaning entirely.

# Chapter 9

# *Wolseley's obsession*

Displaying a bitterness that characterised the feelings engendered at all levels by the Gordon affair, Edwin Egerton, Britain's acting minister in Cairo while Baring was in London discussing Egypt's finances, wrote to a friend on August 31 1884, in denunciation of 'the infernal plan of those Red River men'. It is evidence of the idiosyncracies of 1884 that a river half a world away in distance and a minor military campaign half a generation earlier in time should become an obsessive interest governing decisions on how to rescue Gordon from Khartoum.

The success Wolseley had achieved in his first independent command, in Manitoba, Canada, in 1870, he was now confident he could repeat in a vastly different set of circumstances in the Sudan. His experience in the Red River campaign ruled his strategical planning in what John Morley called 'the battle of the routes', a battle that was fought among Generals and politicians for three to four months even before the British government sanctioned money for a possible expedition on August 5. Wolseley won this first 'battle', but his Red River obsession added delay to delay until his dreams of triumph in the realities of the Nile's cataracts.

There were two obvious route options open to a Gordon relief expedition. One was overland from Suakim on the Red Sea coast, a distance of 280 miles to Berber and thence a further 200 miles up the Nile to Khartoum. The other was the river route, 1,650 miles from Cairo. In the end, the river men's counsel was favoured only after debate that lasted a further two weeks beyond the August vote of finance, and the controversy boiled up afresh in the wake of failure. 'It may, however, fairly be said that, in the history of the world, no expedition has ever been pushed continuously forward with utmost exertion, 1,500 miles into the interior of a country in which accurate information could not be obtained as to the movements of a numerous and fearless enemy, and which was almost devoid of supplies of every sort', wrote Reginald Wingate, who observed affairs with an intelligence officer's eye. The British soldier, he also remarked, 'did a service which has at present no parallel'. Magnificent and unique though the effort was, costly though the sacrifices were, the British soldier came too late. The river route led him to failure.

The case for the overland route was fiercely advocated by General Sir Frederick Stephenson, the Army's man in Cairo commanding the British garrison in Egypt. It was not without glee that his adversaries pointed out that it was precisely Stephenson's own lack of enthusiasm which had prevented General Gerald Graham sending a flying column from the Red Sea coast to Berber in March after the British victories of El Teb and Tamai; Graham was eagerly pressed to detach troops for the task by a dashing cavalryman, Sir Herbert Stewart, who was later to die in the Bayuda desert. Graham said he always regretted not acting on his own initiative and sending troops through to the Nile before he was ordered to withdraw from Suakim in the spring.

Nevertheless, in the late summer of 1884 the port was an enclave where the Khedive's writ still held and it could be reached easily and quickly by troops from the United Kingdom and India. Stephenson argued that the river plan had little hope of success in the time available. He was supported by the advice of a naval team which, under Commander Hammill of the *Monarch*, had spent weeks surveying the Nile. Progress upstream through rock-strewn cataracts and with the river falling would be fatally slow, warned the sailors. The view was backed by others in Cairo, both British and Egyptian.

Gladstone, albeit distinctly unenthusiastic about *any* expedition, was another opponent of the Nile route, if we are to believe the sentiments he expressed in a letter to Queen Victoria on February 5 1885, the day the dreadful news of Gordon's death reached Britain: 'The balance of testimony and authority was decidedly against him [Wolseley], and the idea of the Suakim and Berber route . . . was entertained in preference.'

Against the overland route was the strong argument that the 280 miles of desert lacked adequate wells to water a large force. Moreover, in the wake of Britain's withdrawal of its main forces from the Suakim hinterland in the spring, Osman Digna's star was bright among the warlike tribes of the Red Sea hills. His redoubtable Hadendowa were in alliance with the Amarar, which was not always the case, and united they presented a formidable threat on the road to Berber. Then, on May 26, Berber, the key to Khartoum, fell to the Mahdiists, securely isolating Gordon and establishing a strong obstacle in the path of any British advance.

Wolseley argued that British troops debouching on the Nile from the eastern deserts would have to face an enemy given ample warning of their coming and with time to mass. As Berber dominated the Nile, however, the same problem would have been met by a river-borne expedition. In the event, four months were consumed by Wolseley's river haul and its climax, the Camel Corps' 'march of the forlorn hope' across the Bayuda desert. In 1883 Hicks Pasha, admittedly amid totally different circumstances and against no opposition, travelled from Suakim to Berber in less than three weeks, and from Berber to Khartoum in five days. 'There was no element of chance in the success of the expedition to relieve General Gordon. It was sanctioned too late', declared Wingate catergorically. History must argue with his judgement in one respect. The Nile route was doomed to failure because it was too slow. In the light of hindsight and the knowledge that Gordon's time was so short, the Suakim route offered the only hope there was.

As the debate over the routes raged in Whitehall and Cairo through the summer and into the autumn, the public at large joined in the great 'Save-General-Gordon' game of armchair strategy, led by retired senior officers. 'Volunteer', in a letter to the *Pall Mall Gazette*, warned Wolseley to take an adequate supply of lifebelts up the Nile. An 'experienced desert traveller' advised the same correspondence columns that water problems were no different with camels from those experienced with horses, and exposed the myth of a camel's being a walking water storage tank.

An ingenious and meticulously detailed project to beat the water shortage on the Berber land route was expounded in a letter of inordinate length in *The Times*. It came from Rear Admiral W.F. Ruxton, of Cornwall Gardens, Kensington, London, who believed that in an expedition from Suakim some 3,000 troops could dispense entirely with water-consuming transport animals by drawing carts across the desert themselves. No ordinary carts, these would be constructed of oblong frames consisting of hollow steel tubes capable of containing all the water needed to last from well to well. When pressed, the British Tommy could survive on half a gallon of water a day. He was to be assisted in his overland trek by Zanzibaris and Somalis, specially recruited for the task, it seemed, for their low susceptibility to thirst, and kept in order by gang leaders armed with ten-foot pikes. The carts would not only provide shelter at night but would make 'an admirable defence'. These wheeled ships of the desert, advised the Admiral, should be named by each regiment—'Esprit de corps should be encouraged. The black man soon shares in that.' Once the Cart Corps had opened the route, 'a few stone towers near the wells, a little money and a gallows or two will keep it open'. The Admiral had thought of everything: 'I am aware of the great objection in making the British soldier draw anything but his rations. But he should be paid threepence per hour whilst actually dragging.'

There were other, official, blandishments to help persuade Wolseley to budge from his river route, some of them only a little less unusual than Rear Admiral Ruxton's. One was the promise of a railway to be built from Suakim to Berber. The plan appeared to take little account of the possible reactions of Osman Digna, but for a short time its prospect had Wolseley wavering in favour of the overland route. He quickly cast it from his mind, however, when first work on the railway was put back to June and then the fall of Berber caused all notions of the rail link to be abandoned.

Wolseley painted a beguiling picture of his expedition sailing up the Nile, untroubled about water or food supplies, cool under canvas awnings, unmolested by hostile tribes. He belittled the obstacles to navigation up the cataracts and he stressed the huge logistic problems of collecting sufficient camels for a desert crossing. On this last point his warning was prophetic: when, after hurriedly re-writing his strategy to take in plans for a desert crossing of the Bayuda by the Camel Corps, the camels that were gathered were too few.

In psychological jargon, Wolseley was engaging in 'positive transfer', which should normally have a beneficial effect on the outcome of a commander's actions. Dr Norman Dixon, Reader in Psychology at University College, London, in his work *On the Psychology of Military Incompetence*, defines 'positive transfer' as that which happens when something learned in a situation is utilised successfully in some subsequent, similar situation. In reliving his Red River experience, however, Wolseley fell into perilous ground. Commanders sometimes fail, as Dixon points out, through a tendency to reject or ignore information which is unpalatable or which conflicts with preconceptions. The preconception that deluded Wolseley was that the challenge he successfully met in the suppression of the Red River rebellion was identical to the one that now faced him in his attempt to relieve Gordon.

In the Red River valley, the deep heartland of Manitoba, the eccentric Louis Riel led a rebellion of half-breed fur trappers who believed they were being 'sold out' by a deal between the Hudson Bay Company and the Canadian government. Fenian influences and threatened American incursion stirred Imperial anxiety. Riel's declaration of autonomy would have to be crushed in the bud. Colonel Wolseley commanded an expedition that was sent, successfully, to quell the outbreak.

It travelled 1,200 miles from base by way of Lake Superior to Fort Garry (near present-day Winnipeg), the last 550-mile stretch being by small boats up dangerous rapids and over rugged portages. Unlike the Sudan, Manitoba was a wilderness of forests which provided fuel for burning on those parts of the journey navigated by steamer, and ample material to use as leverage and hauling tackle where boats had to be manhandled through shallows and portages. On the Red River, local help was available from large numbers of experienced Canadian voyageurs, riverwise Indians, and loyal Fort Garry people who came downriver in their own boats to meet the soldiers. In the woods there was little, if any, risk of attack on the river route. In the desert, for the last 500 miles at least, the projected Nile expedition would have to pass through territory peopled by tribes under the Mahdi's sway. In 1870 Wolseley moved 1,200 troops to confront, at the most, 500 discontented backwoodsmen, and the operation ended in a bloodless victory with the rebel leaders running away as the British arrived. In 1884-85 his task was to deploy an army of 7,000 against an enemy consisting of tens of thousands of battle-hardened fanatics dedicated to the philosophy of jehad, and the operation was quite likely to, and did, culminate in bloody battles and heavy losses.

Wolseley's Red River campaign was, incontestably, a triumph. Almost the only blood spilled was in brawls that took place during an epic three-day binge when soldiers, voyageurs and Indians — rigorously kept 'dry' by Wolseley during their long journey — broke loose on the saloons of Fort Garry. (Significantly, Wolseley, not a teetotaller by habit, repeated his 'no drink' order on the Nile expedition, giving rise afresh to the old soldiers' Red River jibe about the 'teapot General', but earning him approbation from an unexpected quarter, the non-conformist lobbyists whose other major passion, the anti-war cause, seldom put them in tune with the General.)

The commander was justifiably proud of having brought peace to the Red River area by not firing one shot and of having completed an expedition of 1,200 miles by a feat of mathematical precision. His soldiers were less happy about being robbed of a good fight at the end of weeks of back-breaking slog. Among them, a burly young Lieutenant who had wielded axe and paddle with as much gusto as the best, the bullish Redvers Buller, complained that he was 'disgusted at having come so far to hear the band play "God save the Queen"'. Wolseley, never short on self esteem, bathed in the praise showered on him by the citizens of eastern Canada. Although he came home to a knighthood, however, his Canadian achievements raised hardly a ripple in the British press, which was totally obsessed with the cataclysmic happenings of the Franco-Prussian War on England's doorstep. The lack of attention rankled with him. After 14 years the Sudan crisis presented him with an opportunity to recoup the triumphs of the Red River. He went to some astonishing lengths to do this.

# Chapter 10

# *A disjointing of noses*

Wolseley fought his 'battle of the routes' from his Adjutant-General's desk and won it by the time he was given command of the expedition, a process of decision which itself was the cause of much rancour. His strongest supporter was Lord Hartington, the War Minister, whose threat to resign had nudged an obstinate Gladstone towards the vote of credit on August 5 that made an expedition possible. Hartington thought that Stephenson, who had declared himself opposed to the Nile route, could hardly be asked to command the force that was to go by that way. It speaks much for the new-found resolution of the normally limp and easy-going Hartington that, within just over a month of the parliamentary vote, not only was the expedition a reality, but his nominee, Wolseley, was in Cairo at its head.

Hartington's diligence in advocacy of Wolseley surprised many who came into contact with him, not the least the Queen and the Prime Minister. Tart telegrams were exchanged between Victoria, her cousin and Commander-in-Chief of the Army, the Duke of Cambridge, and the unwontedly active War Minister. Victoria resented the popular demand of sending for 'our only General' and feared for the effect it would have on the army's morale. 'The despatch of the Adjutant-General to a distant command' was deplored by the Queen. It can be likened in modern business terms to appointing the managing director of a multi-national company to head a sales push in an emergent country.

The Queen's secretary, Sir Henry Ponsonby, had a personal opinion of Hartington which reflected that of his employer: '. . . has talent and tact but terrible idleness. . .he takes things very easy indeed.' Because of his tendency to talk 'a great deal at dinner. . . he was rather set down as a bore. He didn't know where and when to stop'. This lackadaisical, waffling social disaster,

Hartington, was now setting the pace.

Hartington had held a loaded revolver to the government in the shape of his threatened resignation. Gladstone must have felt the threat was still there in Hartington's insistence that Wolseley was the man for the job. It was anathema to Gladstone to sanction the appointment of a General whose thirst for military glory and admiration for Gordon (Wolseley regarded himself 'not worthy to pipe-clay Gordon's belt') were such that a rescue expedition under his command might easily lead to attempted reconquest of the Sudan. Radicals such as Sir Charles Dilke and Joseph Chamberlain, each equally detested by Wolseley, shared their leader's distrust, but they had little say in the matter.

The reactionary Cambridge was peeved at being robbed of his Adjutant-General, but was forced to submit to the appointment when the Queen herself gave way in the face of Gladstone's reluctant sanction. However, Cambridge fought a spiteful rearguard action; he sniped at the Adjutant-General's habit of gathering around him old cronies, known as 'the Wolseley Ring', and succeeded in blocking the appointment of some officers. Negotiating with Cambridge by coaxing, flattering and terrifying him, Wolseley remarked, was like 'dealing with some naughty little girl or some foolish old woman'. Wolseley could hardly guess how true his words were: the Duke was to reserve his most violent tantrum for his reaction when Wolseley sprang upon him a revolutionary plan for a Camel Corps drawn from élite regiments.

On November 15, 1884, *Punch* published a topical cartoon entitled, 'Against Stream; or, The Political Nile Passage'. It depicted desperate attempts to haul the steamer of the government's Franchise Bill through the cataracts of the opposition, a course of the most fearful obstructions. Those in command of the operation were shown in a state bordering on hysteria, bawling advice and conflicting orders. The general impression was one of chaos and an enterprise in which the main participants were at loggerheads with each other. Few readers of *Punch*, or even the artist, Harry Furniss, and the editorial staff themselves, could have known that the cartoon came devilishly near to the true state of military affairs on the River Nile in the closing months of 1884.

Nevertheless, the cartoon's apparently lunatic combination of superhuman effort and the political manipulation represented by ropes and pulleys appeared, on closer examination, marginally capable of getting the craft through the rapids; thus Wolseley's logistic genius — and only he in all Britain could have devised and conducted a military expedition that travelled further than any since Napoleon's march to Moscow — succeeded against all odds in transporting an army and an immense amount of supplies to the borders of the Mahdi's domain in the deserts of the Sudan. Part of the final tragedy, however, must be ascribed to the discord, resentment and jealousies engendered within the upper ranks by the manner in which the command structure was established. These antipathies inevitably caused misunderstandings, breakdowns in communication and serious mistakes that debilitated the strike force and compounded the failure of the expedition.

Prominant in 'the Wolseley Ring' were four names: Buller, Brackenbury, Stewart and Butler. Imported into Egypt by Wolseley, each of these men was given an important role with the expedition. In Cairo — where Stephenson had to be content with command of troops north of Assiut, nearly 1,000 miles from the seat of action — these and other appointments fostered resentment summed up by one garrison officer as 'a disjointing of all our noses here'. The rivalries crystalised in some bitter personal feuds and, worse, in the creation of virtually two armies — the Wolseley Ring, pressing south up river, and the disgruntled Cairo faction on which the former depended for forwarding of supplies, men and animals.

There was an immediate clash over the appointment of the two Generals, Earle and Buller. The Duke of Cambridge had argued for a senior role for Major-General William Earle, who was the Alexandria garrison commander. He wanted him to command troops going to Dongola in the Sudan. This caravan crossroads on the Nile above the third cataract held a charismatic appeal for both Generals and politicians alike. It was almost as though they hoped or half-believed that the placing of a British army there might somehow solve the problem of Khartoum, some 300 miles away as the crow flies and many, many more by river and desert route.

Earle was 51, born in the same year as both Wolseley and Gordon, and senior in rank to Buller. Wolseley, grumbling about 'the sentiments of personal vanity and ambition of the few superior officers in Egypt', riposted through Hartington that the expedition would come to grief if 'ordinary parade officers' were appointed. It would be folly to appoint an 'unknown' like Earle instead of Buller, 'whose name is known to every bugler in the Army'.

That Sir Redvers Buller — 'Gentleman George' — was popular with and respected by the soldiers was beyond question. A brave and dashing officer, he was, in the words of Sir Henry Evelyn Wood (a leading member of the Cairo faction), 'careful of his men's lives, reckless of his own'. Later in Buller's career, Churchill was to assess him as: '. . . a characteristic British personality. He looked stolid. He said little and what he said was obscure. He was not the kind of man who could explain things, and he never tried to. . .he was regarded as a very sensible soldier.'

Buller, however, could be unnervingly eloquent in the written word, as he proved in a famous memorandum issued at Aldershot in 1899. The timing was the eve of the Boer War, a campaign that produced a catalogue of British disasters and the downfall of Buller, who proved a woefully inadequate commander-in-chief. Battles, he declared, were not won by 'jacks-in-boxes' who 'bob up, fire and bob down again', but by resolute, enthusiastic men who stayed on their feet; officers did not bob and such antics were to be discouraged in their men. Such military sentiments among the enemy were music to the ears of the Boers.

Buller loved a fight. In the 1882 Egypt campaign he wrote to his bride on the subject of war: 'I do believe that it is wicked and very brutal, but I can't help it; there is nothing in this world that so stirs me up as a fight'. Paradoxically, he had strong talents for administration. In command he was overly cautious and indecisive; these faults, coupled with his penchant for refusing to accept responsibility for the deeds of subordinates acting under his direction, were to contribute to the demolition of his reputation in South Africa. He was, on his own admission, unfitted for overall command in South Africa: 'I have always considered that I was better as second in a complex military affair than as an officer in chief command', he told Lord Lansdowne, who was Secretary for War in 1899.

On the Nile in 1884, however, Buller, aged 45, was serving as he had nearly always done, under Wolseley, and was one of the brightest jewels in the Ring. Wolseley was determined to see his protégé play a leading part.

Hartington, holding the balance between Cambridge, Wolseley and the Cairo command, found a compromise that seemed to satisfy the protagonists for the time being. Earle was to command the force to go south of Wady Halfa on the Egypt-Sudan border — 'Bloody Halfway' in the soldiers' vernacular — and Buller was to be Chief of Staff. The game was to get farthest south, and in the end Buller won. The irony in Buller's eagerness to be in at the fray was his professed contempt for the man they were trying to rescue, Charles George Gordon. 'The man was not worth the camels', Buller had remarked earlier that year when he was approached to support the idea of a freelance rescue expedition of soldiers and sportsmen. The undisciplined, troublesome and frugal mystic found no fellow feeling in Buller, a stout, red-faced hard liver with gruff manners, whose taste for champagne and rich food necessitated a personal baggage train of 40 camels on his journey up the Nile. His dinner parties were legendary in the expedition; they were always accompanied by gallons of champagne, in a force which was ostensibly 'dry'.

Immensely sociable and a good host, he nevertheless quarrelled with many of his fellow senior officers. He had furious rows with Evelyn Wood, as we shall see, and even grumbled openly about his mentor. He complained of being cut off from Wolseley for two months in Egypt and criticised the Commander-in-Chief's decision to use the Camel Corps in a thrust across the Bayuda desert, the very contingency for which it was formed. His own conduct was not inviolate from criticism, however, as he was soon about to prove by mishandling the supply of coal for the Nile steamers.

If Buller was a candidate for election as the most popular man in the Army, Colonel Henry Brackenbury appears to have been the most disliked officer. The potential chemistry for discord was surely intensified by the importation into Cairo of this Wolseley devotee, a morose and unfriendly man, as Deputy Adjutant and Quartermaster General. He was, however, a brilliant organiser and Wolseley recognised his worth, although irritated beyond measure by Brackenbury's character and appearance. 'Brack', Wolseley wrote home, 'has not improved in beauty. I think he has become yellower and certainly much uglier than ever. He has already the broad expanded figure of middle age [Brackenbury was 47], and as he grows older his legs seem to become shorter.' And in another letter: 'Brack's voice becomes deeper, his tail squarer, his legs shorter, his calves thicker, his hair thinner, his stomach larger and his complexion yellower every day'.

Sir Herbert Stewart was chosen by Wolseley, who regarded him as one of the finest staff officers in the Army and the 'best all-round soldier'. He knew how to use cavalry, and he quickly learned how to use the Camel Corps when, in the January of 1885, he led them across the Bayuda desert in a skilfully handled but tardy attempt to reach Gordon. A tall, elegant figure, he was instantly recognisable to his men, atop his camel, wearing a Guards helmet with distinctive pugaree of orange silk. Two days after the battle of Abu Klea in the desert he fell mortally wounded by a marksman's bullet and died in mid-February at Jakdul while being carried back to Korti by the retreating survivors of the march.

Stewart was capable of detachment bordering on insouciance, even in the midst of battle preparation or the worst adversity. At Korti on the Nile, late in 1884, when the Camel Corps was poised for its desert expedition and Stewart was beset by a host of logistical problems, a war correspondent found him poring over documents, engrossed in the minutiae of installing the new electric light in some houses he had bought in Sloane Street, Knightsbridge: buying, redesigning and converting houses was a passion with him. Even as he wrote his last letter to Wolseley, in great pain a few hours before his death in mid-February, he was cool enough to end it with a reference to some property he had advised his friend to buy: 'Kindest regards to Lady Wolseley. Tell her I am sure the houses will be a success in the end.'

Stewart, simply by the fact of his appointment to the most glamorous task of the enterprise — the flying column — became the target of many jealousies. The one who perhaps resented his preferment the most was Earle, whose original compromise role *south* of Wady Halfa was later changed to command *at* Wady Halfa, the plum Dongola job being given to Stewart.

The Wolseley Ring senior quartet was completed by Lieutenant-Colonel Sir William Butler, a romantic, inventive, loquacious and indiscreet Irishman who was undoubtedly one of the most eccentric of many eccentrics in the expedition. He was 46, had served as a scout under Wolseley in the Red River campaign, and was a passionate advocate of the river route. While the battle of the routes was being waged, he wrote a spirited justification of the river approach and contemptuously rejected the Navy's case, embodied in Commander Hamill's warnings about the Nile. 'I have not seen the Nile above Cairo and its neighbourhood', he admitted. But to him it was as simple as, 'Water is water, rock is rock, whether they be in America or in Africa'. Wolseley rewarded him with command of the boats on the Nile.

Stephenson and some in his circle, once resigned to the Nile route, advocated the use of native boats. Wolseley, however, supported an ambitious scheme for a fleet of specially built whalers to be made in the United Kingdom and shipped out to Alexandria. The planning, the organisation of 47 British firms to do the work, the production of 800 boats, the arrival in Egypt of the first 100 within one month of sanction and the despatch from Britain of the last 400 just over three weeks later was a feat to be marvelled at. Whatever was to come on the Nile, however, Wolseley's Red River obsession and his boats in particular met a rough passage from the press. Of 'that unfloatable flotilla for the Nile', the *Army and Navy Gazette* said, 'A more wicked waste of money was never perpetrated, a more silly quackery never devised. . .'.

The boats, which had to be sturdy enough to withstand the rapids and light enough to be carried by 12 men at the portages, averaged 30 feet in length. Each was self-contained, fitted to carry 6-7,000 lb of stores (as well as ammunition), sufficient to last the crew of 12 soldiers for 100 days. Specified stores in each craft were corned beef, fresh meat, bacon, biscuits, flour, preserved vegetables, rice, oatmeal, cheese, pickles, tea, jam and marmalade (the last two were 'sweets' included at Wolseley's insistence to compensate for alcohol deprivation among the men). 'Luxuries' included tobacco and soap, and lime juice was part of the specification. In the event, few boat crews enjoyed such varied fare, owing to a mix-up of supplies in Lower Egypt.

Colonel Butler scoured boatyards to find a model on which a prototype whaler could be based. When he found what he was looking for, he filled it with the specified amount of supplies and men, and tested it on the water in Portsmouth dockyard. It passed with flying colours, and inspired Butler to lyricise in his memoirs on a vision he had: 'It was of a great river flowing through a desert world, with buried temples and ruined tombs of forgotten kings standing at long intervals on the sand-swept wastes. And, sailing there I saw this frail boat, and scores of others like it, with sails and oars flashing in the sunlight, moving on through that immense land in the grandest effort our generation had seen — the saving of the noblest knight among us all.'

The first of the boats (which cost £75 each) were shipped by the first week in September. But even then, from Alexandria, the flotilla's destination, a correspondent was informing *The Times* readers on September 7: 'Singular unanimity appears to prevail in all circles in Cairo, military, civil, official and unofficial, regarding the expedition and is expressed in the two hopeless words, "TOO LATE"'.

Indeed, time was against every enterprise. Although the 'unfloatable flotilla' justified itself — few whalers were lost entirely while dozens of native boats were wrecked — delays were encountered in repairing damage, closing seams, drying out and replacing gear. The time taken to pass the fleet through the rapids was underestimated: a group of the Staffordshire Regiment, having negotiated the terrible Bab-el-Kebir, or second, cataract — known to the natives as the 'belly of stone' — then averaged less than 3½ miles a day for 11 days on a supposedly 'clear', between-cataracts, stretch of the river which was nevertheless termed in local lore 'womb of rocks'. Belly of stone, womb of rocks. . .the truth was that the Nile offered almost continuous rapids and the Generals deluded themselves by regarding it as a series of separate obstacles embodied in its six cataracts.

In Khartoum, Gordon wrote in his journal on September 17: 'I have the strongest suspicion that these tales of troops at Dongola and Merowe are all gas-works, and that if you wanted to find Her Majesty's forces you would have to go to Shepheard's Hotel in Cairo'.

While the boats were being prepared and shipped to Egypt, a search was going on, 4,000 miles from London, for a remarkable band of men to help handle them. To recreate his Red River triumph satisfactorily, Wolseley decreed that the expedition would require the services of the type of indigenous boatmen who had performed brilliantly in the Canadian backwoods, the voyageurs. The trouble was that, 14 years after the Red River campaign, the species was almost extinct in Canada with the development of railways. Within less than a month, however, 386 men — French-Canadians, half-breeds, Indians and others — were on their way to Egypt, having been recruited as voyageurs on a six-month engagement at the high pay of 40 dollars a month. But they were not the voyageurs of old. Many did not know how to handle boats: they included clerks, storekeepers, cowboys and even some professional men such as lawyers.

They left Canada under the command of a militia, or part-time, officer who was a Toronto alderman and lawyer. Insubordination was common among these civilians, and force sometimes had to be used to keep them away from the medical stores of alcohol. Oddly enough, and despite their partial complement of incompetents, the new-style voyageurs did a good job and were an asset to the expedition. The Wolseley whalers, they complained, were too weak, the rudders were too small and the keels were a handicap in the rapids.

Butler believed that the Navy — which had, after all, been virtually excluded from a major role by the Wolseley Ring — was grudgingly doing only what was necessary. He railed at the Cairo faction of the Army, accusing it of delaying the boats. At the same time he was bitterly jealous of Stewart and his promotion to Brigadier-General in the desert. He even had harsh words for his own men, the 'Wet Bobs'. He later said of their attitude: 'In its normal state it was lethargic; at its worst it was unwilling, careless and even worse. . .simply a clogged, lethargic "hand-down" attitude that was even more hopeless than the most insubordinate refusal'. And from his unenviable seat on the river he fired some critical buckshot at the lordly Camel Corps: 'all the swells are passing up to Korti by camel, too precious to trust themselves in boats apparently'.

Another officer, Sir Ian Hamilton, shared his view of 'the swells'. He noted that the boat soldiers suffered resentfully as 'this band of patricians' rode camels and enjoyed 'the toothsome jam, cheese and boiled mutton'. Hamilton ruefully added: 'My bleeding gums and loosened teeth taught me once and for all the advantages of belonging to the aristocracy'. On the privileged side of the fence among the 'swells', Lieutenant-Colonel Hugh McCalmont, second in command of the Light Camel Regiment, marvelled at the enthusiasm of his colleagues which was such that they acted as if they 'were going to fight the Battle of Waterloo over again'.

What of the 'disjointed noses' of the original garrison in Egypt?

Stephenson and Earle made the most of a bad job. In the closing stages of the campaign the latter found in the river column the action he had been seeking — and was shot dead when, against all warnings of the dangers, he ventured too near to a house full of enemy riflemen at the battle of Kirbekan.

There had been much deliberation over what to do with Major-General Sir Henry Evelyn Wood who had been Sirdar, or commander, of the Egyptian Army and therefore was a prominant member of the Cairo faction. He was outspoken and quarrelsome, a man, in Wolseley's judgement, of 'inordinate vanity'. As Sirdar, he adopted the picturesque Bedouin headgear with a circlet of black goat wool and gold thread to keep it in position, instead of the traditional fez. To him was given the important but unglamorous command of lines of communication south of Assiut.

Although Wolseley tried to keep the peace, Evelyn Wood and Buller quarrelled fiercely. Their main topic of dispute appeared to be whether priority should be given to men or supplies on the river. An argument between the two must have been interesting to watch and hear. Wolseley despaired of Wood's deafness and complained that a conversation with him had to be conducted in a roar. The difficulties were compounded when Wood met Buller, whose front teeth had been kicked in by a horse in China, leaving him with a semi-coherent lisp. Wolseley found Wood unmethodical, unenterprising and deskbound. Like Buller, Wood was the recipient of the Victoria Cross; Wood's was awarded in the Indian Mutiny, Buller's at Wood's own recommendation in South Africa. Like Buller, Wood lived well on campaign: his baggage train contained 96 cases of stores, nearly half of them being wine. 'He evidently intends being comfortable', commented one officer of the voyageurs. Alike in many respects, at loggerheads over their roles, Buller and Wood epitomised the tragedy of the two armies on the Nile.

Wolseley knew full well what was happening. After dinner in Cairo with Stephenson's chief-of-staff, James Charlemagne Dormer, he wrote: 'I wonder there was no arsenic in it, for I am sure he hates me because I have not included him in the list of those to go up the Nile'. He laboured to keep a balance between them warring factions, but it was far from easy. He might be forgiven for detecting a note of malicious glee when Admiral Hay came to tell him that the first steamer had been wrecked in an attempted passage of the Bab-el-Kebir cataract. Privately, Wolseley considered that the Navy's sailors 'were right good fellows at sea, and could, I have no doubt, haul an ironclad up a hill, but they have as much idea of working boats in rapid waters as my big boot has'.

His boot, it seems, could even be directed at his own nominees. Buller probably had some justification for suspecting in his Commander-in-Chief a coolness towards him. From Korti, Wolseley expressed the view that next time in the field he would, in preference to Buller, seek a Chief-of-Staff in Brackenbury who 'has far the longest head of any man out here, and although he is not liked personally, I cannot help that'. In another letter home he wrote of William Butler: 'He is becoming an impossible man for me. He has great natural ability, but no business values. I like him, but I think I shall have to drop him off my list.'

Some of the difficulties undoubtedly arose from the armour with which 'our only General' clothed himself, or at least from the way in which subordinates perceived him. They, aware of his dynamism, were often slow to make decisions; he, aware of others' shortcomings, was often loath to delegate. 'There are now serving under my command some regimental Lieut-Colonels who are entirely unfit for their positions . . . to the Brigadier or General under whose immediate orders they serve, these officers are a source of constant anxiety. Owing to their ignorance of the first principles of tactics or of the military art, it is always necessary for him, in order to avoid disaster, to keep them under his own personal observation, or to send some well-trained Staff Officer to take care of them', he wrote to Hartington in April 1885 when the army was completing its withdrawal from the upper Nile. His condemnation of what he termed 'manifestly incompetent' officers was part of a reiteration of his campaign for a system of promotion by merit rather than seniority in the British army — a campaign implacably resisted by the Duke of Cambridge.

The Duke, in his pique at Wolseley's Nile appointment and his subsequent choler over the formation of a Camel Corps, had been responsible for the inclusion of the expedition of an officer of archetypal incompetence. It arose, as these matters often do, in a round-about fashion. The Prince of Wales was eager to join the great adventure, but there was little Cambridge could do to meet his wishes in the face of blunt opposition from the Queen. He could, however, insist on the inclusion of two of the Prince's friends: Lord Charles Beresford, a naval officer of distinction who was to play a gallant role in the thrust to Khartoum; and Lieutenant-Colonel Stanley Clarke, who was a disaster.

Clarke had no experience of active service. In fact, he had been away from the army for six years when, following Cambridge's insistence, he was given command of the Light Camel Regiment. McCalmont of the 7th Hussars had been promised command and resented serving as number two under a man whose appointment he regarded as jobbery. He lobbied Wolseley in vain, even as late as the end of the year at Korti on the eve of the Camel Corps' Bayuda expedition. Clarke fulfilled McCalmont's and fellow-officers' misgivings. He lost many camels by allowing them to stray and not paying sufficient attention to their welfare; he was careless about water supplied. 'He is useless and a failure . . . he came to get a medal', Wolseley was to write — and he firmly refused to sanction a decoration for him when the campaign was over. Clarke packed his bags and returned to Britain in February 1885 while the army was still on the Nile.

There remain to be named two more members of this disparate officer corps of a campaign planned in controversy, launched in haste when it was already too late, and conducted in disharmony. One of Cambridge's deletions from the list of candidates was Colonel Frederick Gustavus Burnaby, a fearless, resourceful but dangerously independent Horse Guard who had been a prime mover in trying to mount a private expedition to rescue Gordon. Burnaby, however, made his own way to Egypt. In the field Wolseley gave him an important part to play with the Camel Corps; in that role he died with a spear through his neck in the Bayuda. And there was Colonel Sir Charles Wilson. Wolseley chose him to head his intelligence department, an appointment he would regret more than any other. In the shadow of failure and the recriminations that were to come, Wolseley's favour of Wilson would turn to hatred and contempt.

# Chapter 11

# *Circus on the Nile*

To be chosen for the Camel Corps was regarded as a hotly coveted military and social prize by the Army's officers. It was the stuff of high adventure and derring-do, a capital lark. 'One day in September, 1884, on coming off one of those numerous guards in Dublin that make a subaltern's life a burden to him, I found the joyful news awaiting me that I was to go out to the Sudan at once with the Camel Corps detachment of my battalion.' Thus begins the personal record of a 21-year-old Grenadier Guard, Lieutenant Count Gleichen, who penned his adventures in one of those many contemporary best-sellers on the Gordon affair, a rattling good yarn under a title that was irresistible for the Victorian public, *With the Camel Corps up the Nile.*

Wolseley sprang his revolutionary plan for a Camel Corps, made up of units drawn from several regiments, while he was at sea aboard HMS *Iris*, on his way to Egypt. Detachments varying in strength from 40 to 100 men would be taken from regiments at home — the Household Cavalry, 16 other cavalry regiments, foot guards, rifle regiments and marines; a further group of mounted infantry would be made up of troops already in Egypt (the force eventually totalled 86 officers and 1,600 men, divided into the Heavy, Light, Guards' and Mounted Infantry Camel Regiments).

When Wolseley's proposals reached London, the Duke of Cambridge exploded. He called the plan 'outrageous'. In his view it cut right across Army tradition and was damaging to regimental *esprit de corps.* How could units drawn from many regiments — likened by the press to ingredients in a salad dressing — pull together in a cohesive force? The 'principle is unsound' thundered Cambridge, and perhaps with some justification, for some of its officers were later to admit that the Camel Corps lacked a unifying *esprit* in action. But Wolseley's timing had been masterly. By sending his proposals from sea and joining them with the ultimatum that, without a flying column such as the Camel Corps, Gordon could not be relieved, he successfully short-circuited debate and quelled opposition. Wolseley found support among his allies in the government, and the Commander-in-Chief grudgingly gave way. To Cambridge's credit, however, once he was resigned to the idea of the Camel Corps, he put nothing in the way of speedy implementation of the plan. The Camel Corps embarked on September 26 amid a welter of newspaper cartoon comment depicting them riding bicycles, giraffes, zebras and weird hybrids of Africa.

Cambridge never ceased to fulminate about Wolseley's 'Nile circus'. Opposition politicians and newspaper commentators remarked on the 'social circus' aspect of the Camel Corps. Noble names abounded among those officers who accompanied the corps from Britain or subsequently joined it on the Nile — Lord Cochrane, Lord Rodney, Lord Arthur Somerset, Count Gleichen, Lord Airlie, Lord St Vincent, Lord Binning and a constellation of 'honourables'. The unfortunate inclusion of the Prince of Wales' friend, Stanley Clarke, has already been recorded. As a further sop, Wolseley included Cambridge's third son, Major Augustus Fitzgeorge of the 11th Hussars, an officer to whom the field commander referred as the 'diseased offspring' of the Duke. Many of these 'swells' had never fired a shot in anger and were inexperienced in active service; they exacted a fearful carnage from the Nile's crocodile population in pot shots from the banks as they travelled south. But no-one could doubt their eagerness for a fight or their courage when action finally came.

Typical of the young aristocrats was Albert Edward Gleichen, the son of Admiral Prince Victor of Hohenlohe-Langenburg. Gleichen went on to a distinguished career in the Egyptian and British Armies, commanded a division in the First World War, and reached the rank of Major-General. His account of the Camel Corps' journey, in which he shared his men's terrible sufferings in the Bayuda desert, was coloured by a resilient cheerfulness against all odds. He factually recorded the shortcomings of equipment and supplies but was seldom critical of superiors, displayed a respect for the camel, universally reviled by others, and even found good words to say for the flying column's staple and boring diet of tinned bully beef.

In the midday heat of the desert, he observed, bully beef floats in the tin as a red, warm, stringy mass, 'yet it has its period of beauty, in the early morning when the cold night has solidified it into respectable-looking cold beef; at that time a quarter of a pound of it inside you, washed down with hot drink, makes a great deal of difference in the way you are disposed to look at things on a dark and cold morning'.

There is at other times a touching innocence in the young subaltern's account. Of the encampment of the Camel Corps at the Pyramids after the first units arrived at Cairo on October 8, Gleichen wrote: 'The next report was that there wouldn't be room for us in Cairo, and we were to remain at the Pyramids under canvas for the next week or so'. The truth lies in War Office records which reveal that orders were given for the column to lodge in isolation at Giza to avoid the risk of venereal disease in the fleshpots of the capital.

Gleichen thought that the corps looked in their new uniforms more like 17th than 19th century soldiers, the bandoliers, breeches and stocking-like putties giving them an appearance of the English Civil War. The man wore red serge jumpers — or loose tunics, yellow-ochre cord breeches, dark blue putties, brown ankle boots and white pith helmets. Their arms and accoutrements included a rifle, held in a leather bucket attached to the saddle, sword-bayonet, bandolier for 50 cartridges, brown belt, frog and sling, haversack and water bottle. A valise contained a blue-grey serge jumper (invariably worn in the field in preference to the conspicuous red garment) drawers, cholera-belt, prayer book, housewife kit, spurs (which were never used), spare boots, shirts and socks. For protection against sand and dust there were goggles and a veil. Officers were dressed similarly, although they generally sported long field boots instead of putties; their arms were sword and revolver, attached to a brown leather belt with shoulder braces. In the accompanying dust cloud in the desert this camel-mounted host of 'the finest troops in the world', as Wolseley called them, predominantly blue-uniformed, and veiled, must have resembled the Touareg from distant deserts in North Africa.

Thus Wolseley completed the casting for his 'Nile circus' with the acquisition of the Camel Corps. It was to be the show-stopping climax, the grand military finale, the key that would unlock Khartoum. Its brilliant deployment as a flying column would bring the campaign to a successful conclusion and unite everybody in the opinion that, as of old, Britain's fortunes in foreign fields

**Above** *The Black Watch clear the rifle pits at El Teb, February 1884, in circumstances which earned them an unjustified reproof from General Graham. Sketch by Melton Prior, special artist of the* Illustrated London News *(National Army Museum).*

**Below** *The Camel Corps at a watering hole in the Bayuda — a sketch by an unknown participant of the relief expedition (National Army Museum).*

*Osman Digna's men stampede the camels at the 'disastrous affair' of McNeill's Zeriba — a contemporary Victorian view.*

**Above** *The desert column preparing for the final march to the Nile in January 1885. This Melton Prior sketch shows the mortally wounded General Stewart beneath an umbrella on the right* (National Army Museum).

**Below** *Building Gubat's defences; the village houses were eventually linked by breastworks of rubble. A Melton Prior sketch* (National Army Museum).

**Above** *Terence Cuneo's 'The Last Despatch' shows General Gordon handing his journal to the captain of the* Bordein *at Khartoum on December 14 1884. Tuti Island is in the background. The painting was commissioned by The Gordon Boys' School to celebrate its centenary in 1985 and is now in the collection of the Royal Engineers. Limited edition colour prints available from The Commandant, Postal Depot, Inglis Barracks, London NW7 1PX.*

**Below** *The Light Camel Regiment crossing the Bayuda desert, a watercolour by Orlando Norie* (Phillips).

were 'all Sir Garnet'.

The corps, made up of soldiers who were marksmen or good shots, was never intended to fight from camel-back, and never did so. It acted as mounted infantry, dismounting in action and fighting from foot after hobbling the camels. The riding camels and the baggage beasts, known as 'baggles', were needed for the long marches. The corps' opportunity came just after Christmas when it was clear to the Generals, urged to haste by the latest dire news from the beleaguered Gordon, that the delayed river column, stretched out over hundreds of miles of the Nile, would never raise the siege in time. The camels were to strike from Korti on the Nile, 180 miles across the empty Bayuda sands to Metemmeh on the Nile, where some of Gordon's steamers were known to be waiting for the final dash to Khartoum. While the infantry laboriously boated its way round the Nile loop that forms hereabouts a question mark on the map, the Camel Corps would remove any question of failure by a glorious overland thrust. It must have occurred to the defeated advocates of the Suakim-Berber route that Wolseley, arch-priest of the river route, had all the time meticulously planned for and was now throwing all on an overland strategy.

It failed, among other reasons, simply because the Army did not obtain enough camels. Their shortage turned what should have been a 'flying' column into a ponderously slow shuttle which signalled its coming as effectively as if Wolseley had sent an emissary to inform the Mahdi. No serious opposition was expected by the British. Forewarned, however, the Mahdi sent 10,000 of his best soldiers, marksmen, spearmen and Baggara horse. The empty Bayuda desert blossomed with the emirs' black, green and red battle flags and a host of white-robed tribesmen. Outnumbered eight to one, the Camel Corps had to fight what Churchill has described as the 'most savage and bloody action ever fought in the Sudan by British Troops'. And yet, a little over a week before this battle at Abu Klea on January 17 1885, Wolseley in a telegram to Hartington discounted 'absurd rumours that the desert is occupied by large hostile armies'.

# Chapter 12

# *Blunted bayonets*

When the main events of the Gordon affair had run their course — Gordon dead, Khartoum fallen, the relief expedition a failure — and a seemingly irrelevent military sideshow was about to begin in the eastern Sudan, Hartington in London on February 8 1885 ordered Stephenson in Cairo to arrange for the immediate purchase of camels needed in the new campaign at Suakim. It is said that when the Mudir, or Governor, of Dongola was asked if there was any prospect of good camels being supplied, he answered that he 'did not see why not as the English had already bought up all the bad ones'. The anecdote highlights two sources of woe in the relief campaign of 1884-85 — the supply of camels for the Nile expedition and the duplicity of the Mudir, one Mustapha Yawer, a former slave whose autocratic rule held sway in the northern Sudan athwart the British access route to Khartoum.

First, the camels. Misinformed in the early stages about the number that would be needed, Wolseley appears to have shown unwonted complacency when matters began to go wrong. The complacency was shared by Buller and those below him. Indeed, Buller's remark that Gordon wasn't worth the camels was more prophetic than he could have known. At first, only 1,200 camels were ordered; in the end, 8,000 were obtained instead of the 12,000 that were needed. Contrary orders to start and stop buying flew from department to department of the army on the Nile. The expedition received some animals which had taken part in the Suakim campaign of the previous March; they were worn out and past employment. The price rose steadily. Dealers offered useless, under-age camels and many were accepted by inexperienced Army purchasers.

Stephenson misled Wolseley by predicting that adequate

numbers of efficient saddles could be obtained in Egypt. It was not so. Of those found, many were of unseasoned wood. Saddles rested on the bones of the animals and harmed them. Thousands of camels were crippled by improper saddling and overwork.

Another problem was the shortage of grain. In the Bayuda, where two camels on average did the work of three, baggage-train deficiencies meant that only enough grain could be carried to allow two feeds per camel (later, there was no feed at all). The camels had to eat mimosa shoots and dry grass, but Gleichen remarked that a hundredweight would barely produce enough nourishment, and it was obviously impossible to allow the animals to graze over large areas.

In its initial thrust into the Bayuda the flying column of 1,100 men (later reinforced to 1,600) had only 2,200 camels. They were too few, resulting in back-and-forth supply marches which wasted time and allowed the Mahdi's forces to mass. Beresford blamed the lack of camels for the fatal delay. Wilson, the intelligence officer who commanded after Stewart's mortal wounding, declared that the shortage of camels was a principal factor in the expedition's failure. In February 1885, when new strategies were being considered by a government dazed by Gordon's death and the subsequent public outcry, another intelligence officer, Major Reginald Wingate, gave it as his considered opinion that: 'the complete breakdown of the camels and transport, owing to the very severe strain imposed on them in recent operations, rendered an advance on Berber out of the question'. Beyond any doubt, the shortage of camels was responsible for the deaths of British soldiers and brought the Camel Corps and its accompanying troops to the very lip of disaster.

The Mudir of Dongola — an appellation that might have come straight from the pages of a G.A. Henty novel — was seen by many senior commanders to be at the heart of not a few of the Army's supply troubles. He cheated on promises to supply camels, enforced extortionate bargains, and generally engendered mistrust in officers who came into contact with him. Mustapha Yawer was a Circassian who was imported into Egypt as a slave in his youth. He was sent to the Sudan by Khedive Ismail in 1864 and given the province of Dongola to govern as Mudir in 1877.

He was a devout Muslim whose religious zeal — coupled with the incontrovertible fact that he was at one time appointed the *Mahdi's* Mudir — was the cause of deep British suspicion. Wilson blamed him for the camel muddle (to which, it must be said, Wilson himself contributed by ordering purchasing to stop on October 11) and observed: 'If the Mudir had chosen there would have been no lack of transport, but he hated us, and was determined to ruin Gordon'. There may have been some truth in this, for Gordon, on his arrival in the Sudan in February 1884, removed Yawer from his post of Mudir; the Egyptians later reinstated him. Whatever his true loyalties, however, the Mudir threw in his lot with the Egyptian authorities and his irregulars' barbaric excursions among local tribes kept an effective if bloody state of order on the frontier as the British advanced.

The Mudir was rather short in stature. His face was fined down by fasting; his eyes were variously described as dreamy brown and piercing black, above a large prominent nose. He customarily wore a white camel felt cap, a cloak, white or black alpaca trousers, and elastic-sided leather boots. A powerful autocrat who ruled many of his subjects by terror, he nevertheless failed to present an imposing figure of oriental splendour to visitors. Frederic Villiers, the war artist/correspondent, went to Dongola — 'a straggling town of mud-and-plaster houses and half-ruined mosques' — and found the Mudir in a whitewashed building. The great man wore a fez and a frock coat and sat on a bentwood chair under a cheap, stinking kerosene lamp. A servant standing behind the chair used a bamboo pole to ward off swooping tame sparrows.

Major Horatio Herbert Kitchener, a strange, solitary adventurer who roamed the frontier wastes on intelligence missions with a phial of poison in his Arab headdress in case of capture, warned that the Mudir was 'exploiting the English and filling his pockets'. He believed that the Mudir was in reality and avowed enemy. Kitchener was not heeded: Buller often clashed with the younger officer and accused him of running a private war. In the end the intelligence Major reluctantly came round to agreeing that the Mudir's loyalty to the Cairo government could be taken on trust.

Wilson had no doubt that Mustapha Yawer did 'everything he could to thwart us'. He was appalled by one plan that was floated to make the Mudir Governor of the Sudan after Gordon was brought back. 'It was hopeless to attempt to work with him', Wilson wrote. 'What a lot of trouble would have been saved if they had sent him down [to Cairo] at first as I wanted'. And he bitterly complained that Wolseley took four damaging months to realise that the Mudir had been a nuisance from the start, failing to deliver camels, blocking supplies, charging exhorbitant prices for materials and labour. The Mudir treated the British military hierarchy with thinly veiled contempt. He subjected Wilson to discourteous delay when the latter visited him in his whitewashed 'palace'. 'How my blood boiled within me', said Wilson, who had to submit to the indignities for the sake of official relations. Another visitor, Herbert Stewart, was kept waiting two days. And there was little more respect forthcoming even for Wolseley when he called to confer the KCMG on the Dongola potentate (having taken the actual decoration from Buller for the occasion).

The Mudir, despite the growing discontent in the Army's high councils, continued to indulge in his strange behaviour, a mixture of rapacity, obstructiveness and eccentricity. When, because he requested it and the Generals dared not refuse him, he was allowed to use the official telegraph line, he opened every message with a chapter from the Koran. When Wilson met him in the company of a secret visitor, the Mahdi's cousin, Mustapha Yawer proposed that the kinsman should return and murder the Mahdi. That, Wilson riposted icily, 'was not the English way of doing things'. Too late, far too late, the Mudir was considered to have had sufficient lease. He was packed off to Cairo on April 3 1885. To all concerned it afterwards seemed incredible that they had tolerated his sabotage for so long.

The cynical Mudir might have replied with justification that the forces of disruption needed no support from him when the British themselves were proving to be masters of muddle through a combination of bickering, mismanagement, ill judgement and bad luck. No one can denigrate the immense achievement of quartering, moving, provisioning and arming a total of 11,000 British troops as garrison, support and strike-force along a supply line from the Nile delta to the Bayuda. The catalogue of mishap was so lengthy, however, that there is reason for wonder, not that the relief expedition failed, but that the advance force did not meet overwhelming disaster.

The shortage of camels was but a part of this catalogue. Supply difficulties began at Alexandria where many of the landed whalers were separated from their gear, thus defeating the concept of the boats as self-contained units. There were not enough oars, for example. Some of the confusion arose because of a dispute over the responsibility of Thomas Cook, the travel company, for a unique deal had been signed: it was the only time in British history that a commercial firm was given the contract to convey a campaigning army (the fee was £21 per passenger transported from Cairo to Wady Halfa). Cook's, which was chosen for its experience of the Nile, believed its duty at Alexandria was to the boats, not the equipment, and there were frequent arguments with the authorities over divisions of responsibility.

The overwhelming majority of men and supplies had, perforce, to go by river. One hope of circumventing the awesome second cataract by using some 30 miles of the Wady Halfa-Sarras railway was dashed when its locomotives and rolling stock were found to be nothing but scrap iron. The river meant steamers to tow the boats; and the steamers meant coal. Cook's had brought 28 ship-loads of coal from Tyneside to Alexandria, but in October, through a misunderstanding, coal could not be obtained on the Nile. The river steamers ceased to run on October 23. Buller was blamed for not foreseeing the crisis and for not acting more speedily when it arose. John Mason Cook, the head of the travel firm, arrived in Egypt, but it was too late. Some accounts say that the coal famine robbed the expedition of three weeks of vital time.

Faulty packing resulted in half of the tea carried by the river column going bad from damp, and one third of the biscuits were inedible. A quarter of the sugar was spilled or stolen. Theft diminished the medical supplies by half. During Earle's long river haul from Korti to Kirbekan, vast stocks were daily buried in the desert or dumped in the water — tons of damaged biscuits and decomposed preserved meat, the latter ruined by faulty canning. In contrast, the desert column dumped huge stocks of *good* provisions when it was forced to leave the banks of the Nile at Gubat and return across the Bayuda; some officers feared the Mahdi's men would be able to retrieve the food. While Stewart's men formed squares and fought off the dervish, there was whole-sale plunder in the baggage lines. Adeni drivers and other natives broke open boxes, stole arms, and even filched a set of scarlet tunics that was being reserved for a 'flag-showing' march through Khartoum. Staff were found blind drunk on medical supplies of alcohol.

There was bitter irony. The river force suffered from scurvy, cholera, dysentery and typhoid. It was made up of men whose faces were 'like raw beef' and covered in boils, their hair infested with lice, the matting of their boats overrun with scorpions. A force which had to send out an SOS for trousers was described by one reporter in these terms: ' . . . there was literally not a sound garment in the whole column, and the men resembled Falstaff's ragged regiment rather than a body of British troops'. Deprived of essentials, they nevertheless found themselves carrying unnecessary encumbrances such as stocks of coffee mills, pewter measures, bellows and even beer taps (in the medical supplies). The critics at home were to question the anomaly by which a commissariat could fail to furnish the hussars with sufficient horseshoes and nails for their ponies, and yet cheerfully announce in February 1885 when the new operations at Suakim were afoot that 10,000 umbrellas had been ordered from a London firm: 'strong, thick, white umbrellas at once', was Wolseley's explicit instruction.

At Gubat, Gleichen remarked on the profligacy of retreat. He noted that the British threw in the Nile 19,000 lb of flour, 22,000 lb of beef and ham, 3,000 lb of biscuits and 1,100 lb of tea, plus preserved vegetables and coffee. Fine champagne, reserved for the sick, was handed out, and his mess enjoyed two excellent old crusted Tarragona ports. But there were no boots. A fresh stock, sent across the desert from Korti in response to appeals, consisted of sizes that were too small to wear; the boots were as hard as bricks and there was no grease to soften them, so men slit the ends and shoved their toes through them. 'As for the officers, no two had the same foot-covering; field-boots, lawn-tennis shoes, gaiters, putties, and boots in all stages of decay and attempted repairs were worn.' Beresford reported: 'There was hardly a pair of boots in the whole column'. men cut up old rifle buckets and tied them to their feet. The sailors marched barefoot.

Fourteen years later, the lesson of the boots still had not been learned. G.W. Steevens, a war correspondent, reported in 1898 that British troops at Berber, on their way to fight the Khalifa's army at Omdurman, were marching barefoot because their stitched boots had fallen to pieces, while the Egyptians marched in comfort in riveted boots. He wrote: 'We have been campaigning in the Sudan, off and on, for over fourteen years; we might have discovered the little peculiarities of its climate by now . . . It is always the same story — knavery and slackness clogging and strangling the best efforts of the British soldier.'

In the Gordon expedition the water-skin supplied to each man was another source of despair to the Camel Corps. 'How a committee of intelligent officers can ever have selected such an article beats my comprehension!', observed the usually uncomplaining Gleichen. The skins seldom held their full complement of water. 'Even after every visible hole had been carefully sewn up, and the whole skin thoroughly greased, at the end of the first day's march you would find more than half your water evaporated; next day the skin would be a damp, flabby bag, and the day after, a dried, shrivelled-up article without an atom of water in it'. Gleichen and his fellow officers made a few men sew up their waterproof sheets into water-bags, but thorns and sharp stones soon punctured the bags. 'The sailors were better off, for they had brought a quantity of large indiarubber bags, specially made for the purpose. I wish the Government would have gone to the expense of providing every one with them; it would have saved an enormous amount of pain and privation'.

The foresight and resourcefulness of the Navy was seen in other ways during the advance and retreat across the Bayuda desert. Before the flying column left Korti, Beresford asked for boiler-plate, rivets, lubricating oil and oakum — the last being rope fibre used with tar as sailors' caulking material — and the camels to carry these stores. At first, Beresford recalled, Buller refused. 'What do you want the plates for? Are you going to mend the camels with them?' In the end, however, Beresford was allowed his supplies and the hardware saved the day when he sailed with part of Gordon's little fleet on the Nile. To everyone's amazement, he used the oakum to do what Buller had acidly joked about — repair the camels. He plugged holes in the camels, caused by sores and sometimes bullets; the admix of tar, he claimed, acted as an antiseptic. As the overworked and underfed animals fell out, totally exhausted and dying, the Navy camels' survival rate was the highest in the column.

The failure of arms was another item in the catalogue of mishaps, one which affected the soldier more directly than any other when he came face to face with the Mahdi's fighting man in the desert.

*'When 'arf of your bullets fly wide in the ditch,*
*Don't call your Martini a crosseyed old bitch;*
*She's human as you are — you treat her as sich,*
*— An' she'll fight for the young British soldier.'*

Kipling's tutorial made it sound so simple. The young soldiers of the desert column, who lost nearly one fifth of their number in dead or wounded, could have supplied him with much stronger invective. The scandal of guns that jammed echoed round Parliament, War Office and enquiry committee for months to come, and there was bitter disillusion in store for a Victorian public convinced of the invincibility of 'British cold steel'. First, however, we must examine in brief the sequence of events that led to the expedition's baptism of fire.

The advanced force at Korti dined on improvised concoctions of plum pudding on Christmas Day 1884 in a state of great excitement. While the Staffords were to lead the slow boat progress around the great Nile loop, the Camel Corps made ready to strike across the Bayuda desert. At three in the afternoon of December 30, Wolseley, instructed against his wishes to remain at Korti, took the salute at a march-past and said farewell to his flying column which marched off to its adopted tune, renamed 'The Camels are Coming'. Gleichen reported the dusty host singing 'Auld Lang Syne' at New Year in the dark wasteland.

The first march was of 100 miles to Jakdul, the site of a series of rocky pools. These would provide water for the next leg to the wells of Abu Klea, half way across the last 80-mile stretch to the objective of Metemmeh on the Nile. Metemmeh, where Gordon's steamers were expected to be waiting, was just 100 river miles from Khartoum. At Jakdul the Guards entrenched while the main column *returned* to Korti to fetch more men, supplies and camels — a strategy dictated by the shortage of baggage animals. Thus it was not until Wednesday, January 13 — by which time the British had given the Mahdi two weeks' notice of their presence in the desert — that a column of 1,500 men, 2,200 camels and 90 horses left Jakdul, heading south-east towards Metemmeh. Camels were already falling out, worked to death. Gleichen wrote: 'You would see one go slower and slower, till the tail of the animal in front he was tied to seemed nearly coming off; then he would stop for a second, give a nasty shiver, and drop down stone-dead'. Those that fell out alive were left: there were no bullets to spare for them. Some were found still alive on the columns return journey across the desert.

On the night of the 16th, the British waited in square before Abu Klea in the sure knowledge that they would have to fight for the wells: 10,000 of the enemy barred their way, the right led by Abu Saleh, an emir of Metemmeh, the left by Mohammed el

Kheir, an emir of Berber. Long-range markmanship took toll of the encamped troops.

On the morning of the 17th Stewart expected attack but none came. He held back, 'waiting', as he put it, 'to give the niggers another chance'. Then at 10:00 he move out in square, leaving a small garrison to hold a thorn bush zeriba of baggage camels, wounded and non-combatants. There followed the battle of Abu Klea in which the British square, dangerously dented, beat off successive waves of tribesmen. There were heavy casualties among the British and carnage among the attackers. Burnaby was one of nine officers killed. When the British occupied the wells they found evidence that large numbers of Arabs had camped there for up to two weeks.

Again, a small group in zeriba was detailed to hold the wells and guard the wounded and sick while the fighting square pressed on. Because of casualties and the need to garrison the staging posts it was now reduced to '900 bayonets', in Gleichen's words. A running action ensued in which the Mahdi's marksmen accounted for more dead and wounded in the British ranks. Among the killed were two war correspondents, John Cameron of the *Standard*, and St Leger Herbert of the *Morning Post*. Both were in the centre of the square and hit by dropping bullets. Stewart was mortally wounded by a bullet in the groin. Scores of camels were hit. The soldiers, crazed with thirst, reached the Nile at Gubat, two miles from enemy-held Metemmeh, at moonrise on January 19. They had lost 122 dead and 206 wounded in the desert; more would die on the return journey.

The fighting in the desert had severely tested the armaments of the British Army and found them wanting. In the judgement of Lord Charles Beresford, the Mahdi's army, universally regarded in Britain as a heathen host led by fanatics, was better served by its arms than was the army of the richest, most powerful nation on earth. More than a year later, when the wheels of officialdom had ground to produce a special committee to hear evidence from men who had been at Abu Klea, Colonel Reginald Talbot of the Heavy Camel Regiment was asked on what occasion did the rifles jam. 'On all occasions', he replied.

The standard weapon of the British soldier was the Martini-Henry rifle, which had been in service since 1871. It was single-shot, breech-loading and lever-operated. It fired a .45 bullet which had devastating effect, especially at short ranges such as the occasion when masses attacked the square at Abu Klea. Trained men aiming in volley were capable of murderously rapid fire. The trouble lay in the rifle's propensity to jam. The army used a Boxer cartridge of soft brass which was easily dented, and went on using it until 1888 despite the failures experienced and grimly recorded in the Gordon relief expedition. Talbot reported that at least half the rifles jammed at Abu Klea, so that a man would throw down his own weapon and snatch up a wounded comrade's. Beresford told a similar story: 'Nearly half the British rifles jammed, owing to the use of leaf cartridges. The Remington rifles used by the Mahdi's soldiers had solid drawn cartridges which did not jam. . . the officers were almost entirely employed in clearing jammed rifles passed back to them by the men.' It was ironic that the Mahdi's men used rifles captured from the Egyptian army, Remingtons, which were regarded by the British high command with some derision as being outmoded. The committee of inquiry subsequently recommended the adoption of solid-drawn cartridge cases and a more powerful extractor.

The column's heavier weaponry was emasculated by the shortage of baggage camels to carry ammunition. For the three 7 lb screw guns (so called because they were transported in pieces and screwed together for action) there were only 100 rounds per gun. The single Gardner machine-gun was supplied with 1,000 rounds, enough for only ten minutes' firing at the most rapid rate. Beresford enthused that the .45 bullets from the gun's barrels 'cut off heads and tops of heads as though sliced horizontally with a knife! It was the identical Gardner that had jammed at Tamai nearly ten months earlier. 'I was putting in most effective work', said Beresford, when the gun jammed after 30 rounds. The extraction had pulled the head from a discharged cartridge, leaving an empty cylinder in the barrel. The Gardner, too, was subjected to critical scrutiny in the 1886 enquiry.

A widely quoted despatch from Bennet Burleigh of the *Daily Telegraph* helped spur the ordnance department to review its purchase and inspection systems. He had first noticed deficiencies of bayonet and Martini-Henry at Tamai. At Abu Klea, where bayonets 'bent like hoop-iron', the complex, ill-shaped Boxer cartridge was the cause of most of the jamming that occurred. . . 'Many a soldier at Abu Klea saw with dismay his bayonet rendered useless at the moment where there was no chance to reload his rifle. After that fight you might have noticed brawny foot-guardsmen, herculean Life-guardsmen, and the deft fighters of the mounted infantry. . .straightening their bayonets across their knees or under foot.'

The hand-to-hand mêlée which almost brought disaster to the square had soldiers 'cursing as the rifles jammed and the shoddy bayonets twisted like tin', said Beresford. After the fight, Gleichen made a little sketch showing the bayonet atop an infantryman's rifle like a corkscrew. The 18-inch sword bayonets of the British had been blunted by wood cutting. They stuck fast when they were thrust into bodies. Beresford blamed unspecified culprits back home: 'The British bayonets and cutlasses bent and twisted, the result of a combination of knavery and laziness on the part of the those who were trusted to supply the soldier with weapons upon which his life depends. The bayonets were blunt, because no one had thought of sharpening them. The spears of the Arabs were sharp like razors.'

The main weapons of the Mahdiists were a heavy two-sided sword and a broad-bladed spear. But Gleichen found a variety of hardware left on the field — long spears, javelins, hatchets, swords, knives and knobkerries. He picked up a Birmingham trade-marked billhook, sharp as a razor and covered with blood and hair, and 'confiscated it for the mess'. Others, too, took their pick of the battlefield debris. Beresford observed 'that when a soldier was killed, a bluejacket always endeavoured to secure his bayonet; and that when a sailor was killed, a soldier always tried to take his hat, preferring it to the Army helmet'. Officers ruefully recalled the discussions they had held over the mess table on their journey south as to whether the point or the edge of the sword was more lethal. In action they found their light swords were no match for the Mahdi's blades, wielded with two hands.

Despatched too late by an unwilling government, affected by quarrels in the high command all the way back down the line from Korti to Whitehall, badly served by some inefficient officers in the field, beset by shortage of transport and equipment and weakened by arms failures, the isolated desert column was saddled with yet another handicap: lack of communication. It had not been thought necessary to lay a telegraph line from the advanced headquarters at Korti in the wake of the advancing troops. Heliograph, requiring sunlight and relay stations within sight of each other, had limited application. When crucial decisions had to be taken in the field during the closing days of January 1885, the availability of quick means of communication with higher authority might have changed the course of history.

# Chapter 13

# *Fatal delay*

At Korti on the Nile, on March 23 1885, Sir Charles Wilson wrote to his wife, Olivia, a soldier's daughter: 'I see I am to be made a scapegoat for this failure'. The vast controversy over Gordon's death, the fall of Khartoum and the collapse of British policy in the Sudan was like a seething morass made up of interacting layers. There was the record of ministerial vacillation: committment followed by scuttle, hasty action in the wake of irresolution. There was the mutual and total breakdown in understanding between Gordon and government about Gordon's role. There were the military errors, strategic and tactical, accentuated by inexplicable misjudgement and negligence over supplies and equipment. Failure to assess properly the influence of Mahdiism was compounded by the political and moral argument raging in Britain: were we trying to suppress a just movement of liberation, or engaged in a crusade against a tyrannical regime?

On the surface of this heaving debate Wilson was exposed and struggling desperately to preserve his professional reputation. In the way history has of sometimes focusing the course of great events on a horseshoe nail, it now thrust him into harsh examination by statesmen, soldiers, press and an angry and bewildered public. All were seeking someone to blame for the disaster summed up in the *Punch* cartoon captioned 'TOO LATE!', which showed a distraught Britannia helpless as ravening dervish hordes poured into Khartoum*.

In question were Wilson's decisions and deeds on three crucial

---

*The cartoon, published on February 14, was, in fact, a retraction on *Punch's* part. A week earlier, convinced that Khartoum had been relieved, it had published a drawing of Gordon greeting his British rescuers, with the caption, 'AT LAST!'. In the next issue the record was set right.

days at the end of January which he spent by the banks of the Nile near Metemmeh before embarking by steamer for Khartoum. His critics' argument was simple and blunt: he wasted time while Gordon died.

Poor Wilson. The final act in which he was destined to star was one of strong drama. It contained suspense, action and tragedy — and not a small element of farce. It called for a bold man, impetuous of spirit and contemptuous of risk. It needed General Wolseley's professed ideal of the archetypal young officer — a man blessed with a death wish and ready to dare all in the pursuit of victory. But fate had cast the understudy. And Wilson, cautious, analytical, inexperienced in field command, was not up to it.

The advance guard of the British desert column reached the Nile as the moon rose on Monday, January 19 1885. Stewart was mortally wounded, Burnaby dead, and Wilson was in command of a perilously isolated force of exhausted men and animals. On the 20th he dug in at Gubat, an abandoned village of mud hovels, 100 miles downstream from Khartoum. Wolseley had ordered that Metemmeh, a walled town two miles away, was to be occupied as an advanced base to await the arrival of the boat-borne troops of General Earle, battling through the Nile cataracts far to the north. Metemmeh, as Wilson was soon to find out by a reconnaissance in force, was too tough a nut to crack with the troops available to him.

On January 21, he was joined by four steamers, despatched over the preceding weeks by Gordon. They brought conflicting accounts of the state of affairs in the besieged city of Khartoum — both in Gordon's journals and notes and by word of mouth. Wilson's orders were to utilise these steamers to sail to Khartoum, establish contact with Gordon, and return to Metemmeh with a report. Faced with the dilemma presented by these orders and by the unexpected responsibility of command over the column at Gubat, he failed to move on Wednesday, January 21, and spent the whole of the next day on fruitless reconnaissance by steamer along the river; he was deeply concerned by reports about approaching enemy reinforcements. A further day was spent preparing two steamers for the journey to Khartoum. These were the 'wasted' days that later came under fiercely critical scrutiny.

It was not until the morning of Saturday, January 24, that Wilson sailed for Khartoum with a handful of soldiers in two steamers. They arrived off the city the following Wednesday —

January 28, Gordon's birthday. Two days late. Khartoum had fallen to the Mahdi and Gordon had been killed on Monday, the 26th. In a desperate return journey under fire, Wilson's party was shipwrecked and brought to safety by a rescue mission led by Lord Charles Beresford.

There was eventually grudging agreement that Wilson should escape the official censure that would have meant blight on his career and reputation. Even his sternest critics in the Army — some of whom would have been happy for a scapegoat to relieve the pressure on their own beleaguered positions — recognised the need to close ranks in face of an onslaught of public opinion. Wilson's peers, champions to a man of the Victorian military code, also took into consideration the mitigating evidence of his redemption by fire: he did brave the gauntlet of a hostile river in ramshackle steamers, reach Khartoum and, with the timely intervention of the skilful rescue enterprise, bring back most of his men safely.

Alas, all of this is not good enough to exculpate Wilson in the record of history — despite the arguments of colleagues and biographers that his hesitancy had no effect on Gordon's fate, the groundswell of support from friends who sought to shift the blame where it partly belonged (with the strategies of Wolseley, for example), and Wilson's own seemingly sound reasons for his decisions. With maddening hindsight, enraged public opinion in Britain demanded that there should have been immediate embarkation for Khartoum when the advance guard of the desert column met Gordon's steamers near Metemmeh. Unknown to Wilson at the time, fate offered him only hours: hours that might have changed history. But the naturally cautious Wilson was awed by the unexpected responsibilities of command and, like his men, physically exhausted. 'An old woman' in the eyes of the spearhead infantry and cavalry troops who suddenly found themselves commanded by an engineer/intelligence officer, he frittered away the time in what he considered to be commendable activities. If only. . . There were several 'if onlys', but foremost in the minds of Wilson's critics was the thought: if only the decision had been Colonel Burnaby's, the outcome would have been different.

Burnaby, unfortunately was killed at Abu Klea, a spear through his neck in the desperate mêlée of hand-to-hand fighting when the Mahdi's men broke the corner of the British square. Burnaby's orders from Wolseley were to take command at Metemmeh while

Wilson sailed for Khartoum. Those orders — which seemed to take remarkably little consideration of what the enemy might do — presupposed that General Stewart, in overall command, would return to Jakdul, the watering place and staging point in the heart of the Bayuda Desert. But Stewart, too, was out of action, mortally wounded by a bullet in the stomach during the march from Abu Klea to the river.

'What Burnaby would have done', hypothetical as it was, irrelevant as it may be, nevertheless stoked up the contemporary indictment of Wilson's inaction. A huge, hulking figure, scruffy in dress and haircut, Frederick Gustavus Burnaby, son of a prosperous Bedford clergyman, was a rebel and a loner. He was essentially the man of boldness needed at Metemmeh. As a schoolboy at Harrow he caused consternation by writing a protest against the public school fagging system which was published in *Punch*. As a soldier, his outspokeness earned him unpopularity in his regiment, the Horse Guards. The Duke of Cambridge called him a 'bad fellow'.

Burnaby roved the far regions of the world, riding alone to Khiva in Russian central Asia, and following Gordon into equatorial Sudan. 'Freelancing' at the battle of El Teb in 1884, he was 'the first to mount the parapet', blasting away with his double-barrelled shotgun, the favourite weapon of a man who like combat close and hot. 'He seemed to be in his element when there was hard and dangerous work to do', wrote Frederick Villiers, war artist of the *Graphic*. Burnaby's fearful toll of 'fuzzy-wuzzy' victims at El Teb earned him bitter liberal criticism when the huge slaughter by British troops caused a parliamentary furore.

To write him off as merely a hothead and a military tearaway, however, would be unfair. He was accomplished in seven languages, including Arabic, Russian and Turkish. After his famous Khiva ride he wrote a stylish book which has seen reprint after reprint. A keen balloonist, he staunchly advocated the tactical use of balloons in the Sudan in a case which would have been beneficial to Wolseley's campaign had the idea been able to rise above the brasshats' foggy minds. (Later, in the 1885 operations in the eastern Sudan around Suakim, balloon observation *was* put to limited use.) He took to the hustings under Conservative colours in the Liberal stronghold of Birmingham in an unsuccessful campaign that was not without a touch of outrageous hypocrisy. Frederic Villiers recalls the gist of one election speech by Burnaby: 'The widows and orphans of the Arabs who had so heroically fallen in the defence of their country were wringing their hands and tearing their hair, cursing the name of Mr Gladstone, the British Liberal Minister who was responsible for the war'. And yet, observed Villiers, 'Burnaby himself had made many a widow and orphan, "sniping the niggers", in the language of the soldiers, whenever they showed their heads'.

Villiers was with Burnaby near the end when, at the age of 42, the Colonel met his death at Abu Klea: 'I never saw him look gloomier than during that march, for he had a presentiment of his coming end. Yet there was always a grim touch of humour about him. One night I asked him what he thought of our chances of reaching Khartoum in time to save Gordon. "The odds against us are about twenty to one", he replied, and added, "We Britishers are a curious people. Why, do you know, I've been made a commandant of Metemmeh, and we haven't got there yet!"' (British troops did not, in fact, enter the walled town of Metemmeh until Kitchener's reconquest some 13 years later.)

There is little doubt that if Burnaby had reached the Nile, he would have used all his powers to convince Wilson that an immediate dash for Khartoum, thrusting aside all risk, was the course of action to take. To throw all on the glorious prize of relieving Gordon was his burning endeavour. Indeed, he had insinuated himself into the expedition for that expressed purpose. In the months of uncertainty while the government dithered over whether or not to send an army, Burnaby had planned with a colleague in the Army to mount a private relief expedition. Following the incapacity of General Stewart, and faced by exhortations of haste from some aboard the steamers who knew how desperate was Gordon's situation, Burnaby might even have pressed that the official orders should be disregarded and that the dash to Khartoum should become a mission of *rescue*, and not merely one to establish *contact*. What is beyond all doubt is that the mild Wilson — a man 'silent by nature', according to his friend, fellow-sapper and biographer, Colonel Sir Charles Watson — would have found it difficult to rebuff the arguments of the flamboyant and articulate Burnaby.

Perhaps even more important, Burnaby would have been in a position to counter the advice of the naval commander, Lord Charles Beresford, an officer as daring and headstrong as Burnaby, and yet a protagonist who, paradoxically, would now abet Wilson's natural caution and restraint — even actively press for delay — for personal reasons of his own.

In ordinary circumstances, Beresford was not a man to countenance tardiness. On Wednesday, January 21 1885, when Gordon's battered but unbeaten steamers hove to and were met by the hoarse cheers of the British, he had every reason to believe he was at the opening of the most glorious chapter in an already distinguished and active career. As commander of the naval contingent, he was under orders to assume captaincy of the fleet and transport Wilson and a small party of soldiers through enemy-held country to contact Gordon, 100 miles upstream in Khartoum — a duty any officer of the Queen would relish. But now a mundane and humiliating factor came into account. It threatened to rob Beresford of his part in the historic escapade, affected his attitude and, arguably, Wilson's decisions, and injected an element of bathos into the deepening tragedy. If Wilson's 'lost' days on the Nile can be said to have contributed to the events that led to the death of Gordon, then the farcical ingredient in the play of fate was a boil on Beresford's bottom.

In their terrible, fighting march across the Bayuda Desert, the soldiers and sailors of the relief column, beset by swarms of voracious sandflies, had suffered agonies from boils. Men's faces and bodies were covered in black pustules. The noble rump of Charles William de la Poer Beresford was not immune. Days of riding in a galling saddle had produced a painful carbuncle which became so bad that he was unable to walk when he reached the Nile. Had the steamers sailed at once for Khartoum, Beresford would not have been able to accompany them (in the event, he was still in hospital when Wilson eventually embarked, but he was fit enough within a few days to lead a rescue of the river mission).

Faced with the prospect of missing the dash for Khartoum, Beresford capitalised on Wilson's natural caution: he stands accused of an insidiuous campaign of counselling that persuaded Wilson of the wisdom of river reconnaissance (which troops on land could have accomplished just as effectively) and overhaul and restocking of steamers (which, throughout weeks of waiting on the Nile, were maintained at full readiness) before starting on the upriver journey. Beresford's motive would have been to buy time until he recovered from his boil. Wilson lacked the strength of character and the initiative to withstand the blandishments of the persuasive aristocrat. The keys to Beresford's moral ascendancy in this clash of wills are to be found in the contrasting characters and backgrounds of the two men.

Sir Charles Wilson's qualities were what an army needed in an engineer, administrator, surveyor and intelligence officer. He was careful and constructive, meticulous about detail, questioning and thorough, analytical in thinking, and possessing a fund of sound commonsense. Never a doer, he was the thinker who, against contrary judgement of many including Gordon himself, had rightly assessed in an intelligence report the latent strength of Mahdiism and forecast its wildfire spread across the Sudan; who had counselled about the realism of coming to terms with the Islamic ethos of slave-trading, unpopular as this might be with the anti-slavery lobby; who had consistently warned about the duplicity of the Mudir of Dongola, Wolseley's trust in whom was a major factor in the expedition's supplies débâcle.

Born in Liverpool of a family of Quaker descent and scientific background, with business interests in Virginia, Charles William Wilson had had a distinguished but uneventful Army career in administration, survey work and intelligence. At heart he was a geographer and archeologist. He was ill at ease in the social milieu, 'not what could be called a society man', in the words of his friend, Watson, and passionately happy excavating ancient sites in Asia Minor and Palestine. As a brevet-Colonel he was appointed as Chief of Intelligence to the relief expedition, and at the age of 49 he found himself for the first time in his career in field command — deep in enemy country and faced with a task for which he was untrained.

Against this somewhat grey figure is set Lord Charles Beresford, younger by ten years, the impetuous, high-spirited sportsman of noble birth, probably the best known sailor of the day. Possessing many of the virtues and faults of his Irish ancestry, he had a large number of friends in high places but was impatient of authority and lived a life of quarrels with superiors, even up to his subsequent Sea Lord rank. He was personally close to the Prince of Wales and shot elephants with him in India. Queen Victoria thought him 'a trifle cracky'. Rich, handsome, married to Jeromima, daughter of a country MP and a countess of German extraction, he was a glittering star in the social firmament, a lover of publicity. A fascinated British public followed with delight his escapades in society and on the hunting and racing fields. 'Lord Charles', recorded a friend, by way of introduction to his autobiography, 'has broken his chest bone, pelvis, right leg, right hand, foot, five ribs, one collar-bone three times, the other once, his nose three times.' (And countless hearts, he may have added.) On the journey south to Wady Halfa with Wolseley's army, Beresford bought three racing camels, named them Bimbashi, Ballyhooly and Beelzebub, and diverted himself by racing them against the prized champions of local potentates. During his 'march of the forlorn hope' across the desert he rode a little white donkey called County Waterford, until it bolted at the battle of Abu Klea.

A glimpse into the home life of this 'cracky' peer is revealed by an account he gave of a dinner party at his Eaton Square home in London, at which he wagered that 'you can do anything with horses if you understand them'. 'The table at which my guests were sitting was designed with a large tank in the centre, which was filled with running water, in which grew ferns and aquatic plants. Gold fish swam in the water, and little new-born ducklings oared upon the surface. This miniature lake was diversified with spirals and fountains fashioned of brass, which I had turned myself. . . I told my guests that I would bring in one of my horses (a bad-tempered thoroughbred), that I would lead him from the street, up the steps into the hall, round the dining-table and so back to the street without accident. Straw was laid on the steps and passages; and I led in the horse. He lashed out at the fire with one leg, just to show his contempt for everything and everybody; but there was no casualty. The next day, I was driving the same horse in a buggy, when something annoyed the animal, and he kicked the buggy to pieces, upset us in the road, and broke my old coachman's leg.' Lord Charles was sorry he could not emulate the feat of an uncle who had leaped a hunter over the dining-table.

Beyond the idiosyncracies, however, Beresford was a resourceful, brave and caring officer who earned the devotion of his men. He had brilliantly handled the gunboat *Condor* at the bombardment of Alexandria in 1882 and quickly restored order in the riot-torn city after landing. His practical talents won high praise for his feat of passing the boats up the 'impossible' second cataract of the Nile. His bluejackets with their Gardner gun had played a gallant part in the fights in the desert. There, Wilson had already experienced Beresford's strong will when, chafing under an enforced halt in sight of the river, the sailor had sent the soldier a peremptory message to march against the enemy, or 'we are done'.

For Charlie Beresford, the tough, hard-riding achiever, it must have been frustrating and bitterly disappointing now to be incapacitated by a boil just as he was prepared for the most publicly observed race of his career, the dash for Khartoum.

The critical timetable of delay after the rendezvous with the steamers, and Beresford's part in it, demands detailed examination. It encompasses the three days from January 21 to 23.

# Chapter 14

# *Warning voices*

*The first day, Wednesday, January 21*

Wilson had available few more than 1,000 men after drawing on detachments left in the desert. Four hundred of these would soon be needed to escort despatches and transport animals to Jakdul, and thence return to Gubat with provisions—another example of the to-and-fro camel shuttle made necessary by the gross under-estimation of the numbers of transport animals needed by the expedition. The entrenched force was encumbered by more than 100 wounded and many sick. After two weeks of hard marching, searing thirst, sleepless nights and, finally, desperate fighting, few if any of the troops were entirely fit. 'The men were so exhausted that when they came up from their drink at the river they fell down like logs', wrote Wilson. The correspondent, Villiers, recorded a tribute to the discipline of the British soldier: 'Almost mad with thirst and with the water in plain view, there he stood patiently waiting till he was ordered to be watered in companies'.

The animals were in a pitiful state. The camels which survived (hundreds died) had been on one-third rations and without water for a week. They were hardly able to walk; sores pitted their bodies; ribs came through their skin. Count Gleichen reckoned that his camel drank from the Nile for 14 minutes without stopping. Some of the horses of the 19th Hussars had been waterless for 72 hours; all were dead beat.

On the Wednesday morning after 24 hours establishing the base at Gubat, Wilson cobbled up an assault group from his battered army to attempt to take Metemmeh. The British shouldered their Martini-Henrys, marched off the gravel terrace by the Nile bank and crossed two miles of ridged ground to the town identified in Wolseley's orders as the first objective. The General's prepackaged strategy, however, had not bargained for Metemmeh

127

being heavily garrisoned. The Mahdi's men — under the chief of the Jaalin tribe, beaten back by Stewart's little force — manned the loopholed walls in strength. The naval brigade's Gardner and the 7-pounder screw guns popped and rattled futilley against the mud ramparts above which the emirs' battle flags fluttered in defiant impunity.

The defenders had three artillery pieces. Although their shells were largely ineffective, they were coupled with the more accurate fire of the Remington-armed blacks, who inflicted casualties on the British. An early victim was Major William Poë, of the Royal Marines, who fell as the result of a display of lunatic insouciance that characterised more than a few of the socially prominent officers in the desert column. He insisted on wearing a red tunic, saying his other coat was not fit to be seen. His fastidiousness was much appreciated by the marksman who found him, boldly outlined, in his sights. Poë was severely wounded in the leg; surgeons amputated in a mud hut at Gubat. Beresford recorded that Poë eventually recovered, and added that 'he rides to hounds to this day', an attitude which overlooked the fact that the loss of yet another experienced officer — through his own conspicuous folly — further eroded the efficiency of the little force. And by now it was clear to Wilson that the taking of Metemmeh was a hopeless proposition.

Then, across the pale green sheet of the Nile came a sight that gave the British new heart. From a bend in the river where a fringe of scraggy palms rimmed the bare brown desert, there wallowed, one after the other, four broad-beamed steamers, paddle wheels thrashing, funnels coughing huge black clouds, hooters blaring, crews joyously firing their Remingtons into the air. Gordon's steamers, the first two of which had left Khartoum on September 30 and arrived to keep vigil off Metemmeh on October 5, had finally linked up with the advance guard of the army that was the only salvation of the besieged city: the shell-holed *Tel-el-Hoween*; the faithful *Safieh*; the former Governor-General's yacht, the *Tewfikieh*, which boasted the luxury of a commodious saloon cabin; and the indestructible *Bordein*, named after a languid resort in Egypt whose Arabic name means 'the cool of the morning and the evening'.

In the heat of this Wednesday morning when the British column was desperately mired in stalemate before Metemmeh, the arrival of the stammers meant not only a gift of firepower (some of the

Sudanese troops immediately disembarked with guns and cheerfully bombarded the walls), but a brightening gleam of hope that their costly desert mission might yet be successful now the means were at hand to reach Gordon in Khartoum.

Although Gordon's armada had performed prodigious feats up and down the Nile, the bluejackets of the world's mightiest seapower must have looked on their new charges with rueful and sceptical eyes. Gordon, Beresford and Wilson have all referred to the ships as being like 'penny steamboats on the Thames'. The largest was only 150 feet long with 60 hp engines, and the smallest, the *Tewfikieh*, was a 24 hp, 73-footer. Tall thin funnels, jacketed in iron plating, soared over what looked like floating junk-heaps. The sides and bulwarks of a steamer were sheathed with a patchwork of boilerplate, above which was fixed a rail of stout timber, leaving a space through which to fire. The boiler, which projected above the deck, was shielded by logs of wood. This makeshift armour was impervious to bullets but would not stop a shell from the Mahdi's Krupp guns, captured from the Hicks army and Egyptian garrisons throughout the Sudan. In the bows, a 9-pounder brass howitzer fired ahead from a timber turret, and a central turret housed a gun that lobbed shells over the paddle boxes. Astern, on the roof of the deckhouse, an enclosure of boilerplate protected the wheel and riflemen.

Below decks was a seething, smelly and verminous chaos of military and domestic life, from which, somehow, a ruthless and buccaneering efficiency emerged when the lumbering old rust-bucket went into action. Everything was filthy, except the engines. Two holds were a jumble of ammunition, durra grain, wood, coal when it was available, bedding, women, babies, wounded men, goats and chickens. Laughing jet-black slave girls from Equatoria endlessly cooked durra cakes on fires perilously near to the 9-pounders' magazine. Loot, gathered during weeks of piracy and mayhem along the Nile's banks, was stuffed in lockers and crannies. The captain kept his booty hidden away in the aft hold. In the *Tel-el-Hoween*, black Sudanese regulars who were freed slaves fought alongside bashi-bazouks, irregulars, made up of the loyal Shagiyeh tribe. The latter were officered by Turks, Kurds and Circassians. The sailors were black Sudanese, the engineers Egyptians. Whatever this motley horde of humanity did — fighting, relaxing, winning, losing, quarrelling, copulating — it did it in a din of screaming and yelling. Rats swarmed everywhere, and a ripe stench heralded a vessel's approach on the sluggish breezes of the river.

The ragged flotilla now delivered Gordon's final messages, entrusted by the General to the *Bordein* on December 14 after the steamer had made a hazardous last run upriver to the invested capital. It was only by a stroke of extreme good fortune that the *Bordein*, its crew and the messages survived to reach Wilson's force. Nushi Pasha, a trusted Turkish-born lieutenant of Gordon, in command of the steamers and fretfully awaiting the arrival of the British, with food running low and crews becoming dispirited, had grown anxious about the non-return of *Bordein* as he cruised near Metemmeh. His wait had been costly: one of his ships, the *Mansureh*, was hit by a shell below the waterline and sank; shells pierced the boilers of the *Tel-el-Hoween* and *Safieh*, but these were repaired within a few days. As there was still no sign of the British, Nushi decided to sail up to the sixth cataract at Shabluka, some 40 miles nearer Khartoum. It was fortunate that he did. He found the *Bordein* stuck on a rock and in danger of becoming a wreck. Superhuman efforts by Nushi's band of Egyptians, Sudanese and bashi-bazouks succeeded in repairing the stricken *Bordein*, pulling her free and battling through the rock-strewn rapids, generally regarded as impassable at this time of the year when the Nile falls dramatically.

In the midst of failure and blunder, the record of the men of 'Gordon's navy' shines out as an epic achievement. There was little real appreciation of their efforts, either official or public, in London where the press was obsessed with the doings of the Army's 'heroes on the Nile'. But the troops of the desert column came to hold deep respect for their floating allies. They did their job — and at what terrible price. Many lost families by butchery or abduction into slavery in the final holocaust at Khartoum. At the end of the day when the vessels were scuttled the crews were given the choice of trekking across the desert with the retreating British column, or staying to take their chance at the hands of the vengeful Mahdiists.

The imminent arrival of the steamers was signalled to Wilson while he was engaged in his attempt on Metemmeh. That sufficient time should elapse for some of the blacks and Shagiyeh to disembark and join the attacking force before Wilson found it necessary to board the *Bordein* and receive Gordon's messages bears witness to his lack of sense of urgency. It was now, by his

own account, the afternoon of the 21st. Why, his critics were to
ask, did he wait hours after the arrival of the boats before
apprising himself of what Gordon had to tell him about the state
of affairs in Khartoum? Even then, another piece of news heard
from the lips of Khasm el Mus, the leader of the Shagiyeh,
appeared to cause him more immediate concern.

The chieftain told him that large forces of Ansar under Feki
Mustafa had been seen marching *north* on the left bank from
Omdurman, which lies across the Nile from Khartoum. The
information confirmed a similar report received the previous day
and coincided with news of reinforcements moving *south* from
Berber, downriver. If these forces were to link up there would be a
very real threat to the British. Wilson, who argued that his cavalry
horses, were too 'done up' to tackle the task, decided on a
reconnaissance by river — but not before consultation with a
group of senior men including Colonel E.E.T. Boscawen, of the
Coldstream Guards, the second ranking officer. For Wilson had
allowed a fatal disease to infect his command: decision by
committee. '. . .everyone gives their opinion and advice in the
free-est manner, from the junior subaltern upwards, and the man
who gets Wilson's or Boscawen's ear last, his advise is followed,'
wrote one officer.

It would have been no surpise to Wolseley. Before he knew of
Stewart's wounding, Wolseley wrote with foreboding to his wife,
Louisa, that his loss would 'at this moment, be a national
calamity'. And before January was out he opined that Wilson's
first dose of fighting 'has entirely hurt his nerves'. Boscawen he
described as lacking nerve, determination and experience. If only
he had commissioned Beresford, 'that splendid fighting man', to
succeed. . . But Beresford, incapacitated by his boil and
bargaining for time, was playing his own Machiavellian role in the
'committee'. Beresford was for reconnaissance.

What cause for debate, deliberation and doubt within the
committee must have been provided by the parcels of messages
and journals which were handed over in the *Bordein*, wrapped in a
variety of handkerchiefs and cloths. There were six volumes of
Gordon's diaries, containing a record of the period from
September 10 to December 14 (no account in his own hand of the
final weeks of Gordon's life has ever been found). The journals
ended with the memorable words: 'Now, *mark this*: if the
expeditionary force, and I ask for no more than two hundred men,

does not come in ten days, *the town may fall*: and I have done my best for the honour of our country. Good-bye'. The warning was followed by one more sentence, typical Gordon. 'You send me no information, though you have lots of money.'

A letter, also written on December 14, repeated Gordon's forecast of a disaster around Christmas: 'I think the game is up, and send. . . my adieux. We may expect a catastrophe in the town in or after ten days' time.' Recriminations were the theme of another letter: 'I will accept *nothing whatever* from Gladstone's government. . .'. A third letter declared: 'I own I consider the position extremely critical, almost desperate. . . '. This, too, was written on the 14th. There were, in addition, instructions to the desert column commander to remove from the steamers all the Egyptians, Turks, Kurds and Circassians, leaving only the more reliable Sudanese: 'I make you a present of these hens and I request you will not let one come back here to me'.

From the general tone of these messages, Wilson — with the support of his advisers, including Beresford — believed that a few days more would make no difference allowing for the fact that Khartoum was still holding out nearly a month after Gordon's Christmas deadline. It was a tragic mistake. But Wilson defenced his decision with vigour when the matter subsequently became a public debate. 'There was nothing', he explained in a report to Wolseley, 'to show that the expected crisis which had been delayed so long would occur within the next few days.' A first priority before moving was to ensure the security of his troops.

There was yet one more communication, written on a scrap of paper and signed by Gordon, to be taken into account. Dated December 29, it had been handed to one of the steamer captains by a runner from Khartoum and was similar to another message received at Korti on December 30. It read: 'Khartoum all right. Could hold out for years.'

Any intelligence man, such as Wilson, would immediately recognise that this message was meant merely as a ruse to mislead the Mahdi in the event of the messenger's capture — and Wilson read it as such. It was significant that in the subsequent enquiry, when under great pressure, he never once alluded to it, although he allowed the British correspondents with the force to make use of it. Its publication in Britain caused immense rejoicing and led to a welter of headlines across the world prematurely announcing the relief of Khartoum and the rescue of Gordon.

The officers of Gordon's steamers pleaded in vain with Wilson. They had first-hand knowledge of the plight of Khartoum and were ready to embark immediately on the Wednesday to return to the city, risking all that the Mahdiists could hurl at them from the entrenched banks at Omdurman. If vessels were needed for reconnaissance, surely two would have been sufficient, while the other two went all out for Khartoum. The British may have felt that the steamer men's pleadings stemmed from their vested interests in the safety of their families in the city. Their case for action, however, was impressive.

Abd el Hamid, the captain of the *Bordein*, told how, when bidding him goodbye on December 14, Gordon had urged great haste. Having given his advice, which was diregarded, Abd el Hamid later sailed a steamer up to Khartoum with Wilson and, on the way back, deserted to the Mahdi when, shipwrecked and despairing of rescue, he judged his allegiance to the British was at an end. Nushi Pasha produced a letter written to him by Gordon: 'I hope you will inform His Excellency, the Chief of the English troops, that they should hasten to arrive at Khartoum, as this is important, for if they delay any longer, there is fear of the city being lost, which God forbid, for it is now in great straits.'

Khasm el Mus was appalled at the delay. Not yet middle-aged, but grey-bearded and dignified, he was short in stature but of immense standing as a leader of influence among his Shagiyeh people, a brave fighter, and staunchly loyal to the Egyptian government. He declared himself bitterly opposed to losing time in reconnaissance on the river — a fact admitted by Beresford in his memoirs. The chieftain argued that the moment was ripe for swift and decisive action while the Ansar were demoralised and confused by their defeat at Abu Klea. He was eager to leave for Khartoum at once. (When, taking part eventually in Wilson's steamer expedition, he discovered that they were too late, he rolled himself in a rug and curled in a corner in stupefied grief; two of his sons died in the Khartoum massacre.) And there was Guku, a Greek to whom Gordon entrusted his journals, who swore afterwards that he urged Wilson in vain not to lose a moment as every one was of inestimable value.

Wilson, bowed down by his committee and worries about his command's safety, ignored the please for haste. He called off the useless siege of Metemmeh and resolved on the morrow to take his navy cruising up and down the river.

In Omdurman to the south, where the people mourned the toll of their dead at Abu Klea, the Mahdi, unaccustomed to defeat, contemplated flight and hourly expected the approach of the victorious British. Across the Nile, Gordon went up as usual before dusk to the roof of his palace and scanned an empty river through his telescope.

# Chapter 15

# *Reconnaissance*

*The second day, Thursday, January 22*

In the harsh light of the desert morning, Wilson, who by now could have been a quarter of the way to Khartoum, set off in the opposite direction in the *Tel-el-Hoween*, with two companies of mounted infantry. They were accompanied by the *Bordein*. Beresford, in much pain from his boil, insisted on accompanying Wilson. He lay on a couch in the *Tel-el-Hoween's* cabin 'and chatted to Khasm el Mus, who became a great friend of mine'. Beresford contributed his advice that the ship's engines required attention, which was a further possible cause of delay.

At Shendy, a slaving and trading crossroads town of 6,000 people six miles downstream, a few shells were exchanged with the enemy. A Shagiyeh came aboard and reported that the force advancing from Berber had met fugitives from Abu Klea and had come no further. Later, another tribesmen confirmed this. Troops sent to investigate in the other direction returned with the news that the threat from Feki Mustafa and his army had evaporated.

Both tasks of reconnaissance could equally have been carried out by soldiers marching along the banks, avowed an intelligence officer with the force, Edward Stuart-Wortley, when, many years later, he was asked for his views. Stuart-Wortley, a Lieutenant at the time, was convinced that Beresford played an insidiously influential role in the decision-making and that it would have been more to Beresford's credit if, in the subsequent enquiry, he had shouldered some of the blame himself instead of allowing it to fall wholly on Wilson without admitting his own part.

At Gubat two forts were built. A detachment of the enemy, occupying a small island, was driven out by infantry sharpshooters and ship's guns. Wilson returned to base, much reassured that there was no immediate threat to his force. And still he did not move towards Khartoum.

The Mahdi could hardly believe the news that was brought to him by his scouts. The British, having reached the Nile, were doing nothing to exploit their success. Relays of fast camel riders could carry tidings from Metemmeh to Omdurman within the day and the council of khalifas and emirs was kept informed of Wilson's doings. The reverse at Abu Klea had caused consternation. The arrival of wounded in Omdurman spread more alarm. After the Mahdi's glittering record of victories he was so convinced of his invincibility that he was sure that the 'Turks' or, for that matter, the English, would not dare send against him another army, to be mown down by the rifles of his formidable black jehadia and minced by the swords and spears of his Ansar. And yet, out of the awful wastes of the Bayuda desert had appeared a handful of English, rolling back before them the flower of his army, and poised now for the final thrust up the Nile.

On the night of Tuesday, the 20th, as the weary British dug in at Gubat, the Mahdi had called a council of war of his khalifas and senior emirs. He told them that he, the guided one, had received a vision informing him that the moment was opportune for a hegira, or flight. He had little stomach for a direct assault on Khartoum, and months of pressure had failed to bring about the city's fall by starvation. The signs were propitious for a withdrawal to El Obeid, the scene of past victories in the inaccessible regions of Kordofan, from where the Ansar could gird themselves ready to strike the final blow. As the council met, a salute of guns was fired as a signal of victory in an attempt to deceive Gordon. But from the rooftops of Khartoum across the river, watchers with telescopes could see knots of women weeping for their fallen. The customary elaborate wailing over the dead was one of the habits that the Mahdi's stringent religious laws had failed to stamp out; another was the wearing of amulets.

Only one voice in the council was for immediate and direct action against Khartoum. It came from the Mahdi's uncle, Mohammed Abd el Kerim*, who argued: 'If Gordon, a single Englishman, has caused us all this trouble, what will our condition be if an army of his countrymen join Gordon?' The council broke

---

*In 1891, six years after the death of the Mahdi, his successor, the Khalifa Abdallahi, banished Abd el Kerim, together with a kinsman and two other emirs, to Fashoda for championing the cause of the Ashraf, or Mahdi's family, against the dictatorship of the Khalifa. At Fashoda they were all killed.

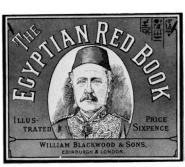

"Stand not upon the order of your going,
But go at once."
*Macbeth.*

**Above** *A satirical booklet of 1885 which made fun of the government* Blue Book *of correspondence in the Gordon affair. It was dedicated to ridicule of the 'Do-Nothing Government' and Gladstone, 'The Grand Old Weathercock' (Stephen Dance).*
**Right** Red Book *cartoon: Wolseley struggles under a load of Gladstone Jam and other goodies in 'The Nile Picnic'.*

THE NILE PICNIC.

*The Gordon drama fascinated Europe. A French version in 1935 is contrasted with Italian heroics of similar vintage; Emilio Salgari was a leading writer of children's stories and Gordon's Italian connection through his lieutenant, Romolo Gessi, was not lost on his readers (Remigio Gennari).*

JACQUES DELEBECQUE

# GORDON
## ET LE DRAME DE KHARTOUM

LIBRAIRIE HACHETTE

EMILIO SALGARI
# L'EROE DI KARTHUM

N. 51
**RACCONTO ILLUSTRATO**

**Above** *Sentimental Victoriana:* The Queen, God Bless Her, *an oil by John Evan Hodgson exhibited at the Royal Academy in 1885, idealises two soldiers of the relief expedition* (Forbes).

**Below** Red Book *cartoon: Granville, the Foreign Secretary (left), and Gladstone turn their backs on Gordon.*

Gladstone's parliamentary tribulations related to the Nile cataracts in a Punch cartoon of November 15 1884.

LEAP-FROG IN THE SOUDAN;
OR "OVER THE WAR-TAR FOR CHARLIE!"

*A* Punch *view of the popular Lord Charles Beresford who led the naval contingent. It was published on January 24 1885 before news came that the expedition had failed.*

up without reaching a decision. So irresolute were the emirs that a bold move by the British might have had dramatic results, according to Feki Medawi, who was at the siege of Khartoum. In a later account of the Mahdi's dilemma, he observed: 'If they had come at once, when we were all alarmed at the defeat of Abu Klea, the Mahdi might have carried out his intention of making a hegira south, but this delay strengthened Abd el Kerim'.

A prisoner in chains in the Mahdi's camp, Rudolf Slatin, heard the women's wailing all night long: 'What news! My heart was literally thumping with joyous excitement.' And again, when stories of the fight before Gubat filtered through to Slatin and other prisoners, they looked forward to imminent deliverance. But the 21st passed. . .and the 22nd. . .with no forward movement by the British. Hope turned to anxious bewilderment.

In the British camp, too, Sir Charles Wilson was weighing the effect of the desert battle on the Mahdi's strategy. Later in a report to Wolseley (on March 23) he wrote: 'I rather hoped that the result of the battle of Abu Klea. . .would have delayed the crisis'. And, reaching a mistaken conclusion, he added: 'Unfortunately, it appears to have had the opposite effect'. In truth, if Wilson had embarked on the forceful course of action, he would have unwittingly taken advantage of a yawning gap in the Mahdi's defences — the almost total breakdown of confidence among the Ansar high command. And it was Wilson's own tardiness that eventually helped spur the Mahdi to order the final onslaught.

# Chapter 16

## *The redcoats sail*

*The third day, Friday, January 23*

'Why did the long-expected steamers with the English troops not come?' wrote Slatin. 'Did their commanders not know Khartoum and the lives of all in it were hanging on a thread? In vain did I, and thousands of others, wait for the shrill whistle of the steamer and for the booming of the guns announcing the English had arrived.'

Why did the English troops not come? On January 23 the English troops were cutting wood and counting 'hens'.

Following Gordon's instructions to remove the Egyptians and assorted allies from the steamers, Lieutenant Stuart-Wortley and Captain Frederick Gascoigne toiled all day at this task. Even this operation seemed to offer an unnecessary distraction to the British command. Where were they going to put Gordon's 'hens'? At Beresford's suggestion they were allocated a camp on the Khartoum side of Gubat, 'so that in the event of a force advancing from Khartoum, and the consequent revolt of the 'hens', we should not be placed between two fires'. The military committee deliberated whether or not this arrangement would foul the water; Beresford had two wooden piers built to take fresh water from midstream.

By this time, the naval commander appears to have succumbed to the debilitating effects of his boil — he entered hospital, where he stayed two days — and to the realisation that he was not, after all, going to be able to accompany the expedition to Khartoum. But still Wilson was not ready. While the ships' crews were being sorted out, work gangs under the direction of soldiers ransacked the riverside settlements and spent hours sawing up the gigantic sakiehs, or water-wheels, for firewood. Ammunition and food were carried aboard the two largest steamers, the *Bordein* and the *Tel-el-Hoween*, chosen for the expedition. A naval artificer

142

completed an engine-room overhaul in each vessel.

Khasm el Mus was placed in command of the *Bordein,* and Abd el Hamid of the *Tel-el-Hoween.* Wilson was to go in the *Bordein,* together with Gasgcoigne, ten non-commissioned officers and men of the Royal Sussex, one Petty Officer and one artificer of the naval brigade, and 110 Sudanese soldiers. In the *Tel-el-Hoween* were to go Captain L.J. Trafford in command of ten Royal Sussex, Stuart-Wortley, one naval artificer and 80 Sudanese; the vessel towed a nuggar, or sailing boat, holding about 50 Sudanese; and a cargo of durra, or grain, for Khartoum. Wilson arranged for Colonel Reginald Talbot to take a column to Jakdul to forward supplies, and for the command at Gubat to be under Boscawen; within two days this last officer was down with a raging fever and command passed to Colonel Mildmay Willson of the Scots Guards.

In Wolseley's original orders, the ships were to be manned by the naval brigade. This was no longer possible because of the severe casualties it had suffered in the desert. Fifty men of the Royal Sussex were to go. Sir Charles Wilson, fretting about the safety of his main force, decided to take a much smaller number of Britons, and to trust principally to some of Gordon's black troops. The opportunity passed to mount what could have been a powerful thrust, strong enough if necessary to *rescue* Gordon, on the initiative of the desert commander who would have to take into account the dramatically worsening circumstances in Khartoum. On paper, Wilson had, indisputably, no mandate to carry out such an operation, as passionately as the British public would have wished it. As his biographer, Watson, pointed out, there was not the least intention of using the desert column for the relief of Khartoum. But the *rescue* of Gordon would have been uppermost in the thinking of Burnaby and, possibly, Herbert Stewart. Whether rescue would have been advisable or possible would have depended on a number of factors: the Mahdi's reaction — flight, hesitation, or assault; the strength of Wilson's own conviction: and finally, but not least, Gordon's willingness to leave. On the last point, however, if one is to judge from Gordon's writings on the subject, his views were unequivocal:

'I declare *positively*, and *once for all, that I will not leave the Sudan until evey one who wants to go down is given the chance to do so, unless* a government is established, which relieves me of the charge; therfore if any emmissary or letter comes up here ordering me to come down, I WILL NOT OBEY IT, BUT WILL STAY HERE, AND FALL WITH THE TOWN, AND RUN ALL RISKS.' November 9.

'I altogether *decline* the imputation that the projected expedition has come to *relieve me*. . .I am not the *rescued lamb* and I will not be.' September 24.

It would appear, then, that any rescuer would have succeeded in removing the stubborn Gordon from Khartoum only by force or by the General's being incapacitated (in the event of any enemy breakthrough a group of Greeks, devoted to Gordon, had nursed a plan to carry him off forcibly and spirit him away by steamer, kept waiting for the purpose; it came to nothing, of course).

It has been argued that Wolseley, a servant of the Queen, had no authority over his friend, Gordon, a servant of the Khedive, to order his retirement from Khartoum. Wolseley, however, was empowered by the British government to undertake a mission of 'rescue and retire', the object being to bring away Gordon, his officers and whatever Egyptian soldiers and civilians wished to return (the main, Nile-borne force was to be used for this task). Bearing in mind Gordon's possible, and probable, refusal to leave, London asked the Khedive in Cairo to give Wolseley a secret firman that would allow him, if necessary, to supersede Gordon.

All this, for the moment, was hypothetical. Wilson's immediate instructions were to communicate with Gordon. 'Orders have been given to Sir H. Stewart [mortally wounded] to send a small detachment of infantry with you to Khartoum. If you like you can, upon arriving there, march these men through the city to show the people that British troops are near at hand. If there is any epidemic in the town you will not do this. I do not wish them to sleep in the city. They must return with you to Metemmeh. You will only stay in Khartoum long enough to confer fully with General Gordon. Having done so, you will return with Lord Charles Beresford in steamers to Metemmeh.'

Of the steamers' tiny complement of British soldiers, the contemprary critic of the campaign, barrister Charles Royle, observed (*The Egyptian Campaigns*): 'Of course, little more than a *demonstration* could have been made with any force such as the steamers could have carried. . .Still, the singular reduction from 14,000, the total of the British Army in Egypt, to 7,000, the force told off for the expedition, then to 1,800, the number of Sir Herbert Stewart's column, finally to twenty, the number of Sir Charles Wilson's forlorn hope, cannot fail to strike the reader.'

The sun set before the steamers were ready. Wilson resolved to move upstream the next morning, arguing — with some justification — that to sail by night might court disaster on sandbanks or rocks.

One further interlude had delayed the expedition's final preparations. It was Wolseley's expressed wish that the British infantry should make their 'demonstrations' wearing red tunics. Some had been specially sent with the column for the purpose, but they had been stolen in the desert. Now a search through the force was made for any red tunics that could be found. The only ones available were jumpers borrowed from the Guards' camel corps. The Royal Sussex put on the oversize jumpers, grumbling eloquently that they had 'thrashed the niggers in grey' and that now they had to fight dressed as if for a circus. Wolseley's idea, however, was more than an empty gesture: visibility was the aim of the operation and he judged that news of 'the redcoats of Khartoum' would spread rapidly.

The redcoats sailed at eight the next morning. Beresford described the departure thus: '. . .the two steamers started, flying the Egyptian flag, the slave girls frying durra-cake under the fore turret, old Khasm el Mus smoking and drinking coffee on the cabin sofa, both vessels crammed with yelling and joyous savages among whom were a bare score of British soldiers'. Khartoum was four days' voyage distant. The Nile was falling and, with it, Gordon's last chance. Within 48 hours an unexpected opportunity for the Mahdi was to expose the city to fire and sword.

# Chapter 17

# *Blood-letting*

Wednesday, Thursday, Friday. . .

On Saturday despair seized both the besieged and the captive. The appearance of the redcoats, 'no matter how few', would have given the garrison fresh heart to fight 'tooth and nail against the enemy', averred Slatin. Father Joseph Ohrwalder declared: 'Had twenty redcoats arrived at Khartoum, it would have been saved . . . Many survivors of Khartoum often said to me, "Had we seen one Englishman, we would have been saved." '

In his account, *Ten Years' Captivity in the Mahdi's Camp*, compiled with the help and, presumably, sympathetic attention of the intelligence officer, Wingate, Ohrwalder laid categorical charges against Wilson: *the unaccountable delay of the English was the cause of the fall of the city, the death of Gordon, and the fate of the Sudan.* The Mahdi, Ohrwalder stated, made up his mind to attack only when he heard of the delay at Gubat. He did not begin to put his troops across the river until January 24, and it was not until Saturday night, the 25th, that the crossing was complete. Some said that the English General was wounded at Abu Klea and lying insensible 'and that those who were acting for him did not dare to undertake any operations until he was sufficiently recovered to be able to give his own orders'. The Sudanese wondered why Europeans, who generally took precautions for every eventuality, should not have done so in this case. Others thought that Khasm el Mus must have urged the English to attack Metemmeh and Shendy in revenge for the persistency with which the Ansar had attacked and harrassed the steamers. 'Even to the present day', Ohrwalder wrote in 1892, shortly after his escape from captivity, 'people in the Sudan cannot understand the reason for the delay.'

When the British did not come, confidence grew in the camp of the Mahdi. His decision to attack was confirmed by a sensational piece of news, brought to him by a deserter from Gordon's lines, Omar Ibrahim. Unknown to the besieging army, the river in its fall had left exposed a ridge of land, little more than a sandback but enough to give access to the ramparts near the junction of the White Nile and a hitherto impassable water ditch on the south side of the city. Unaccountably, the defenders had not realised the importance of this development and had done nothing to repair the potential breach. This was no vision, but in it Mohammed Ahmed saw the hand of Allah.

After darkness on Sunday, the 25th, the Mahdi summoned his three senior khalifas and together they crossed the White Nile by rowing boat from Omdurman to the vast war camp arrayed in a crescent round the now vulnerable southern bastions of Khartoum. Wilson's two steamers with their Sudanese and twenty Royal Sussex were 60 miles to the north at uneasy and watchful anchorage; they were poised for an attempt in the morning on theformidable Shabluka cataract, its gorge of soaring black cliffs a nightmare of ambush possibilities. The Mahdi must have known that the British had, at last, moved, but any threat they posed was now outweighed by the tactical gift of the sandbank, the key to Khartoum.

No roar of acclaim, as was usual, greeted the Mahdi's arrival among his warriors. The Ansar, gathered in a half circle, had been ordered to keep silence less the defenders should be alerted. But the announcement of Khartoum's new-found weakness brought a low growl of delighted anticipation from the host: Dongolawi from the north, with more reason than most to hate the oppressive and corrupt 'Turks': riverine Jaalin, some of whom had been mauled at Abu Klea and who now looked forward to an awful vengeance on their neighbours, the Shagiyeh lickspittles of the English; Baggara cavalry, the spoiled and fanatical adherents of Khalifa Abdallahi, who had ridden a path of blood from distant Darfur and whose fearful reputation would ensure them the juiciest pickings in women and loot; and the black Sudanese jehadia, the slave force of captured riflemen honed to murderous efficiency by Abu Anga, who relished any opportunity to turn their guns on their former masters.

The great commander, Abd el Rahman el Nejumi, who had learned to develop more than a little liking for the worldly fruits of holy war, particularly when it came to augmenting his harem, headed a group of 20 emirs, arranged in a tight cordon around their leader and his khalifas. The Mahdi stood beneath a tree, a tall and powerfully built figure in a simple white jibbeh sparsely decorated with patches. On his head was a white skull cap, wrapped round with a broad white turban. He had perfected a gentle manner of speech, which exuded an air of piety, but now his words were warlike and penetrated the ranks of the assembled Ansar.

'The Prophet has ordered me to attack Khartoum at dawn. Are you ready to go through their forces not caring for the consequences of what will happen?'

'Yes!', came the suppressed shout in reply.

'Do you look forward to the jehad with true belief and strong hearts?'

'Yes!'

'Will you stand steadfast even if two-thirds of you are killed?'

'Yes!'

In response to a signal from the Mahdi, the host repeated with him the fatiha, the first chapter of the Koran. The Mahdi then drew his sword, waved it in the air three times, and shouted, 'Allahu akbar' (God is great). In a ring of upheld torches so that all could see him, the Mahdi made a last theatrical gesture. He raised his arms and face to Allah and roared: 'Come on, come on to Khartoum'.

The assault was made an hour before the dawn. The treacherous Nile loosed on the city a tidal wave of 50,000 Ansar, outnumbering Gordon's starving soldiers ten to one, outnumbering even the population of Khartoum. Resistance ceased within two hours.

Gordon was done to death at the top of a flight of steps leading from a balcony down to the palace gardens. Victorian popular tradition pictures him immaculately uniformed in white, sword and pistol in hand, defying the dervish intruders who pause in awe and trepidation before releasing an avalanche of spears. Whoever was responsible for killing Gordon risked the retribution of the Mahdi who ordered before the attack that Gordon should be spared. No such protection extended to others. The Mahdi, who customarily granted mercy to unbelievers who agreed to espouse the Muslim faith and recognise him as the promised one, had told his followers on this occasion: 'Whomsoever you encounter in battle, kill him. God has said, "Their belief in Me only after they have seen my might profiteth them nothing".'

Gordon's head was hacked off and taken to the Mahdi. He is

said to have been angry when he saw it. Nevertheless, after sending it, wrapped in a cloth, to Slatin for identification, he allowed it to be hung in a tree in a public place where it was reviled by the mob until it withered to a skull. Gordon's body was thrown down a well.

Ohrwalder estimated the deathroll at about 10,000 in the first few hours after the city fell. It is a subjective assessment coloured by his intense hatred of the Mahdi and all connected with him. Certainly, the bloodletting was extensive and often indiscriminate until the Mahdi ordered the survivors to be spared.

In Britain, outrage and prurient fascination were fed by writers' accounts based on the knowledge that massacre and rape on a massive scale had taken place, and embroidered by imagined details in the absence of immediate eye-witness evidence. It was a production that would run and run, the great Victorian peepshow with classic crowd-pulling ingredients: an epic last stand by the God-fearing hero, alone against the heathen mob; the forlorn hope of the redcoats; the slaughter of the innocents; the defilement and abduction into bondage of Christian women by barbaric hordes. The story was retold many times in the ensuing 13 years of the 'Sudan crisis' as survivors' accounts reached London and former prisoners such as Ohrwalder and Slatin published best-selling editions on their ordeals. What they had to tell often plumbed deeper depths of horror than the journalists' imaginings.

Swordsmen severed the hands of the Greek consul, Nicolas Leontides, before the coup de grâce by decapitation; of him, Gordon (who preferred to call him Leonidas) wrote during the siege that he had 'behaved worthy of his ancestor of Thermopylæ, on a smaller scale'. The 62-year-old Austrian consul, Martin Hansall, who had enjoyed the attentions of seven female attendants and earned the contempt of Gordon for considering as early as September desertion to the Mahdiists, was also beheaded — then they burned his body, his dog and his parrot in alcohol and threw them into the river. Having seen an Austrian tailor called Klein make the sign of the cross, they cut his throat from ear to ear in front of his wife and children, and speared his 18-year-old son to death. A Greek woman saw her 12-year-old son cleaved by an axe. She saved her six-month-old boy by saying he was a girl. The woman was reserved for the harem of the commander Nejumi. Aser, the American consul, fell dead on seeing his brother beheaded. Seven Greeks who had escaped the slaughter by hiding for eight hours, were being taken to a place of safety by George Clementino — a trusted prisoner captured at El Obeid and sometimes used by the Mahdi to carry messages to Gordon — when they were stopped by Dongolawi tribesmen who were rampaging through the streets, spearing any wounded they found and routing out fugitives. Despite Clementino's pleas, the Dongolawi beheaded the seven Greeks in the street.

The unfortunate Shagiyeh tribespeople who had stayed loyal to the government, though the despair of Gordon, were hunted mercilessly for days after the Mahdi's 'amnesty'. It was customary to kill them on sight. Thus genocide gave birth to a Sudanese proverb: 'The Shagiyeh, the Egyptian, the dog, no rest shall he find in the Mahdia'. According to Mahdiist doctrine, dogs, considered unclean, were to be destroyed.

Women were herded into thornbush enclosures: one *zeriba* for young and good looking, fair women; one for unmarried Sudanese; another for black slave girls suitable for concubines; and so on. The Mahdi reportedly took the first choice, including girls from the age of five who would be destined for his harem. The khalifas then had their choice, and next, the emirs. The remaining women were given to the Ansar. Old women were herded to Omdurman to fend for themselves; many died of starvation. Some townsfolk, eager to seek favour with their conquerors, betrayed young girls who were in hiding, or others who had cut their hair short in order to pass as boys: after the first orgy of bloodletting, it was deemed safer to be male in Khartoum.

Strict regulations governed the apportioning of material spoil. By the Mahdi's law, it belonged to the treasury, and severe punishment — even death — was meted out to transgressors. Nevertheless, many an emir enriched himself on the loot of Khartoum. The hippopotamus-hide kurbash was used freely to extract information about hidden treasure from the wealthier and more secretive citizens. With no small sense of outrage, Ohrwalder recorded that Ibrahim Pasha Fauzi, 'the favourite of Gordon', was tied to a date-palm for several days and flogged until he revealed the whereabouts of his money. The old widow of Mustafa Tiranis, a rich merchant, was whipped 'nearly to death'. In each case discretion might have been the better part of greed.

Militarily, the victory gave the Mahdi fresh stocks of arms and one million rounds of ammunition, and refurbished belief in the Ansar's invincibility. Economically, it solved few problems for the

Mahdi. The absorption of the city's population, forcibly moved across the river to Omdurman, into a seething, disordered collection of makeshift hovels, added to the chaos in the new capital of the new state, which already lived under the twin threat of starvation and disease. One immediate and visible benefit to the triumphant Ansar was totally cosmetic. Large stocks of cloth were found, and the tattered jibbehs of the victorious army sprouted a crop of many-coloured patches.

# Chapter 18

# *Inquest*

Early on the morning of February 5, 1885, an astonished maid who opened the door of Osborne Cottage in the Isle of Wight was brushed aside by a totally unexpected visitor who had descended on the doorstep in unwonted haste, a short black-garbed figure seething with indignation and the suppressed desire to impart what could only be momentous information. In the drawing room where they were sitting after breakfast, Mary, wife of Sir Henry Ponsonby, her elder daughter, 20-year-old Betty (Alberta), and the younger Mags (Magdalen) heard voices in the hall and were equally startled when the door burst open and the caller entered, unattended and unannounced. Mary Ponsonby beheld her sovereign pale and trembling, and hardly had time to curtsy before Victoria, standing and without preliminaries, intoned: 'Too late! Khartoum has fallen. Gordon is dead.'

The Queen drove the quarter of a mile from Osborne to her private secretary's house, adjoining the royal grounds, seeking someone with whom to share her grief and anger, as soon as she heard the news that had reached Whitehall by telegram from Wolseley in the early hours of that morning. Later, in her journal, she enlarged on the feelings she had so eloquently expressed to Lady Ponsonby: 'It is too fearful. The Government is alone to blame, by refusing to send the expedition till it was too late.' And the message was made only too clear to her mininsters — or anyone else who cared to read it — when she threw constitutional niceties aside, abandoned the use of cipher, and telegraphed in plain words to Gladstone, Hartington and Granville: 'These news from Khartoum are frightful, and to think that all this might have been prevented and many precious lives saved by earlier action is too frightful.'

Gladstone regarded the telegram as public censure on his

152

government. Unrepentant and willing to be convinced that Gordon had brought on his own death, he riposted with a lengthy justification, respectfully rejecting 'the conclusion which your Majesty has been pleased thus to announce', and admitting only to the mistake of sending troops south of the Egyptian frontier.

Nothing elicited from Victoria harsher words, reflecting the distaste she felt for Gladstone and his Liberal government, than did the death of Gordon. Much is on record in her journals and letters and in government papers. The true acidity of her feelings, however, is to be found in written exchanges she had with her secretary, Sir Henry Ponsonby, a conscientious and diplomatic servant who tended to water down his employer's vintage tartness when decanting her views for official consumption. Alarmed at Gladstone's reaction to the telegram and fearing ministerial resignations, Ponsonby drafted a letter of explanation to the Prime Minister's secretary, Edward Hamilton, and asked the Queen whether he might send it in her name. A note followed from Victoria:

'Quite right but you might add that the Queen's feelings are so strong for the honour of her Grt Empire that she with difficulty abstained fr saying *much better*.

'The humiliation of this *defeat* NO one feels more keenly than she does but *dear Mr. Gladstone's* feelings are *much more thought* of than the Queen's suffering! This is too bad, wd be glad if it *was* known.

'Mr. Gladstone has no chivalry, no sense of the *real* honour and dignity of his country. Mary P. (Ponsonby) wd quite agree with the Queen. Sir Henry is not half indignant enough. She cannot excuse her anger.'

This was followed by a full letter to Ponsonby on the same day. For the insight it opens into the Queen's thinking — that she cared not a fig for resignations, Gladstone's own if necessary, and that she regarded herself (with some justification) as arbiter of popular feelings — it is worth quoting at length. The Queen wrote:

Osborne, Feb. 7, 1885
'The Queen . . . *meant* that Mr. G. should remember what SHE suffers when the British name is humiliated as in the present instance — & he can go away & resign but she MUST REMAIN & she was suffered so cruelly from humiliation & annoyance from the present Gov$^t$ *since* the unlucky day when Mr. Gladstone came

in — that she was boiling over with the indignation & horror which *everyone* in this country felt & feels! Mr. G. *never* minds loss of life etc. & wraps himself up in his own *incomprehensible delusions & illusions* refusing to read what is in every paper & everyone's mouth.

'She makes no secret of what she thinks & w^d repeat it to Mr. Gladstone. How c^d she be silent when the news came & how c^d she NOT say what she did? She named *no one*. Sir Henry stated the exact fact to Mr. Hamilton. Is it possible that Mr. Gladstone's *adulators & worshippers* (who do him much harm) *ignore* the universal feeling? Some of the newspapers even fear L^d Wolseley may not be aware of the real feeling & that he may still be influenced by Cabinet views. She *thinks* not.

'In the Queen's heart (& in that of many others she knows) she holds *Mr. Gladstone responsible* by imprudence, neglect, violent language for the lives of many 1000^ds tho' unwittingly. The Queen w^d not object to making him a peer but she will not give him the Garter, not from personal but from public motives as she honestly thinks he has *done such incalculable harm* to the country. Look at our relations abroad! No one trusts or relies on us & from '74 to '80 especially the last 3 or 4 years of that time England stood very high.

'It is a terrible grief to her. The Queen blames Lord Granville very much for he is as many people truly say "quite past" — weak & indolent & not able to work hard.

'Sir Henry must speak very seriously to L^d Hartington as to eventualities but without making him *think* that he *is certain* to be Mr. Gladstone's successor. We cannot tell what may happen.'

While the monarch censured her Prime Minister for months of delay, the Nile commander whose river-obsessed strategies had cost weeks blamed the officer he considered responsible for wasting vital days. 'He might have started on the afternoon of the 21st, and did not start till the morning of the 24th', was how Wolseley summed up Sir Charles Wilson's error. In a letter home to his wife, Louisa, he wrote: 'I hate to see Sir C. Wilson because I cannot help remembering that he *might* have been at Khartoum easily the day before it was betrayed'. On the day the dreadful news broke on Victoria and her subjects, Wilson was riding despondently back across the Bayuda Desert from Gubat to Korti with an escort of Coldstream Guards on camels.

A storm broke in the press when Charles Williams, who had

been a correspondent in the desert for the Central News Agency, accused Wilson of 'hanging about at Abu Klea' in a bitter indictment published in *Fortnightly Review*. Faced with allegations of military incompetence, Wilson made the mistake of replying, which spread the controversy in the public domain. Williams quoted an officer saying that Wilson had lost his nerve, and added: 'If I differ from this it is only in wondering whether he had any to lose.' Wilson and his 'committee', argued Williams, 'had no more notion of what could or should be done than a bugler'.

It was bitter stuff, which would have brought a sensational libel action down on the writer's head today. Curiously, however, the only one to resort to the law was Williams, the biter bit. When *Saturday Review*, in the course of criticism of *both* protagonists, cast doubt on William's personal and professional motives, the journalist sued for damages of £2,000. The court found in his favour, but awarded only £300 — and the public might be forgiven for reading in the judgement indirect condemnation of Wilson's dalliance.

Wolseley confined his official judgement to a dismissive and damning note which he sent to the War Minister, Hartington, on April 13, enclosing a letter in which Wilson attempted to explain his decisions at Gubat. 'I do not propose to add any remarks of my own to this letter', wrote Wolseley. 'The reasons given by Sir Charles Wilson must speak for themselves.' Such comment by ommission was a source of lasting bitterness to Wilson, who had ended his report with the words: ' . . . I do not think that any action of mine could have saved his [Gordon's] life or averted the fall of Khartoum'.

Wilson could guess what was being said in influential circles behind the scenes by Wolseley, who was under fire in the press for his strategies and the 'social circus' flavour of his camel corps. Sir Henry Ponsonby has left a record of a meeting with the Nile commander at Osborne in July. 'Do you think you could have saved Khartoum,' asked Ponsonby. Wolseley looked round and said: 'May I speak confidentialy?' Ponsonby said: 'Yes'. Wolseley replied: 'I haven't a doubt we could have done it. Wilson was useless as a military commander and lost his head. He lost nearly three days. If he had gone on at once a rapid move would have encouraged our friends and Gordon would have been saved.'

Two days later, Ponsonby observed: 'The Queen told me that Wolseley was low when he talked to her, his expedition was a failure. He had gone to rescue Gordon, and his garrison had not done it. Checked by the Government at home, delayed by Ministers and badly served at the critical moment by a good man but inefficient soldier, he missed his object by 48 hours. When he spoke of Gordon his voice broke . . . '

To Wilson's support came a close friend, General Sir Lintorn Simmons, who was then the Governor of Malta. In a letter to Wilson he described the tone of Wolseley's official remarks to Hartington as 'contemptuous, and intended to let the blame of failure rest on you'. Simmons wrote 'in the firm belief that the dastardly act of trying to make you the scapegoat will, ere long, meet the reward and exposure it deserves'. He unequivocally placed part of the blame on Wolseley himself in these words: 'The "too late" policy, for which I suspect Lord Wolseley is largely responsible, and the political mistake of abandonment, to which I attribute by far the greater measure of the cruel fate of Gordon, are the real causes of total failure of the expedition'.

Wilson (who was further exonerated by Gordon's brother, Sir Henry Gordon, in the edited version of the Khartoum Journals) declared in a letter to a friend that 'under the same conditions, I believed that I should act again in the same way' — and delivered his own harsh indictment of the policies and decisions that led to the Sudan debacle.

Listing a catalogue of contributory factors, Wilson first blamed the government's delay 'which obliged everything to be done at high pressure'. Second, the government and Wolseley erred in treating with the wily Mudir of Dongola who hated the British, was determined to ruin Gordon and 'who has, throughout, done everything he could to thwart us, and prevent our getting supplies and transports'. Next, bad management on the line of communications delayed the boats at least a month. But the chief reason for failure, in Wilson's opinion, was 'the different views of the boat and camel men' which resulted in vacillation and disorganisation in acquiring camels when finally a desert column was decided upon. The shortage of camels caused critical delay at Jakdul which allowed the Mahdi's troops to mass in the Bayuda; if Stewart had had sufficient transport animals to go straight across in his first march he would have met no opposition in the desert and only slight resistance at Metemmeh, which he would have reached by January 3 or 4 — 'so, for want of a thousand camels . . . the game was lost'. And, in passing, Wilson argued that the faulty composition of the Camel Corps, Wolseley's brainchild, caused the loss of many lives, if not time.

In high and lower echelons the debate over Wilson's responsibility rumbled and spluttered indecorously, until it was gradually lost in the louder argument about what Britain was going to do with its Sudan troops, extended, fragmented and exposed over several hundred miles of river and desert. Wilson sought Army permission for a public enquiry into the allegations against him but was firmly advised not to press the matter. He had an interview with the Commander-in-Chief, the Duke of Cambridge, who — no admirer of Wolseley — congratulated him on his gallant action on the Nile. In the Commons vote of thanks to the soldiers, Hartington spoke in glowing terms of Wilson's 'perilous and romantic expedition up the river to Khartoum'. There was even apparent blessing from the Queen — who could see but one arch-villain, Gladstone — by her receiving him in audience at Buckingham Palace. His feelings thus assuaged, Charles William Wilson, subsequently promoted Major-General, stepped off the public stage into the obscurity of the Ordnance Survey.

What *was* Britain going to do with its troops on the Nile? The answer was to be found in the government's reaction to the tide of public odium which now engulfed Gladstone and his ministers. The result was a policy — or rather a series of changing policies that veered from one extreme to another — summed up in Wolseley's own description as 'butcher and bolt'. Under the torrent of indignation after Gordon's death, government motives, no less than those of governments in the next decade, were steered by the reality of unashamed capitulation to popular demand for revenge.

In letters from the Queen, in newspaper editorials, in the streets, in the music halls, Gladstone was reviled. It became popular to reverse the initials G.O.M., for Grand Old Man, to M.O.G., for Murderer of Gordon. Wolseley, who consistently adopted this practice, taught his dog to growl at the word 'Gladstone', and kept a bust of the statesman on his mantlepiece so that he could have it turned always towards the wall and tell visitors that he could not stand seeing the face of the 'old crocodile'.

To Wolseley's surprise, he was informed early in February that the government intended to smash the Mahdi. No prospect could afford him greater pleasure. 'If I can only kill him, it will be a very happy finale to our expedition up the Nile', he told his daughter, Frances. At the opening of Parliament on the 19th the public was assured that the British Army was going on to Khartoum to break the dervish empire. Wolseley knew it could not be done without substantial reinforcements. With the Nile falling and the Sudan stoking up to unbearable temperatures, no major campaign could be attempted before the autumn. First, however, he planned to take Berber by a pincer movement using General Earle's river contingent and the desert column at Gubat, now commanded by Sir Redvers Buller and reinforced by 600 Royal Irish and the Light Camel Regiment.

Buller, however, reported that the desert column's precarious river bridgehead could not be held. There were rumours of 50,000 dervishes massing for attack. He disabled the two remaining steamers (they were subsequently reintroduced into service by the Mahdi's resourceful river men), dumped stores in the Nile, and allowed (much against his gentlemanly inclinations) the code of the desert to be infringed by spoiling the wells. Then he successfully extricated the battle-worn, exhausted column in a series of hair-raising piecemeal shuttles across the Bayuda, harassed and sniped at by Ansar skirmishers, but inexplicably unmolested by the Mahdi's main force.

Bootless, clothes in tatters, reduced to eating their camels, the men who made up the column of 'the forlorn hope' footslogged the 180 miles to safety carrying their wounded and sick. That Anglophobe, the future Kaiser Wilhelm II, had wished: 'May the Mahdi chuck them all in the Nile'. The great German strategist, General Count Helmuth von Moltke, said of them, however: 'They were not soldiers, but heroes'.

The main British force on the Nile destroyed 2,000 Ansar at Kirbekan, an action in which it pleased William Earle to have the South Staffordshires dressed in scarlet tunics and the Black Watch put on their kilts. Its clockwork meticulousness was impaired by the death of Earle when he imprudently ventured near a house held by enemy riflemen. The force, now under General Henry Brackenbury, pushed on past the wreck of Colonel Stewart's steamer, the *Abbas*, to Abu Hamed, the high point of the boatborne expedition's progress. Abu Hamed lies at the very top of the huge 'question mark' formed by the Nile as it sprawls round the escarpments of the Bayuda Desert, and was an objective regarded by the soldiers as 'half-way house' on the river haul from Dongola to Khartoum. There, on February 24, Brackenbury was ordered to retire and the Nile soldiers sailed and marched down the river that had cost them months of back-breaking effort to conquer.

Why the Mahdi allowed the vulnerable river and desert columns to retire almost unmolested has been the subject of much mystery and speculation. Preoccupation with the establishment of his new capital at Omdurman and the Ansar's natural inclination to rest on their laurels after the costly siege of Khartoum have been put forward as reasons. The fall of the city, however, made available — by some estimates — 100,000 fighting men, and more were flocking to the Mahdi's flag every day in the wake of his success. More simple but plausible is the theory that the unsought death of his Christian adversary, Gordon, with whom he had strong spiritual affinities, profoundly moved, awed and unnerved the Mahdi and brought on one of his characteristic crises of indecisiveness.

At the Red Sea port of Suakim in the eastern Sudan, a remarkable two-month 'sideshow' was about to begin. With the object of crushing Osman Digna's tribes and building a railway to support an overland advance towards Berber, the government despatched an expedition of 12,000 British and Indian troops, a force even stronger than Wolseley's Nile expedition. To the surprise and dismay of many observers military and civil, command was handed to Gerald Graham, whose tactical mistakes had given cause for grave alarm the previous year despite his victories. After several indecisive dervish-killing actions, including the near-disaster of McNeill's Zeriba and the subsequent whitewash by the Generals, Graham announced that he had taught Osman Digna 'a severe lesson'. As the British troops, under yet another change of Gladstone policy, halted the railway-builders, withdrew from the field and sailed away before the end of May, the Mahdi's champion understandably hailed the outcome of the confrontation as victory for his generalship. Uncrushed and far from chastened by Graham's 'lesson', Osman Digna* claimed that once again he

---

*Osman Digna remained free until the 20th century. It would have been an observant reader of the London press who discerned a paragraph tucked away among the columns of Boer War news in January 1900. It revealed that 'the slippery eel' was betrayed by tribesmen in his old stamping ground of the Red Sea hills and captured by Egyptian troops under an officer of the Gloucestershire Regiment, Frank Burgess. Thus, nearly 20 years after he joined the Mahdi's holy war, the last and greatest of the Ansar generals ended his career. Reporting on March 21 his imprisonment at Rosetta, near Alexandria, *The Graphic* assured its readers: 'In place of the barbarous Dervish rule, absolute order with a sense of security is manifest everywhere, and one can even book a ticket from Charing Cross to Khartoum'. Osman Digna devoted his later years to religious contemplation, made a pilgrimage to Mecca in 1924, and died at Wady Halfa in 1926 in an odour of sanctity. He was 86.

had driven out the British and he gained fresh popular support in the wake of 'butcher and bolt'.

Simultaneously, the Army of the Nile was engaged in an inexorable movement northwards, down-river, which was to culminate in the total abandonment of the Sudan. The Queen railed in vain at Gladstone for his perfidy. *'No change* or *withdrawal must take place* immediately', she wrote to Ponsonby in April from holiday in Aix-les-Bains, where she thought she was being deliberately kept out of policy-making. Britain must not 'scuttle out' after killing thousands. She even suggested buying off Osman Digna and his tribes. From Darmstadt, a few days later, she declared that Gladstone 'cares not how many lives are sacrificed or how civilisation is advanced provided his Franchise & (. . .) Bill pass'. Furiously and hastily written, abbreviated, Victoria's words to Ponsonby were often indecipherable as they ran into the broad black mourning edge of her notepaper.

Gladstone had found a heaven-sent reason for abandonment, however, which solved two problems for him at one blow. While an Anglo-Russian commission was trying to settle the disputed areas of Afghanistan, Russia took advantage of Britain's Egyptian distractions and attacked the remote village of Pendjeh. The Prime Minister thundered at this 'unprovoked aggression' and alerted the Army reserve. The 'Pendjeh Crisis' enabled him to justify the total withdrawal of the Army in the Sudan on the grounds that the troops might be needed to defend India. Cartoon art depicted Wolseley's lion cubs marching to tackle the Russian bear. The crisis also presented Gladstone with the opportunity eloquently to divert public wrath from himself to the Tsar. In June, after the Liberals resigned — nominally on a budget motion but arguably as the result of the Sudan débâcle — a Conservative government came to power. Though the Russian crisis blew over, however, Lord Salisbury found it impossible to reverse the previous administration's policy of abandonment in the Sudan.

The Mahdi outlived his adversary, Gordon, by less than five months.

On June 22, 1885, Mohammed Ahmed died in the cement hut which he occupied at Omdurman. He was not yet 40 years of age. There were stories, eagerly given prominence by the British press, that he succumbed to poison administered by a concubine whose husband and children had been murdered at Khartoum. The evidence, however, points to a natural death. Slatin believed he died from typhus. Ohrwalder ascribed death to fatty degeneration of the heart, brought on by a 'debauched and dissolute mode of life'.

The Mahdi's principal wife, Aisha, and other close relatives washed his body, anointed it with sandalwood oils, wrapped it in a plain shroud and buried it beneath the bed, a piece of loot from Khartoum, in which he died. He was suceeded by the Khalifa Abdallahi, who ruled at Omdurman for 13 years — during which several millions died by pestilence or the sword — until Kitchener's Anglo-Egyptian army destroyed the power of Mahdiism on September 2 1898, in a set-piece battle which left 11,000 Ansar dead on the field.

There were some tidying-up operations to be undertaken — such as the dislodgement of an opportunist French expedition from the upper Nile at Fashoda and the trapping of the Khalifa Abdallahi, who escaped from Omdurman — before Anglo-Egyptian government settled in to rule the Sudan for more than half a century. Anglophobes who observed that the rebuilt Khartoum was in the shape of the Union Jack missed the point: Kitchener's meticulous mind recognised that radiating avenues could be effectively controlled by strategically-placed machine guns in the event of another rebellion.

At large in the wastes of Kordofan for a year, the Khalifa was hunted down and cornered by a force of Egyptians and Sudanese under Sir Reginald Wingate on November 25 1899. The place where the Khalifa fought the last stand of Mahdiism was a valley of stunted scrub and trees only a short march from the holy Abba Island on the White Nile where the Mahdi first proclaimed his mission. The war drums and the long booming notes of the Khalifa's elephant-tusk horn were heard for the final time. There was a short, sharp action by dawn's half-light in which Ansar brothers bound themselves together to fight and die as one. When the machine-guns stopped, grinning soldiers of the Sudanese IX and XIII Battalions probed with bayonets and kicked their way through the dead and wounded seeking the leader of their enemy. They found his bullet-riddled body on a sheepskin prayer rug where he had seated himself to receive the onslaught in the van of his men. Close around, in blood-soaked jibbehs with their symbolic patches for poverty and piety, lay the corpses of his emirs and his devoted Baggara warriors.

The avenging of Gordon was complete. The Mahdia was over.

An astute Churchillian observation put the net monetary cost of reconquest, the gaining of military prestige and 'the indulgence of the sentiment known as "the avenging of Gordon"' at £800,000 for the British taxpayer. At that price, wrote the future Prime Minister who had ridden with the 21st Lancers at Omdurman, 'it may be stated in all seriousness that English history does not record any instance of so great a national satisfaction being more cheaply obtained'.

The war correspondent, George Warrington Steevens, found less cause for congratulation: 'The poor Sudan! The wretched dry Sudan! Count all the gains you will, yet what a hideous irony it remains, this fight of half a generation for such an emptiness.'

# Interlude

# *The margin of fate*

The men whose spears ended the life of Charles George Gordon on the morning of Monday, January 26 1885, have never been identified precisely and satisfactorily beyond all doubt. From time to time history has arraigned various accused — a group of blood-crazed Dongolawi. . . Jaalin warriors under the banner of Emir el Nejumi. . . a disaffected former follower, and so on. 'Arrivals from Khartoum', victims of or panderers to Victorian newsmen's appetite for detail, have conveniently supplied the names of three wretches, all with motives of revenge for Gordon-inspired executions of their fellow tribesmen. But whether or not one of these three — Awlad el Mek, Mussa Agha Tayallah and Ali Wad Rahma — delivered the mortal thrust is unimportant. Responsibility for the killing of Gordon lies elsewhere.

Decades of Turkish and Egyptian misrule prepared the ground for the religious and nationalist magnetism of the Mahdi's cause. His holy war against the unbelievers aroused panic in Cairo and passions in London. In Britain the public and press bayed for action and the establishment sought and found its *deus ex machina*, and sent Gordon to Khartoum. With deplorable cynicism and calculation, the Prime Minister allowed the wrong man to be sent on a hopeless mission with an ill-defined mandate. When things went wrong, as they were destined to do, vacillation and miscalculation worsened matters.

Too late, cried the Queen whose hatred of her Prime Minister blinded her to the insufficiencies of Gordon. Too late, complained the Generals whose own mistakes in strategy piled delay upon delay. Too late, whined the British people whose force of opinion had stage-managed the whole débâcle and whose imperial dreams of glories turned to ashes and lust for revenge. And at the heart of the matter Gordon, guided as if by a death-wish, helped seal his

163

own doom by a series of actions and pronouncements that could lead to only one conclusion. When Awlad el Mek and his brethren are placed in the dock for the death of Gordon they should be joined by a host of fellow-accused: Queen and Khedive, Prime Ministers and pashas, Generals and their staffs, public and press, the Mahdi and Gordon himself.

Once Khartoum was isolated, Gordon trapped, and his rescue the object of British government policy, the margin between success and failure was such that 'a little neglect may breed mischief'. Franklin's observation would have appealed to Wolseley who held Sir Charles Wilson to be the horseshoe nail for want of which Gordon was lost. Wolseley was, of course, a principal contributor to the misjudgement about route and supplies that compounded delays caused by the government's irresolution. (On performance in the field, the British Army's record in the Sudan is of the highest merit, but even here commanders such as Graham and McNeill are accused of acts of foolishness which, had fate loaded the Mahdi's hand a little more generously, could have resulted in historic British catastrophes.) Wilson's counter-accusations in his own defence have detailed the political, strategic and logistic failings. Remove one or several of these factors and the relief expedition might have been on the Nile at Gubat weeks or even months earlier than late January. Gordon could have been saved. Equally, he might have survived had the Mahdi adhered to his visionary belief in a hegira to El Obeid, had the emirs rejected the forceful counsel of Abd el Kerim, had the secret of the gap in Khartoum's defences not been known to them, had the Nile not fallen to create that gap.

In the case of Wilson, whatever the justice of it, he remains exposed for his own bad judgements at the peak of a pyramid of mistakes and miscalculations which had its broad base in politics and public opinion at home. At Gubat on the Nile in the closing days of January 1885 history might have been changed if Herbert Stewart had not been mortally wounded, if Frederick Burnaby had lived, if Charles Wilson had been more aggressive. Would those vital three days have been lost if the impetuous Lord Charles Beresford had been well enough to take part in an immediate dash to Khartoum by steamer? We have seen the evidence to show that he abetted a policy of delay in the hope that he would recover from his boil in time to join the attempt. Wilson, prodded by Beresford's determination, almost certainly would have acted differently. It is the irony of history that epic events sometimes stem from prosaic beginnings. Thus, it may be argued, Beresford's boil was a banal but accountable factor in the death of Gordon.

W.H. Auden wrote:

*'History to the defeated*
*May say Alas but cannot help or pardon.'*

Let history have the disastrous political decisions and vacillation of 1884, the errors and inconsistencies of General Gordon, the doubts and hesitations of the Mahdi, the misjudgements of the Generals, the elimination of Burnaby and Stewart in the Bayuda Desert. Let the battle-weary British column keep its appointment on the banks of the Nile no earlier than moonrise on Monday, January 19 1885. But what if, in the 'committee' councils of the hesitating and colourless Wilson, there is now a powerful, arrogant and aristocratic voice for action, that of Charlie Beresford, fighting fit and impatient to embark without delay on the rescue of Gordon the moment a rendezvous with the steamers is accomplished?

In helping and pardoning Gordon we are stirring 'that great dust-heap called "history"'. Who knows what fearful things may happen before the dust settles?

# BOOK TWO

## *As it might have happened*

# Chapter 19

# *Go for Khartoum*

*The following is an extract from the journal of Lieutenant Count Gleichen, written up and edited later by a member of his family from notes the Count made as an officer of the Guards Camel Regiment at Gubat on the Nile early in 1885. Gleichen, of the Grenadier Guards, was killed in the battle of Gubat on February 14 of that year when an overwhelmingly large force of the Mahdi's army annihilated the British garrison. Gleichen's notes were lost for more than a decade. They came to light during the 'grand advance' up the Nile of the Anglo-Egyptian forces during the reconquest of the Sudan. Some of these forces, troops of the 15th Egyptian battalion under Major T.E. Hickman, were towed in boats by the gunboats* Zafir, Naser *and* Fateh *and landed at Shendy (six miles from the old battle ground of Gubat) where the emir, Mahmud, had established a depot in which he kept surplus stores, a large number of wives of emirs, and the loot of years of depredations up and down the Nile by Ansar troops. There was a short, sharp engagement in which 150 tribal irregulars attached to the Egyptians took part. Disregarded by the irregulars in their haul of loot from Mahmud's depot was a small green leather valise. It was retrieved by Major Hickman who discovered that it had belonged to the young Count Gleichen and contained his journal notes. The valise had been removed from the Gubat battlefield after the Mahdiist victory of 1885. Hickman restored the valise and its contents to the Gleichen family. Through Lieutenant Gleichen's account historians were able to illuminate the course of decision-making at Gubat on the Nile in late January 1885, a chapter which had remained clouded by the deaths in action of many of those who acted as principals in the affair.*

'Gubat, Wednesday, 21st January. The camp is alive with rumour and anticipation this evening. We have been established here for

169

almost forty-eight hours in what seems to be a remarkably tricky situation, with the enemy at Metemmeh entrenched and apparently impregnable before us, and God only knows what behind us between our small number and Khartoum. What is important, however, is not the delicacy of our position, but the great news that, following the timely arrival of General Gordon's steamers today, Colonel Wilson has decided to move in them on the river immediately to the relief of the General.

'Even the humblest observer has been aware that Colonel Wilson is not the most decisive of commanders: he appears invariably to hold consultative councils before committing himself to even the simplest course of action, though this is perhaps not to be deplored in an Intelligence officer who has enjoyed little or no experience of isolated command in the field. Some of the men call him an old woman. It is a harsh and unenlightened judgement, for caution is not a quality to be eschewed in a commander, given the pickle in which we find ourselves.

'Lord Charles Beresford has been pressing ardently for vigorous action. This is not a secret confined to the Staff. He is a strong-minded officer, with all the best and worst of his Irish race. He is all for cracking a few heads, and, if the shaves [*unauthenticated reports*] are to be believed, he will start with Sir Charles Wilson if he does not get his own way. This Beresford is no devious, diplomatic fellow who fights round corners. He says what he thinks, right or wrong, and has made no secret of his belief that Wilson is given to excessive caution. The news are bad from Khartoum, according to what we hear of the contents of Gordon's messages fetched in the steamers. Beresford from all accounts has won the day in the Staff councils. He is itching to go to Khartoum. What a triumph it would be in an already distinguished career to be the man who brings succour to Gordon! There is not an Englishman in the column who would not give his right arm to be part of the glorious mission at his side.

'Since the arrival of the steamers this forenoon, Beresford, though hampered by the fact that he does not have a combatant officer left in his gallant Naval detachment, has toiled untiringly to provision and prepare two of the vessels for the enterprise. The brave little fleet of 'penny steamers' has been maintained in a most commendable condition of readiness by Nushi Pasha and his skilled captains, and this has made Beresford's tasks the easier. The Egyptians and assorted bashi-bazouks among the crews have been unceremoniously kicked out and will be placed under careful watch in a camp upriver from our forts. The ships are now Bristol-fashion and readied for sailing by nightfall. In ordinary circumstances, navigation by night on the Nile is not the wisest course to be adopted, but the reach immediately upriver from Gubat is relatively clear of dangerous sandbars and rocks and the native commanders of our 'Nile Navy' are confident of the outcome. Under the hand of Providence, a combination of seamanship, moonlight and the famous Charlie Beresford luck should see them through and afford the fleet a headstart tonight before the enemy wakens up to our strategy. For none of us have any doubts that they are watching every move we make, and the Mahdi, wherever he be, soon gets to know what we are up to.

'As done up as we are, all would support Beresford's contention that resolute action is required. We can see to ourselves here, though we expect a 'slating' from the niggers before reinforcements can reach us from Korti; surely, apprised of Sir Herbert Stewart's wounding, Buller has already started on his way. Trafford, Gascoigne and Stuart-Wortley, chosen for the steamers, are the most envied officers in the force. We have been given a part, if only in the humblest, commissarial way. In his messages, Gordon had repeatedly said that the presence of a few red-coats in Khartoum would work wonders; so the twenty men selected from the Sussex, as having been longest up country were rigged out in red jumpers belonging to our men as they had none of their own. They were not, as might be expected, a particularly good fit.'

*There is one further paragraph in Gleichen's notes for the 21st, written as a footnote, in haste, when news spread round the British camp that Beresford would not, after all, accompany Wilson to Khartoum with the* Tel-el-Hoween *and the* Bordein:

'It must have required the noblest of sacrifices for Beresford to forego his place by Wilson's side in the steamers. After his forceful advocacy, without which they would not have sailed this evening, we all expected him to accompany the mission, which indeed had been the Commander-in-Chief's expressed intention. The reasons behind Wilson's decision to leave Beresford with us at Gubat are sound, however. He is the only Naval officer remaining alive and unwounded. If we are attacked (and the shaves variously tell of ten, twenty and thirty thousand Arabs approaching from north and south) we will need all the support we can get from the two remaining steamers and from Beresford and his Gardner. Duty notwithstanding, Charlie Beresford must be the most disappointed man in the column tonight.'

A French view in a contemporary sketchbook of cartoons: Gordon's military activities, a grand ball for the children of the Sudan, and the Mahdi's entry into Berber (Phillips).

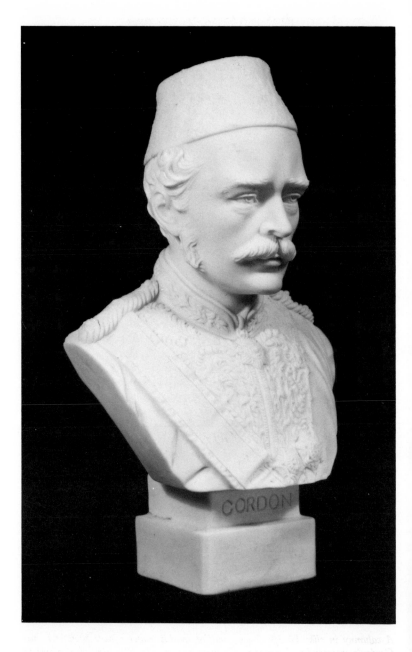

*Commemoratives of Gordon abounded, such as this Parian-ware bust from Stoke-on-Trent* (Phillips).

*A calumny in silk: Faragh Pasha, vilified in this contemporary bookmark, was Gordon's commander of troops at Khartoum; he was later exonerated of blame for opening the gates to the Mahdiists (Stephen Dance).*

*Generations of British boys played with Camel Corps troopers and Sudanese infantry, produced by Britain's, the toy soldier manufacturer* (Phillips and Forbes).

# Chapter 20

# *The rescue of Gordon*

*Walter Ingram was 28 years of age in 1884 when he joined the Gordon relief expedition in the role of newspaper observer. He was an accomplished big game hunter and sailor, the youngest son of the late Herbert Ingram, founder of the* Illustrated London News. *Having arrived at Gubat, he was commissioned in the field as acting naval officer and took part in Lord Charles Beresford's rescue of Wilson's contingent after it was shipwrecked. From Luxor in Egypt on Thursday, March 5 1885, he wrote to his brother, William, the proprietor of the family newspaper. The following extracts are taken from his combined letter and news despatch.*

'It is both painful and difficult for me to enter the indecorous public debate which has attended General Gordon's return to the bosom of the civilised world. Some of the statements he is reported to have made to the correspondent of *The Times* in Cairo, however, reflect such an inelegant light on those who cannot speak for themselves, that the cause of decency deserves an answer. Wilson, Stuart-Wortley, Gascoigne, Trafford and other brave men are dead because they answered the call of duty; through their duty England's honour was saved and Gordon lives. It ill befits a man of his standing, however diligently he sought the martyrdom from which he has been saved, now to infer that the "human glory" of these men is composed of "twaddle". For of such is the import of his indiscreet recriminations.

'In writing this account of the events pursuant to January 25th, my motive is to present the facts as they were related to me by those parties who played such a gallant role in those events and who, alas, are no longer here to speak up for themselves. Water with discretion, if you must, my more fervent personal observations, but let our readers know that there is another version which differs from recent messages emanating from sources tinged with hysteria in Cairo.

'You will have received my earlier account of how the *Bordein* and the *Tel-el-Hoween* went unmolested past Wad Habeshi, some 40 miles from Gubat. It was here that Sir Charles Wilson expected Feki Mustafa, the Mahdi's emir, to be lying in wait with Krupp guns; in fact, it was not until the flotilla had safely passed upstream that Mustafa moved into position with 3,000 riflemen and his Krupps, locking the Nile behind Wilson. The ships remained untouched through the potential perils of the sixth cataract and the Shabluka Gorge, and it was not until they had reached Halfaya, a dozen miles from Khartoum, that the first cannon and rifles were fired at them. More fire was directed from the Mahdi's fort at Omdurman on Wilson's starboard side as he rounded the wedge-shaped mass of Tuti Island, which sits opposite Khartoum at the confluence of the Blue and White Niles. It was by now the afternoon of Sunday, the 25th. In the heavy firing which greeted the steamers' entrance into the Blue Nile channel at Khartoum, Wilson received a flesh wound above his knee from a spent bullet; it troubled him little, for there was great excitement on board the *Bordein* where all could see Gordon's flag still flying over his palace on the distant skyline.

'In its heyday Khartoum presented no great picture of civic magnificence to the approaching traveller. Wilson found it an unprepossessing sight as his two steamers forged their course between the muddy urban agglomeration on the starboard quarter and the grey, ramparted forts, swamp-rooted palms and the occasional water-wheel, or sakieh, of Tuti on the port, the setting sun a crimson orb astern of them over the still smoking guns of Omdurman.

'Flags appeared, little miracles of colour in the dun dreary scene. From the decks of the ships bluejackets and Sussex sent a volley of hoarse cheers rolling across the shell-splintered palms of Khartoum's waterside. Wilson's blacks, no doubt relishing the prospect of meeting families they had given up for lost, danced with glee and discharged their rifles. Above the decks of the *Bordein* a lookout called out his sightings as buildings of substance hove into view above the trees and ramshackle defence works of the river front. Khasm el Mus identified for Wilson the garden of the Austrian Mission, the Mission Convent and, nearer the water's edge, the square shape of Government Buildings.

'Renewed outbreaks of fire, raining shrapnel on the roofs of the city, appeared at first to have no chastening effect on what were presently large numbers, soldiers and citizens alike, who gathered noisily on the waterfront in the neighbourhood of the Governor's Palace, the headquarters occupied by General Gordon. The building, though not large by western standards, presents an imposing frontage to the river. It is basically of two main storeys, its facade being graced by arches cut into the stone and stucco walls, the central arch being directly beneath a squat tower surmounted by a flagstaff. A line of thin acacia trees screens the front of the palace from the river. To provide clear lines of fire, Gordon had ordered the boughs of trees to be cut back, and a conglomeration of wattle and daub hovels which habitually occupies Khartoum's riverine "promenade" was hereabouts removed for the same reason.

'This expanse of mud, broken paving stones and rubble — it can hardly be termed an "esplanade" — was now occupied by a beseeching horde of humanity, many in the last stages of starvation, their faces a fearful mixture of hope and despair. The British had come to a scene so daunting that it must have seemed to the handful of men of the desert column that their bayonets, baptised at Abu Klea, would now be needed, not to fend off more of the Mahdi's warriors, but to deter this seething mass of townsfolk which threatened to overrun the two small steamers and end their voyage in floundering, overladen disaster at Khartoum's waterside.

'The vast throng contained an overwhelmingly large proportion of the city's remaining fighting men, the very soldiers who should have been defending Khartoum's ramparts to the south, west and east. Alas, in the gathering dusk, the glow of torches held up by many revealed the red tarbooshes of Egyptian officers and the tattered and muddied, but still recognisable, white military tunics of huge numbers who had deserted their posts on the city's walls. And as if to emphasise the awful proximity of the enemy, fresh outbreaks of shellfire from the Omdurman guns announced themselves like a distant roll of thunder on the evening air.

'Of Gordon there was no sign on the quay, although the lookout of the *Tel-el-Hoween* had reported seeing a group of figures peering through telescopes from the flag tower of the palace.

'General Wolseley's orders had included an instruction to march the Sussex Regiment through the streets in their red jumpers as a patriotic gesture to refurbish the morale of the population; but this

179

resort was to be abandoned at the commander's discretion if he considered that there was a danger of serious epidemic in the town. That danger was most apparent. It was clear to most observers on board the steamers that starvation had reduced the townspeople to dire straits and, in such circumstances, there was every reason to believe that infectious diseases were rife; typhus being a most likely probability and, at worst, cholera.

'A Shagiyeh, sent by Khasm el Mus to gather intelligence, returned to report soldiers' and townspeople's statements that Gordon Pasha had not been seen in public for several days. The gates of the palace were barred and guarded, and the building appeared to be as much under siege from the mob as were the newly arrived vessels.

'In the cabin of the *Bordein* Wilson held a conference by candle light with his officers and captains. What none could predict with certainty was how the Mahdi would react to the events of the last few hours. There were frequent and persistent reports of large volumes of felucca traffic on the White Nile; these indicated that the Mahdi was transferring considerable numbers of troops from the Omdurman bank to reinforce el Nejumi's legions on the southern flank of Khartoum.

'While the various preparations were being made for a party to disembark, a small group of prominent citizens and officials thrust its way through the multitude on the quay and was received by Sir Charles Wilson on board the *Bordein*. Among them was Bordeini Bey, a leading merchant of Khartoum. This worthy, in the short time at his disposal, was able to furnish the British officers with information about the state of the city and the garrison, and about the well-being of General Gordon himself. Disturbing as was the former, what Bordeini Bey had to impart on the latter subject could only give cause for alarm.

'Bordeini Bey was regarded with some esteem by Gordon as being of sounder stuff than some of his fellow merchants. His account, corroborated by those with him, of General Gordon's actions and general demeanour in the days up to this fateful Sunday should be set on the record as it was given to the British officers who accompanied the steamers. It is of particular import in the light of the subsequent controversy, much of which rests on General Gordon's version of his dealings with Sir Charles Wilson and his comrades in the last few hours of Khartoum's freedom. All but Gordon are dead. This is the testimony of those who cannot speak for themselves.

'Bordeini Bey asserted that, of recent, Gordon withheld from his people the greatest boon he could bestow on them: his personal presence. Councils were summoned by Gordon, but they were addressed by the Governor's chief clerk, Giriagis Bey. In the last week no Gordon Pasha was seen inspecting the defences which faced el Nejumi's encircling force; lamentably, his practised engineer's eye was not turned on the place where the falling tide had eroded the ramparts. Bordeini Bey feared that Gordon was sick and recounted examples of behaviour which critics may construe as abberational.

'One incident took place during the period of the Mahdi's rapidly tightening investment of the town when projectiles from the guns, rockets and all types of firearms were falling on the garrison and terrorising the people. Bordeini's account illustrates Gordon's bravery — which, it cannot be said too strongly, has never been in doubt — but, weighed with other evidence provided by the deputation, this fresh insight could reasonably support suspicions that Gordon's judgement was under severe pressure owing to the increasing burden he bore alone. As reported to this correspondent, the following was Bordeini Bey's version of the event:

'"In spite of all this danger by which he was surrounded, Gordon Pasha had no fear. I remember one night some of the principal men in Khartoum came to my house and begged me to ask Gordon Pasha not to light up the rooms of the palace, as they offered a good mark for the enemy's bullets. When I mentioned this to Gordon Pasha he was very angry, saying, 'Who has said Gordon was ever afraid?' A few evenings afterwards I was with Gordon in the palace, and as the rooms were still lighted up I suggested that he should put boxes full of sand in front of the windows to stop the bullets. Gordon Pasha was then more enraged than ever. He called up the guard, and gave them orders to shoot me if I moved; he then brought a very large lantern which would hold 24 candles. He and I then put the candles into the sockets, placed the lantern on the table in front of the window, lit the candles, and then we sat down at the table. The pasha then said, 'When God was portioning out fear to all the people in the world, at last it came to my turn, and there was no fear left to give me; go, tell all the people in Khartoum that Gordon fears nothing, for God has created him without fear'".'

'The scene, as described by Bordeini Bey, now shifts to the night of the 20th, some five days before the arrival of the British. Gordon summoned a council meeting at the home of Faragh Pasha ez Zeini, the commandant of the troops. With Faragh Pasha there were present Bordeini Bey and other notables, who were astounded when they were addressed on matters of great import, not by Gordon Pasha, but by the clerk, Giriagis Bey, an official junior in rank to several of those at the meeting.

'Gordon's message was that the British were approaching and would arrive within two or three days; but the council must remember that the officer commanding the British force was of very high rank, and that Gordon Pasha's rank was in comparison very small (allowing for Gordon's hyperbolic licence, this was probably a reference to the Commander-in-Chief, Lord Wolseley). It was not probably the intention of the British force to enter Khartoum; the principal officers would come in a steamer and would moor off the palace, and they would order him [Gordon] to come on board the steamer to meet the English Commander-in-Chief.

'Gordon Pasha, therefore, wished the officers present to put on their full uniforms when the steamer approached and attend at the palace. When the English officers should ask Gordon to accompany them, the Egyptian officials were to protest against his leaving the town. If the English officers insisted, the official should protest violently to the Commander-in-Chief that they would not permit Gordon to leave Khartoum. Should the English soldiers still decide not to come into Khartoum, the garrison and people might rest perfectly satisfied that Gordon Pasha would not leave them.

'Whilst Sir Charles Wilson understood that such a declaration of intent on Gordon's part was by way of allaying the fears of his lieutenants, he also knew that Gordon had declared in his journals his determination not to leave Khartoum without those he had gone to save. No possible equivocation could be read into the Journal entry for September 24: "I altogether *decline* the imputation that the projected expedition has come to *relieve me* . . . I am not the *rescued lamb* and I will not be". In that respect, Bordeini Bey's account of the meeting told Sir Charles nothing he did not suspect; although, by reading between the lines, Wilson and his colleagues must have been forewarned of Gordon's intention to attempt to involve the British advance guard in the defence of Khartoum. What aroused concern, how-ever, was the increasing evidence which pointed to the fact of Gordon's self-imposed seclusion during the last few days of gathering storm. Sir Charles's misgivings were not eased by further news from Bordeini Bey of events on that very mornings, Sunday, the 25th.

'The council had again been summoned, this time to the palace, and all expected to be addressed by Gordon. Considerable movement had been observed in the south which denoted that the enemy was collecting in enormous force around the village of Kalakala, which would be the strategic pivot of any concerted attack on the landward side of Khartoum. Much to the officials' consternation, it was again Giriagis Bey who met them. He told them that Gordon Pasha wished them to make a determined last stand, as the English would be here within the next 24 hours. If, however, they preferred to submit they were at liberty to open the gates and let all join the rebels.

'Bordeini Bey was amazed and distressed that such a message should be delivered by an intermediary and should not come direct from Gordon's own lips. He demanded to see the pasha and was admitted to his presence. Bordeini Bey was appalled at the state of nervous disturbance in which he found Gordon, who, though given to outbursts of anger on occasion, was renowned for coolness and calm in the face of adversity. The following, as noted by Captain Gascoigne, is Bordeini Bey's version of the brief meeting with Gordon:

'"I found him sitting on a couch; and as I came in he pulled off his tarboosh, and flung it from him, saying, 'What more can I say? I have nothing more to say. The people will no longer believe me. I have told them over and over again that help would be here, but it has never come, and now they must see I tell them lies. If this, my last promise, fails I can do nothing more. Go and collect all the people you can on the lines and make a good stand. Now leave me to smoke these cigarettes.' (There were two full boxes of cigarettes on the table.) I could see he was in despair, and he spoke in a tone I had never heard before. I knew then that he had been too agitated to address the meeting, and thought the sight of his despair would dishearten us."

'Bordeini Bey's news was a matter of especial consternation and perplexity for Captain Gascoigne, an officer who had the highest personal regard for General Gordon; one who had not a shred of

ulterior motive in passing on to others anything false or of a
denigratory nature about the General. Gascoigne further recalled
that Bordeini Bey warned his listeners to be prepared for a
disturbing physical change in Gordon Pasha. The vicissitudes he
had undergone had turned his hair to a snowy white.'

*At this point several paragraphs of Walter Ingram's handwriting were
defaced by water damage on their journey down the Nile. It is apparent that
the defaced text dealt with Wilson's landing in search of Gordon. Wilson, it
seems, went ashore by small boat, accompanied by Trafford, six of the
Sussex, a signaller, Khasm el Mus and a company of the chieftain's
Shagiyeh irregulars, leaving the steamers under the command of Gascoigne
and Stuart-Wortley. The landing was covered by the rifles of those of the
Sussex, bluejackets and Sudanese who remained on board. The narrative
regains legibility after Wilson's party had gained access to the interior of the
palace.*

'In contrast to the disorder outside on the wharfs and in the
streets, a calm reigned inside the palace. Wilson and Trafford,
however, were surprised to discover that no apparent attempt had
been made to fortify the building.

'Gordon was some time being fetched. When he appeared at the
door of the first floor ante-room which led to his divan, he was
dressed in the full uniform of the Governor-General; at his side he
wore his sword. Wilson and Trafford, although forewarned by
Bordeini Bey, were shocked by his physical appearance. He was
bareheaded, and his hair and mustache were entirely grey, almost
white. His steel blue eyes were lined and tired, evincing the
adversities he had under gone during the months of uncertainty
and isolation. His cheeks were hollowed and showed signs of
having been hastily and recently shaven. He smoked the inevitable
cigarette, and replenished it, one immediately after another.
Trafford noticed that his hand trembled.

'A torrent of questions poured from Gordon's lips. Where was
the British Army? What was the strength of Wilson's force? How
many ships had he? Which of his, Gordon's, messages had been
received? What was the truth about Colonel Stewart and the
*Abbas?* Had the British brought food and supplies for Khartoum?
When would Wolseley arrive? Had the steamers met opposition
on the Nile? The questions poured forth in haphazard order.
Wilson, sitting with Trafford across a table from Gordon,
attempted to answer them, but often their interlocutor would

interject with another question before Sir Charles had the opportunity to complete a reply.

'Gradually a note of recrimination began to creep into Gordon's questioning. It was now that his two colleagues recognised a disturbing facet of his demeanour: Trafford believed that the General was suffering from severe mental stress. Gordon, smoking furiously, began to pace the room. He flung questions and Biblical quotations at his listeners. His tirade left few unscathed — the British Government, its ministers in Cairo, the War Office, the Army.

'Why had the British forces tarried while Khartoum starved? Why had they not come earlier? ". . . in the land of Egypt, when we sat by the flesh pots, and when we did eat bread to the full . . ." Trafford recognised a quotation from *Exodus*, delivered by Gordon in sonorous tones as he stood by a broken window, gazing out towards the river front.

'It would be invidious and not productive to attempt to reconstruct at length the exchanges which ensued. Suffice it to say that Wilson and Trafford each received the impression that General Gordon's burden, borne so bravely in his isolation, had produced in him a state of mind which prevented him seeing the realities which surrounded him, the people of Khartoum and his would-be rescuers. He demanded that the entire contingent of British troops, fetched in the steamers, should disembark and enjoin themselves in the defence of the city. In vain did Wilson argue that, not only were they too few, but such a course of action was expressly against the Commander-in-Chief's orders. Gordon's riposte was to quote from his favourite book of the Bible, *Isaiah:* ". . . I have nourished and brought up children, and they have rebelled against me."

'When Sir Charles, summoning all his resources of tact, attempted to test the truth of Bordeini Bey's assertions that Gordon's absence from public view in the last few days had been the cause of despair and perplexity among his followers, Gordon exploded in wrath. Khartoum was safe, he averred. Had he not said the city could hold out until the end of January? That time was now imminent, and the British had arrived. Together they would push back the Mahdi's host. In his solitary counsel of the preceeding days he, Gordon Pasha, had communed with God; ". . . the Lord of Hosts, shall lop the bough with terror: and the high one of stature shall be hewn down . . .".

'It had rapidly become apparent to the newly arrived British officers that Gordon did not recognise the full extent of the peril in which Khartoum was placed. In acrimonious exchanges, Sir Charles Wilson was forced to explain that, *in extremis,* he carried — by writ of the Commander-in-Chief — the Khedive's firman to supersede Gordon's own authority. The only right and proper course for the small expeditionary force to adopt at this time, in view of the swiftly enclosing investment of Khartoum, was that of withdrawal. It was Wilson's duty to request General Gordon to accompany him back to the safety of the lower Nile.

'The suggestion produced a fresh attack of choler. Had he, Gordon, not vowed that he would never, *never* be the rescued lamb? His mission had been to retrieve the garrisons of the Sudan and to bring them, and those who wished to accompany them, down to safety. (The reader may well remark that over the course of the several months before Khartoum's isolation, General Gordon had provided remarkably little evidence of attempting to carry out this mission.) No one would convince Gordon Pasha of his duty to leave, while his people in Khartoum remained in peril from the false Mahdi.

'Whilst these acrimonious arguments, which consumed more than two hours of time, were taking place, an uneasy calm had overtaken the city beyond the palace walls. The shelling and rocketing had ceased; there was only the erruption of sporadic rifle fire in the distance, such as would be exchanged between opposing pickets; the noise of the crowd in the streets was now subdued, and a messenger from the *Bordein* reported that all was quiet on the river. Trafford confessed to a deep feeling of disquiet, finding in the comparative calm a presage of violence. In retrospect, his fears are proven to have had grounds. Gordon, on the other hand, chose to interpret the lull as a sign that the Mahdi had lost heart. All they had to do now, he declared, was to await the morning when the sight of redcoats on the walls of Khartoum would finally decide the enemy to abandon the siege. He then astonished his listeners by informing them that he was going away to "smoke some cigarettes and attend to some papers of state".

'Trafford noted that he delivered a valedictory quotation from *Isaiah* ("Therefore as the fire devoureth the stubble, and the flame consumeth the chaff, so their root shall be as rottenness, and their blossom shall go up as dust . . .") before going into his divan and closing the door.

'Wilson and Trafford took the opportunity, in Gordon's absence, of questioning Giriagis Bey and a small group of other Egyptian government officials who had been for the most part silent witnesses to the exchanges between the senior British officers. Then, having dismissed the officials, the two Britons held counsel alone. Both were of the opinion that, in his present state of mind, Gordon's judgements were not to be trusted and that he must be persuaded to leave, by force if necessary. Their deliberations were soon to be cut short in the most violent fashion.

'Over the rooftops of the city came a sound which began in small, staccato explosions and quickly swelled into a continuous roar. Wilson and Trafford immediately recognised it as massed rifle fire. There was no accompanying cough of cannon and scream of shells; these were to come later. Such an explosion of fire from what must have been hundreds, perhaps thousands, of rifles could only mean what the officers feared most: a surprise attack on the defences of Khartoum, a swift and determined rush unheralded by artillery fire. The time was shortly after midnight. Whatever conclusions Wilson had reached about withdrawal, with or without Gordon, the actions of the British force were now about to be dictated by rapid events.

'Trafford was sent to call Gordon from his divan. The door was unlocked. The young officer found the General seated at a writing desk on which were an open Bible, several pages of handwritten text (which subsequently turned out to be Gordon's Journal covering the previous weeks), a glass, and a half-emptied bottle of brandy. A box of cigarettes lay at Gordon's elbow and a wreath of smoke hung in the hot night air. Trafford remembers Gordon's words when the import of the rifle fire was pointed out to him. "He was dismissive, almost casual, explaining the noise away as 'the Mahdi's nightly fire-work show'," Trafford later told this correspondent.

'Word was brought to the palace that the worst had happened. There were conflicting and muddled reports, but their general gist was that the Mahdi's followers had broken the defences in the west. Here, Fort Mukran stands, ramparted, on a promontary of land between the Blue and White Niles. At high water the two streams present impassable obstacles on either side. The falling waters of the White Nile, however, had exposed dangerously vulnerable sandbanks, over which the enemy had crept in the darkness. They came in their thousands, riflemen in the van, supported by masses of sword and spearmen, carrying angarebs, or straw couches, to fill up the ditches.

'The starving and demoralised defenders were no match for the attacking hordes. A few fought back bravely. Many surrendered. Great execution of the Egyptians took place, but the blacks were mostly spared. The Arabs were quickly on the ramparts and running along them, thus obtaining access to the city. Here and there on the desolate plain between Khartoum and the White Nile, which is dotted with powder magazines, cemeteries and slaughter houses, a few desperate squares were formed in the darkness; but resistance was in vain and the bare flatlands became a charnel house for the defenders. These news were delivered to Wilson within the space of little longer than half an hour. It was evident that the ships' companies had also been apprised of the incursions, for three piercing blasts of a steamer whistle were heard in the palace over the rattle of musketry and the now rising tumult of a frightened people in the city streets.

'The Arabs have reached the Messalamieh Gate in the south; Faragh Pasha (commandant of the whole line in this sector) has surrendered; the gate is open and the enemy is pouring in; Buri has given way in the east; resistance is useless: alarming rumours, some to be believed, others to be discounted, flooded into the palace. If Wilson required further confirmation that the enemy had broken through, he received it in the crimson glow of flames over the western part of the city.

'And now, according to Trafford, the Colonel was distracted by a spirited, even vituperative, argument with the General. Wilson argued that it was his duty to take Gordon immediately to a place of safety in the ships on the river; as holder of General Wolseley's mandate, he had the authority to *order* Gordon to leave, if necessary. Gordon maintained that it was his duty to remain and die with his people: a courageous and noble stand, but one from which the other officers knew he must be dissuaded.

'Trafford said afterwards: "We had each been forced to the conclusion that we would have to arrest General Gordon if we were to save him. He appeared to be confused and, in the circumstances, I formed the opinion that he was unfit to issue any commands or decide the course of any actions." Trafford's misgivings were confirmed when Gordon issued orders for a slow match to be lit to destroy the powder arsenal in the Catholic church. Wilson countermanded the order and told off the

Corporal of the Sussex to ensure that his wishes were observed, as an explosion of the magazine might have seriously harmed the ships on the river, lying in close proximity to the church.

'Surprise having succeeded in the west, el Nejumi's Krupp guns in the south and east began to bombard the city. The explosion of their shells increased the panic in the streets and quickened the defenders' desire to submit. The palace and its grounds came under heavy fire. In the first floor chamber, Gordon was fuming at Wilson for cancelling his orders. His words were cut short by the thunderclap of an explosion. Whether the projectile was aimed by the Mahdi's forces from Buri in the east or from the old North Fort across the Blue Nile will never be known; it struck the facade near the window where Gordon had once arranged his defiant candelabra and poured down a rain of plaster and other debris on the small group of British and Egyptians inside the room. A servant was killed, a Private of the Sussex and several palace officials were wounded. When Sir Charles and Trafford shook themselves, dusted the plaster from their uniforms and took stock, they discovered Gordon unconscious on the floor; he had been struck on the temple by a piece of falling masonry. It was, remarked Trafford, a heaven-sent opportunity to resolve the problem of removing the General to a place of safety without resorting to arrest.

'There was no time to act on ceremony. Gordon was borne out by two Shagiyeh in a makeshift hammock. The small party had to fight its way back to the landing stage through a terrified horde of soldiers and citizens. On board the *Bordein* the insensible Gordon was laid on a couch in the cabin.

'Wilson's steamers, with no lights showing, hugged the Tuti shore, thus to present a minimum of target, until they reached the confluence of the Blue and White Niles. Astern, Khartoum glowed and flickered with the fires of hell. It was now eerily quiet apart from the occasional burst of rifle fire. Where the rivers meet the two steamers changed course north-eastwards, carrying Gordon Pasha back to his own people. Off the starboard bow, a thin gold rim on the horizon announced a new dawn breaking, awakening both friends and enemies on the river ahead of them.'

*Thus ends Walter Ingram's account of the happenings at Khartoum, as reconstructed by him from statements made by Wilson, Gascoigne, Trafford and Stuart-Wortley.*

# Chapter 21

# *Shipwreck*

Wilson knew that the steamers' flight from Khartoum would be no gentle cruise. There were enough witnesses in and around the palace to vouch for Gordon having been taken away alive, and the Mahdi's pleasure in capturing the city would be marred by the news that his great adversary had slipped through his hands. Ambush could be expected, most probably at the Shabluka Gorge and cataracts, or farther down at the Wad Habeshi fort. On the first day, however, with Khartoum a smoky blur on the horizon astern, the only gestures from the Mahdi were random shots from both banks and the appearance of a camel rider from the direction of Omdurman, pacing the steamers and flourishing a white flag. He was ignored.

That night a paddle wheel had to be repaired, bullet and shell-holes plugged, durra grain dumped overboard. Both ships, laden with guns and armour plate, were heavier than anything that would normally be taken down the cataracts at this time of the year. The two captains and four reises, native pilots, said it was impossible. A promise of £100 to each captain and £50 to each reis persuaded them to attempt one boat at a time. At mid-day the next day the *Tel-el-Hoween* bumped and scraped its way down a rapid, stern first, followed by the *Bordein*. Then, in a stretch of clear water, the *Tel-el-Hoween* hit a rock and began to sink; the men and two guns were transferred to Wilson's steamer, now mightily overladen.

An evening event was the reappearance of the camel rider with his flag of truce, one Feki Abd al-Rahman bearing a letter from the Mahdi. A feature of war in the Sudan was the amount of paper involved — on both sides. It was the custom to exchange long letters, demanding submission, offering surrender terms, threatening retribution, or merely purveying misleading

190

information. The Mahdi, Khalifa Abdallahi and lesser emirs were particularly prolific letter writers; their messengers roved the desert miles, bombarding their enemies with a barrage of closely written Arabic texts, often running to dozens of pages.

Furthermore, the Sudan conflict — despite the horrors of campaigning in the desert and the cruelty on both sides — was one of the last of the 'gentlemen's wars'. Emissaries were received and listened to; they were often allowed to mix with the potentially disaffected and put to them the case for going over to the other side (in Khartoum, Gordon regarded it as a means of being rid of mouths to feed). Generous terms of clemeny were common — acceptance of the Muslim faith was the Mahdi's main condition — and soldiers and tribes switched sides when expedience demanded. Most of Abu Anga's blacks of the jehadia rifle corps had soldiered under the Egyptian flag; irregulars working for Nile potentates under British control had fought for the Mahdi.

The messenger, Abd al-Rahman, a minor chief and holy man of the Dongolawi tribe, was received aboard the *Bordein*. The Mahdi, he said, had been sent by God to convert the world and he intended to march straight to Stamboul. The Mahdi's letter was addressed to 'Gordon Pasha, representative of England and the Khedive, the British and Shagiyeh officers and their followers'. It told them: 'Surrender and you will be spared . . . As you have become a small remnant, like a leaf within our grasp, two alternatives are offered to you. If you surrender and prevent the shedding of blood . . . grace and security from God and His Prophet and security from us will be upon you . . . but if you refuse you shall taste evil . . . '

Wilson had seen many letters like this one and decided there was no advantage in sending a reply. Gordon, ill with fever, had no say in the matter. Khasm el Mus, however, received Wilson's permission to write a letter that was a ruse to ensure the steamer was unmolested through the remaining rapids and the Shabluka Gorge. If a safe conduct were promised for the Shagiyeh leader and his followers, Khasm el Mus wrote, he would deliver the ship and the English to Feki Mustafa who was waiting at Wad Habeshi. Abd al-Rahman departed with the letter — and also the first of the deserters, a fact which little worried Wilson who regarded defection as good riddance.

The Shabluka Gorge, where the Nile slices through the Jebel Rauwaya, was passed without incident on the third day. The vertical cliffs of water-polished basalt, streaked with silt from previous high floods, were empty of life except for the occasional eagle. Flat rock shelves, jumbled masses of granite piled high, and banks covered in thorny acacia offered endless ambush possibilities, Khasm-el-Mus, who had been prostrated by grief at the probable fate of his family in Khartoum, was relieved that his stratagem had apparently worked. He cheered still further when the last of the rapids was behind them. Gordon passed his 52nd birthday in fitful fever.

Disaster overtook the *Bordein* on the fourth day, Thursday, January 29. Ahead lay the river, running pale green, wide and clear apart from some rocky reefs and verdant islands; there was only the gauntlet of Wad Habeshi to be run, then it was plain sailing for nearly 40 miles to Gubat. Off Mernat Island, four miles from Feki Mustafa's guns, the *Bordein* hit a submerged rock which ripped open her bottom.

Wilson landed his men and the four guns and built a zeriba of acacia thorn and timber on Mernat island. Gordon, between bouts of deep sleep and delirium, was made comfortable with the wounded in the centre of the encampment. The Sudanese were restive, an increasing worry to Wilson who knew it was impossible to ask them to march downriver. So at 6:35 on the Thursday evening, he despatched Stuart-Wortley, four Sussex and eight Sudanese in a ship's rowing boat to seek help at Gubat.

The arrival of two improbable and totally unexpected visitors broke the tedium of the next day. A sister of Khasm el Mus, who had followed the steamer from Khartoum, came with news that most of the Shagiyeh's and blacks' families had been murdered: the details she gave did little to bolster the sagging morale. Then, hailing the marooned party and waving a white flag on the left bank, there appeared none other than Feki Mustafa, accompanied by a sheikh. They were allowed into the zeriba. Their message was to the point: surrender or be killed. Wilson rejected their overtures but, astonishingly, allowed them to talk to the already deeply disaffected natives.

The immediate result of Mustafa's pleading — following close on the terrible news from Khartoum — was the desertion of Abd el Hamid, who had captained the *Tel-el-Hoween*, and 17 of the Shagiyeh. A pilot, a most valuable commodity on the river, also fled. Wilson was working to the book, following the code of honour which applied to parleys under the white flag, even if this meant allowing the enemy to disaffect one's own troops. In Abd el Hamid's case, the defection was potentially immensely damaging to the British as he had been party to the staff councils at Gubat and knew the strengths and weaknesses of the isolated desert column and its detailed prospects of reinforcement. Trafford and Gascoigne urged Wilson to sieze Feki Mustafa as a hostage against the party's safe conduct, but Wilson refused and let him go. He did, however, put a Private of the Sussex to watch each of the remaining pilots, Dongolawis all, with orders to shoot to kill at the first sign of attempted desertion or treachery. The British and their allies dug in and waited for rescue.

# Chapter 22

# *Telling the news*

*At dawn on Friday, January 30, Bennet Burleigh finishes writing by
lamp light in his tent at Gubat, breakfasts on his last tin of Leibig
soup and a powerful shot of whisky, and mounts the horse that has
been saddled by his servant. (It was a constant source of amazement
and envy to commanders that the gentlemen of the press managed to be
well mounted while the cavalry had to soldier on worn-out nags.)
Before his colleagues in the press lines are awake, Burleigh is through
the pickets and heading north-westwards across the Bayuda desert. He
carries with him a few provisions, his Navy Colt revolver and a story
that will scoop not only the other newspapers, but the British
government as well. His destination is Jakdul Wells, 80 miles away,
where, being a true newspaper man, he has laid his lines of
communication. From Jakdul a camel rider of the Kababish tribe,
bought with baksheesh and the guarantee of more to come on delivery,
will carry the despatch to Korti where an agent will send it on to the
telegraph head at Dongola. Burleigh must return from Jakdul to
Gubat; for big as the story is, it is still unfinished — as readers of the*
Daily Telegraph *learn in a special edition on the morning of
Wednesday, February 4.*

Gubat, January 30

'General Gordon is alive and has been taken by Sir Charles
Wilson's relieving force from Khartoum, which, as was feared,
has fallen to the Mahdi's forces. The joy which the news of
Gordon's rescue will bring to the civilised world is tempered by
the knowledge that the General, Sir Charles and the complement
of the two steamers which left Gubat on the 21st are isolated and
in some peril south of Wad Habeshi on the Nile.

'The information reached the relief column at Gubat in
dramatic circumstances in the early hours of the 30th. Every night

194

it is Lord Charles Beresford's custom, as naval commander, to haul off the steamer *Safieh* into mid-stream, where he sleeps on deck. At three o'clock on this morning he was awakened by a voice hailing the *Safieh'*. He ran to the rail, and there, in the first half-light, was a boat and Lieutenant Stuart-Wortley's face was to be seen.

'"Khartoum has fallen; Gordon is saved," was the burden of Stuart-Wortley's announcement. This officer was last seen when he sailed with Wilson's small flotilla. He was now accompanied in a rowing boat by four men of the Sussex Regiment and some Sudanese. They had been despatched by Sir Charles to fetch assistance after both the *Bordein* and *Tel-el-Hoween* were holed by rocks and sunk in the river and the party marooned in zeriba on Mernat Island, 40 miles up stream from here.

'General Gordon was slightly injured and concussed by the results of a shell explosion in the Governor's Palace at Khartoum, and has been suffering from a high fever, but is otherwise fit and well. The news of Khartoum's fall had been presaged for the British expeditionary force at Gubat by the sound of tom-toms and night-long celebrations in Metemmeh during the last few days, and by unconfirmed reports of a Mahdist victory brought in by friendly tribesmen. Now we know those reports to be true.

'Your correspondent's first intimation of Stuart-Wortley's arrival came as his colleagues of the London press still slept. A voice was heard calling at the neighbouring tent occupied by Lieutenant Douglas Dawson. It was Stuart-Wortley, asking to be shown to Colonel Boscawen. The latter has been confined to hospital with an illness, and command has passed to Colonel Mildmay Willson. Stuart-Wortley was directed to the acting commander with his remarkable news, but not before he furnished the following detailed account of happenings at Khartoum and on the river for the benefit of *Daily Telegraph* readers.'

*Burleigh's despatch here includes a résumé of the timetable of principal events from Wilson's arrival off Khartoum to the sinking of the* Bordein, *and is followed by Stuart-Wortley's own story of his journey by rowing boat to Gubat.*

'"Our start in the evening was timed to enable us to pass the enemy's fort at Wad Habeshi under the cover of darkness. We rowed to within about half a mile of the fort, and then, shipping oars, I ordered the crew to lie down in the bottom of the boat, which gradually approached the enemy's position on the current of the river. So near did we drift to the shore that the dervishes' faces could easily be distinguished as they sat over the camp fires, and they were heard discussing whether the black object they saw upon the stream was a boat or not.

"'Suddenly their doubts were dispelled by the rising of the moon on the eastern horizon in a straight line behind the boat, which was at once rendered plainly visible. The shout which followed this discovery soon warned us that further concealment was useless. We applied ourselves to the oars with a will amid a rain of bullets which ploughed up the water on every side, but fortunately did no damage. A few hundred yards brought us to an island, by following the right hand side of which we were enabled to continue our journey under cover for a considerable distance. Again emerging into the main channel, we found that we were followed only by a few camel men apparently unarmed with rifles. And thus we came to Gubat unscathed."

'Before embarking on a journey across desert country still infested by small bands of roving Mahdiists to deliver this despatch to a courier, your correspondent ascertained that Lord Charles Beresford is making urgent plans to sail the *Safieh* to the rescue of Gordon and Wilson; the remaining vessel, the *Tewfikieh*, a mere 24 horse-power and only 70 feet in length, is far too small to be used for anything other than ferrying duties. Even so, Lord Charles describes his *Safieh*, strengthened by boiler-plating, as nothing more than "a penny steamer in a packing case", through which bullets and shells will easily pass.

'She has been armed with two brass four-pounder mountain guns and two Gardners, which Beresford now has available following the arrival, among reinforcements, of the other half of the Naval Brigade. For officers he can draw on Lieutenant E.B. van Koughnet, Sub-Lieutenant Colin Keppel and Surgeon Arthur May. He is also using the services of Mr. Walter Ingram, of the *Illustrated London News,* who was commissioned as an acting Lieutenant in the Royal Navy at Beresford's request when casualties at Abu Klea had robbed Lord Charles of all his officers. The *Safieh* is to sail packed to the gunwale with marksmen drawn probably from the Mounted Infantry. Chief Engineer Harry Benbow can be relied on to obtain every ounce of power from the engines. There is no doubt amongst any of the British here at

Gubat that Charlie Beresford's "penny steamer" will give good account of herself on the hostile river.'

Bennet Burleigh may be forgiven for injecting a note of self-congratulation into his despatch. His lone ride across the desert to Jakdul was a hazardous venture not to be taken lightly, in which Burleigh risked death, if not from Mahdiists, then from wandering bands of robbers looking for easy pickings in the wake of an army. The route, along which Buller was now moving the Light Camel Regiment and the Royal Irish towards Gubat, was kept open by a tenuous link of zeribas at the wells, and shuttles of massed herds of decrepit baggage camels under escort. Death, in the form of Ansar corpses between Abu Klea and the river, and a trail of worn-out camels, marked the route with a stench of decay; a solitary traveller and a good reporter, Burleigh remarked airily to his chagrined colleagues on his return, had merely to follow his nose.

The *Daily Telegraph* story created a sensation in London, and brought forth a burst of national rejoicing, hardly tempered by the news of Khartoum's fall or the fact that Gordon was not yet 'home and dry'. But there was dismay in Army circles that Burleigh had beaten them to it. His despatch reached Korti before the news came through military channels. Wolseley did not quite know what to make of it, by which time Burleigh's message was on its way by camel rider to Dongola. The Army's machinery in Korti was loath to commit itself to an announcement that Gordon was free while he was still deep in enemy territory, and while it still knew precious little about the circumstances, anyway. Ideally, Wolseley would have preferred to stop Burleigh's message, but a speedy and enterprising Thomas Cook clerk in Dongola, 'softened' some weeks earlier by Burleigh's promisory notes drawn on a Fleet Street bank, used similar persuasion on the telegraph operator: if the Mudir could telegraph the Koran, the clerk argued, surely the telegraph could bear the news of Gordon Pasha's rescue.

Too late, Wolseley rushed a guarded, short message through to the War Office. The official version, tantalisingly bare of detail, was relayed to Osborne House. It arrived on Queen Victoria's breakfast table simultaneously with the morning's copy of the *Daily Telegraph*. Acidly, she asked in telegrams to Gladstone and Hartington: 'Why must the Queen learn the news of General Gordon's merciful release from a special correspondent in greater detail than the Government can provide? What is General Wolseley doing to keep us informed?'

Wolseley was furious. Burleigh had hitherto enjoyed good relations with the Army: neither he nor his newspaper were inclined to publish anything in the least detrimental to the British soldier or the imperial cause. After the battle of Tamai in the eastern Sudan in the previous year, however, some military noses had been put out of joint when other correspondents gave Burleigh the credit for helping mend the broken British square with his stentorian shouts of 'Give it the beggars!' and 'Let 'em have it, boys!' — an intervention which several observers claimed rallied the 65th and the Marines. Now, Wolseley was more than ever convinced of his long-held dictum that war correspondents were the 'curse of modern armies'. He commanded that existing orders prohibiting the independent movement of correspondents were to be strictly enforced.

Burleigh's prediction of the make-up of *Safieh's* complement, based on a hurried early morning conversation with Beresford, was correct. The reporter shrewdly defined that Beresford was strong enough to have his own way in deliberations with the temporary commander, Mildmay Willson.

Sheathed in extra boiler-plate (the supplies Buller had tried to refuse Beresford) and laden to capacity with wood for fuel, the *Safieh* sailed at two in the afternoon, eleven hours after Stuart-Wortley's arrival. The young Lieutenant was aboard. Within 40 hours the steamer was off Wad Habeshi, in sight of the *Bordein*, and engaged in a howitzer and musketry slogging match with Feki Mustafa's fort. A shell pierced the *Safieh's* boiler, temporarily crippling the ship. The engineer, Benbow, toiling incessantly for ten hours, made repairs which enabled Beresford to move his ship close to the right bank, to a point reached by Wilson's party on foot and in a nuggar. On a crowded deck of a crowded ship, Beresford shook hands with Gordon, weak but now able to walk, and said: 'Welcome aboard, sir'. After spraying the last of 5,400 Gardner rounds and lobbing its 126th howitzer shell at Feki Mustafa's men, the *Safieh* wallowed downstream and arrived off the jetty at Gubat at 5:45 pm on Tuesday, February 3.

Thus, a little over a week after the fall of Khartoum, Gordon was safely delivered to the British garrison at Gubat by a triumphant but exhausted Wilson. Rescuer and rescued were in poor shape. Wilson was in great pain and partially crippled by the wound he had received from a spent bullet when the *Bordein* arrived on the Blue Nile; disregarded as a minor flesh wound, the lesion had festered so that he could walk only with the aid of improvised crutches.

Edward Gleichen, in his journal, recorded Gordon's landing at Gubat: 'His progress from the ship along the jetty which the Sappers and Navy had built was in the nature of a triumphal homecoming. Sergeant-Major Borthwick called for three cheers, and the Guards responded, raising a hundred sun helmets in the air as one. The blacks could scarce forbear to join in. Even the Adeni drivers, of whom not one man is given to the slightest exertion except under duress, were roused to a state of enthusiasm, I swear. And yet, no Roman hero presented such an appearance at his homecoming. Gordon Pasha's head was swathed in bandages, atop which sat his tarboosh at an unmilitary and raked angle. His face was gaunt and clothed in several days' growth of beard. His uniform, once white, was stained and torn, but no more so than that of many another scarecrow who walked off that ship; nor, indeed, was he worse dressed than any in the reception committee. His bearing, however, was proud, and a fierce light danced in his blue eyes. On stepping ashore he refused the proffered medical attention and requested immediately to hold council with Colonel Mildmay Willson, our acting commander.'

Having spent most of the downriver voyage incapacitated by a raging fever (somewhat to Sir Charles Wilson's relief), Gordon had sufficiently recovered to reopen battle with the British Establishment. Sir Charles was content to surrender himself and his throbbing knee to the ministrations of Surgeon Magill of the Coldstream Guards. It was no longer his battle.

# Chapter 23

# *The Mahdi's army*

The killing had ended in Khartoum. The city and its inhabitants were stripped of their wealth and it was placed in the beit-el-mal, the official treasury from which the Mahdiists financed all the activities of their emergent state and people's army. One million rounds of ammunition and a hoard of rifles were distributed to the arsenals of the Ansar who waited now, flushed with victory, for word from the Mahdi.

It had been his custom every Friday to hold a review of his troops, but an urgent summons had gone out to the emirs to attend with their men on the Wednesday, nine days after the fall of Khartoum. The place chosen for the parade was the flat ground beneath the low hill which gives Omdurman its name — on the land where the new capital would be situated. In front, the two Niles meet and, beyond, the roofs of Khartoum could be seen above a belt of palm trees.

The forces of the Mahdi were composed of three divisions, each under a khalifa who had his own flag, or raya. The line of the Black Flag division, the Khalifa Abdallahi's own, was drawn up in its usual position of honour for the Mahdi's review — facing east to the morning sun. At the front, under the black banner which proclaimed in white script 'The Mahdi is the Khalifa of the Prophet of God', stood Yakub Mohammed, short and thick set, a Baggara like his brother Abdallahi. Across a wide expanse of stony ground the Green Flag faced Yakub's division under their commander Khalifa Wad Helu, who had been one of the first of the Baggara chieftains to follow the Mahdi. Joining the two files, and facing north, were the Red Flag headed by Khalifa Mohammed Sherifa, the son-in-law of the Mahdi, whose fame throughout the army was that he had killed Hicks Pasha.

Other great battle leaders, each known as 'emir of emirs', stood

200

before their cohorts: Abu Anga, short, dark and leonine-headed, the half-breed former slave who was raised by the wild Baggara and whose black jehadia had no equal; el Nejumi, the Jaalin who had led the assault from the south on Khartoum; Abu Girgeh, first to reach the Governor's Palace where, in the cellars, he had slaughtered the servants unmercifully in his fury at Gordon's escape. And behind the emirs of emirs stood their subordinate emirs, and behind these their under-officers, each with a battle flag representing 100 men or more; thus the Ansar counted their army in flags, or rayas, 100 rayas being 10,000 soldiers. Over this host, then, there must have fluttered nearly 300 flags, each one hailing the Mahdi and proclaiming extracts from the Koran. The brazen drums thudded and the immense host, wearing to a man the patched white jibbehs of Ansar faith, formed three sides of a square, the fourth side of which was left open for the coming of the Mahdi.

The men owed allegiance to their emir, who usually raised his troops from his tribal group. He furnished them with durra, a mere few handfuls of grain per day, but otherwise the Ansar had to fend for themselves. The uniform consisted of the simple jibbeh of cotton twill, drawers, straw girdle, skull cap, turban and sandals. Every man carried two goatskins — one for durra, dates, onions, and rarely pieces of roasted meat, the other for his drinking water. Pay was not issued regularly, except to the black jehadia corps who received a pittance monthly (in theory). The blacks' pay was a source of resentment to the Arabs; ill feeling was common among the blacks who complained they were always put in the front of any action.

The emir was responsible for seeing that his men supplied their own donkeys and camels. These were usually put to transport use, for the Ansar in the main fought on foot. There was no organised cavalry arm: if cavalry were needed the emirs were supposed to provide horses, which were scarce, or camels. In his preaching of self-denial, the Mahdi had insisted that horses were to be ridden only in battle. The lordly Baggara, of course, ignored the edict. These 'manliest of men in the Sudan... inured to war, and in chronic readiness to plunder' (as Wingate described them) were employed much as light cavalry — in scouting, as lookouts, and in harrying retreating troops or the fringes of enemy columns.

The Ansar Arab carried into battle a formidable and heavy armoury of weapons consisting of a two-edged, cross-hilted sword, a long lance with a blade broad enough to take off a man's head at one thrust, four small spears which were effective in close fighting, and a dagger. The lance and spears were weighted with a roll of iron at the extreme end of the shaft to give them greater momentum and piercing power. A boomerang-shaped club of mimosa wood was employed to break the legs of horses. Some warriors carried circular shields of hippopotamus or rhinoceros hide. These, however, were discouraged by their religious leaders who taught that a man's shield was his faith; in the beginnings of the rebellion firearms were eschewed, even if they were available, and the early Mahdiists fought only with spears and sticks. On the field after fights British soldiers found some unconventional hardware far removed from that stipulated in 'Mahdi's regulations' — vests of chain mail, breastplates, greaves, and Saracens' helmets with ostrich plumes. Hauls of musketry ancient and bizarre included 18th century flintlocks and a one-inch calibre elephant gun which fired spherical iron bullets. There were products of Wilkinson, the swordmakers in Pall Mall, supplied to a former khedive's bodyguard.

The firepower of the Ansar was, of course, mainly in the capable hands of Abu Anga's blacks. Their Egyptian Army Remingtons had less tendency to jam than the more modern Martini-Henrys of the British. Each man carried 40 rounds in the field. After Khartoum the Mahdi had available more than 12,000 Remingtons and 9,000 other rifles; the artillery included about 30 brass mountain guns, several Krupp howitzers, half a dozen machine-guns and some rockets, but not all were in working order and the Sudanese were not expert artillerists.

Discipline was strict, being based on the Mahdi's religious code, and the harsh penalties for a soldier who infringed the code were the same as in civil life. Sixty blows of the kurbash were given to anyone convicted of drinking alcohol, usually marissa, a foul and potent native beer. Such a beating would frequently end in death; Ohrwalder wrote of a drinker who was beaten until his bowels fell out, and people in Omdurman would tell of the lips being cut off smokers and the noses cut off those who took snuff. The use of hashish was punishable by a lethal beating, and sodomy by beheading. Death was the penalty for blasphemy and murder. Less drastic deterrents restrained men and women from wearing fine clothes: it was only by gradual evolution that purely decorative coloured squares replaced the black repair patches on the Ansar's jibbehs, and later the patches became uniform.

The tacticians of the Mahdi's army had learned a great deal about fighting the English from Osman Digna's battles at El Teb and Tamai — to attack squares at their vulnerable corners, to use ravines and dried water courses as concealment, to take advantage of a column's lack of mobility caused by its customary encumbrance of a slow-moving herd of baggage camels. The enveloping onslaught in the shape of a crescent was still the Ansar's chosen method of attack — it was carried out with the bravest warriors at the front, and others of them held in reserve at the rear, with a middle mass of second-rate troops who would rush forward to complete the slaughter once the spearhead had broken through. They were learning new tricks, however: at Abu Klea they had dug earthworks for riflemen in the path of the English; at the same battle Nur Angara, an emir who had been a soldier in the Egyptian Army, had taught them not to raise a great shout before attacking — which was their custom — because it simply warned the enemy to be ready.

Experience gained in the eastern Sudan and in the Bayuda had been costly in lives, but the Ansar army was now mightier than ever, gorged with victory at Khartoum, strengthened by recruits who flocked to the Koranic banners in ever increasing number every day, and armed with an arsenal of new weaponry captured from the 'Turks'. Would the Mahdi show them how to put all this to use in exacting vengeance from the English who had spirited Gordon out of their grasp? The troops were eager to know why they had been called together.

A blast on the 'umbaya', the great ivory horn that was guarded by the Black Flag, announced the arrival of Mohammed Ahmed, the Mahdi. He entered the vast square on a white racing camel — the Guided One, white himself from head to foot in cotton skull cap, turban, jibbeh and pantaloons, and the ordinary people sighed and knelt and kissed the sand as he passed by. Behind him rode the Khalifa Abdallahi at the head of the retinue whose broad lance blades reflected the eastern sun.

The Mahdi raised his arm as a signal for the drums to stop. Then in a silence broken only by the occasional snort of a camel, a shuffling of hooves and the faint jingle of harness, he called out in a clear, deep voice: 'Allah yebarek fikum' — 'May God bless you'. The host answered back in echo.

Mohammed Ahmed, in his 38th year, had a tall, broad-shouldered figure with an inclination to stoutness. His face was light brown, his eyes dark and limpid, his beard neat and black. Three slits, ritually applied, marked each cheek. His regular features gave him a handsomeness by western standards; when he smiled, he revealed a V-shaped aperture between two front teeth that the women among his people found especially attractive — there was also lore that when the Guided One came he would have 'separated teeth'. Nature polished by practice had endowed him with a dignified presence. People said that he moved in an odour of sanctity: it was true that he habitually wore a personal fragrance, produced from sandalwood, musk and attar of roses by the women of his harem — a large establishment with a polyglot population ranging from eight-year-old creamy-skinned Turks to fulsome black beauties from Abyssinia. After his appearances on ceremonial occasions such as this stories would circulate of wonderful apparitions: the Prophet was seen riding by the Mahdi's side; a passing cloud formed into angels' wings to give shade to the faithful; voices from heaven called blessings on the Ansar and promises of victory. The Mahdi would weep rolling tears of compassion and love for his people: the infidel Gordon had given currency to the opinion that he concealed pepper beneath his finger nails to induce the tears.

After various Koranic exhortations and responses, the Mahdi called for his soldiers' silence and close attention. Then he spoke in slow, deliberate tones. So large was the throng that he delivered a sentence or two at a time, enabling the emirs to relay his words to the remote ranks.

'We are angry that Gordon Pasha has gone, angry for his own disgrace. Where are his brave words now? A man who does not stand on his fur is no man.' (A Sudanese warrior who 'stands on his fur' takes the sheepskin from his saddle, lays it on the ground and fights there to the death.)

'We knew of his innermost thoughts. We know he has joined the English soldiers.

'He brought the English here to steal our right. Gordon must not go unpunished, nor the English army which came to challenge the law of God.'

A huge acclamation rose from the assembled army. The Mahdi waited for the last echoes to fade. Then he recited the names of emirs who had died in recent battles with the English: Mussa Wad Helu, a leader of the attack at Abu Klea and brother of the khalifa commanding the Green Flag ... Mohammed Wad Billal, a Dongolawi who died in the same fight ... Ahmed Wad Faid, 'our dearest brother who died at Wad Habeshi two days ago when the English steamers attacked our forts' ...

It was virtuous to fight in war and be killed, martyrdom in battle was victory, but the Mahdi was calling for vengeance on the English. 'We are the hurricane of God in Africa. The hour of the jehad was set for us before our very birth.

'Osman Digna broke the back of the English in the eastern lands. He showed us the way to lower the mighty English.

'Their water skins will be pierced by God's intervention. Their corpses will clothe the desert. Gordon welcomed them here for a mission from the Devil. Our enemy is a pale, thirsty hyena from a cold land who would not hesitate to steal our sun. But he is sick with fear. We shall go north with 200 rayas and destroy the English.'

The Mahdi's intentions to destroy the British would come as no surprise to his European prisoners, such as Slatin and Ohrwalder on whose testimony this account is based. Although in durance, they were remarkably well informed about the doings and thoughts of the high command. News of what went on in the councils of the Mahdi and the khalifas was often common knowledge within a very short time in the vast, warren-like townships of straw huts and palisaded compounds which made up the Ansar camps at El Obeid, Rahad and now Omdurman. Slatin, especially, had close personal contact with the leaders, although around the time of Khartoum's fall he was in disgrace and chains for having concealed messages in correspondence he wrote to Gordon at the Mahdi's orders. At Omdurman it was well known on the grapevine of this huge village that the Mahdi was deeply angered by Gordon's escape. All men said that he had offered Gordon clemency; it had been refused; had Gordon come over to him, he would have let the English troops go. His last letter to Gordon had promised: '... should you wish to rejoin the English we will send you back to them'. But the choice was the Mahdi's prerogative and now Gordon had pre-empted it. Loud in the councils for smashing the British had been the Mahdi's uncle, Mohammed abd el Kerim, whose lone and persistent voice had urged resolute action before Khartoum. Following that victory, he was closely listened to.

By the Wednesday evening the advance guard had started down

the left bank of the Nile. Its object was to alert the Ansar at Wad Habeshi and Metemmeh; to seal off all the routes into the heart of the Bayuda and to Gubat so that no news would seep through of the great force that was coming; to play tricks to deceive the English. Ahead of them, on the right bank, camel-riders were speeding the Mahdi's orders to the mudirs of Shendy and Berber who would ready their tribes.

Khalifa Abdallahi was appointed overlord of the attacking force. Under him, Abu Anga and el Nejumi were chosen to command in the field, the former to make the most advantage of his jehadia riflemen, the latter as a mark of honour to a Jaalin who might now avenge his tribal brothers killed by British guns at Abu Klea.

To Nur Angara, the emir who had been a soldier in the Khedive's army, was allotted a special task. The career of Nur Angara, who was now nearing 50, had been many-sided. A Dongolawi, he had been a cavalry Private for the Egyptians, a slave-raiding freebooter for Zebehr and his son, Suliman, and then a soldier for Gordon who made him a bey, an official of senior rank. He surrendered to the Mahdi in 1882 and was created an emir. And, of course, he had been blooded against the English a month ago in the desert. On this new expedition to the Bayuda he was given stewardship of a valuable property — Abd el Hamid, the steamer captain from Gordon's fleet who had deserted when the *Bordein* ran aground at Mernat Island in the previous week.

Abd el Hamid, although a detested Shagiyeh, was pardoned by the Mahdi who had immediately recognised his worth. As a captain he had been privy to the British commanders' deliberations at Gubat, so he knew the nature and plan of the defence works, the number of men and armaments in the garrison, the arrangements for reinforcements, the state of the remaining steamers. It was explained to Abd el Hamid that, in exchange for his co-operation in supplying this intelligence to the Ansar generals in the field, the Mahdi would return to him the women-folk of his family in Khartoum who had been distributed around emirs' harems. As an added incentive, the deserter was given the leech-like attendance of Nur Angara whose way with recalcitrant prisoners was famed throughout the Sudan: he once personally cut off the head of a rebel sultan he had been sent by Gordon to capture.

On the day following the Mahdi's review, the main force of 200 rayas — more than 20,000 fighting men — trekked northwards out of Omdurman, filling the gravel slopes between the black hill of Surgham and the Nile with a shimmering white host, and raising an immense dust cloud which could be seen from Khartoum. At the rear where the dust was thickest 150 captured Egyptian soldiers, considered to be artillery specialists and thus spared execution, shuffled in chains alongside a camel train of mountain guns.

# Chapter 24

# 'A pretty hullabaloo'

When Buller, half-way across the Bayuda desert and moving at the pace of the foot-slogging Royal Irish, learned that Gordon had arrived at Gubat, he sent ahead a peremptory order to Mildmay Willson: 'Get him out'. Buller had understood enough from Willson's brief but frantic signals to realise that the sooner Gordon was safely passed down the line and placed under the control of Wolseley the better it would be for all concerned. 'Gordon is pressing for an attack on Metemmeh and strongly counselling action towards Khartoum. His manner is assertive. He is not responsive to reason and I believe we have an increasing problem on our hands the longer he remains in the forward theatre. Sir Charles Wilson, who is sick and in hospital, concurs with my assessment.' Willson had written in a despatch.

On Buller's mandate, and exercising the authority of his command, Willson placed Gordon under the orders of Colonel C.R. Rowley of the Grenadier Guards who was to convey him on the first stage of the journey to Korti with an escort of 30 men of the Guards Camel Regiment commanded by Lieutenant Gleichen. They left Gubat on an early morning, accompanied by a motley band of camp followers whose departure afforded almost as much relief to Willson as Gordon's. These were the newspaper correspondents and artists — rigorously segregated from Gordon in the camp — who had decided on a general exodus: their 'story' was moving back down the line, angry, unpredictable and likely to explode into sensational 'copy' at any moment.

Of the newsmen, only Walter Ingram, commissioned as a Lieutenant in Beresford's naval detachment, remained in the camp. His colleague and employee, the special artist Melton Prior, took from him his eye-witness account of the *Safieh's* rescue dash, in which Ingram had participated. It contained a straightforward description of Beresford's action and the *outline* details of Wilson's mission to Khartoum, which Ingram had gleaned from Trafford, Gascoigne and Stuart-Wortley during their close association on the return voyage of the *Safieh*.

Ingram was no hardened, experienced correspondent with an acute nose for news and scandal. He had in his possession first-hand from Trafford the evidence of Gordon's disconcerting behaviour in the palace, supported by Trafford's affirmed suspicion that during the exchanges Gordon had been intoxicated by something more material than guidance from *Isaiah*. It was knowledge that some of his more mature colleagues would have sought in some way to convey to their readers — if not the ultra-conservative Bennet Burleigh, then surely the less fastidiously establishment-minded Harry Pearse of the *Daily News*. Ingram was constrained by two considerations, however — his sense of proprietorial responsibility as part-owner of the *Illustrated London News*, and his commission as an acting naval officer. His secrets stayed in his notebook; for the time being.

Buller, moving south towards Gubat with the reinforcements, met Gordon on the old battleground of Abu Klea wells, a broad sandy valley, dotted by tussocks of yellow grass and rocky knolls and rimmed by steep black hills. Gleichen, returning to the scene for the first time since the battle three weeks earlier, wrote in his journal: 'Scores of bodies were still lying about the country, all in a mummified condition, and smelling horribly. The air was so dry that they would not decay properly, but simply dried up in the hot sun and stank. On the actual scene of the fight, to the left of the track, there were still piles of bodies, though hundreds had been taken away and buried.' Several forts had been built, one of them together with hospital tents 'surrounded by a dangerously close zeriba of thorn-bushes'; Gleichen considered it a fire hazard in the event of an attack.

Buller, who shared Wolseley's distaste for the 'curse of modern armies', ordered the war correspondents to be placed in the hospital lines and for there to be no contact whatsoever between them and Gordon.

The meeting between Gordon, who had accused the Army of tarrying in Shepheard's Hotel, and Buller, who had declared 'the man was not worth the camels', was icy. It was held in Buller's tent, in the presence of Colonel Rowley and Gleichen. The young Guards officer's journal left the following record:

'General Gordon was in a sombre mood, demanding to know under whose authority he had been "placed under arrest", as he put it, unflinching in his demand that he should be allowed to return to Gubat and insisting that our force should move without delay to smash up the Mahdi. General Buller was equally obdurate in his refusal to accede to these last two requests. Gordon remarked, "I cannot too much impress on you that this expedition will not encounter any enemy worth the name in the European sense of the word". Buller's answer was to refer General Gordon to the large cairn of stones which had been built not a hundred yards away over the column's dead, and the hospital tents full of our wounded, including General Stewart. Buller was awaiting orders on future operations, upon which a great deal hung in the balance, especially the progress of General Earle's column on the river.

'He seriously doubted whether the troops at Gubat, exhausted, depleted by casualties and sickness, and with done-up camels, could really attempt offensive operations, notwithstanding his re-inforcements of a battalion of Royal Irish and the impending arrival of the Lights [the Light Camel Regiment]. The meeting ended as it began with the two Generals extending only the most formal of courtesies to one another. Gordon at one stage in the proceedings had intimated that he would address the gentlemen of the press. Buller strictly forbade this. In the event, Gordon went to his tent where he remained, alone, until the next morning. We saw that his lamp burned all night. On the following day, Gordon went down to Korti with some of the Mounted Infantry taking despatches and a convoy of some of the less seriously wounded. I returned to Gubat with my men, taking almost two days as we travelled at the pace of the Royal Irish on foot. We saw nothing of the enemy.'

A less privileged observer than Gleichen, the reporter Harry Pearse, provided a footnote to Gordon's one-night sojourn at Abu Klea. Confined to the hospital lines with the other press men and kept away from Gordon, he nevertheless gleaned some fragments of information from an orderly on Buller's staff whom he softened with a bottle of whisky and some tobacco — just as his investigative talents had enabled him to tap some rumours in the messes at Gubat. Having arrived at Korti, still 'quarantined' from Gordon, the newspapermen went down the river to file their despatches. Pearse telegraphed the *Daily News*:

'Your correspondent understands that the meeting between Generals Buller and Gordon, held in private and under close guard, was less than cordial.' Pearse's message continued in the same paragraph: 'There were unconfirmed reports among officers of the force at Gubat that General Gordon's later days in command at Khartoum were marked by prolonged and unexplained absences during which he shut himself away from his subordinates in deep seclusion. Having apparently gained little or no satisfaction from his interview with General Buller on the 7th, General Gordon sought similar seclusion in the privacy of this tent in what, in a lesser man, might be described as "a fit of the sulks", and refused to mess with the other officers. It would be invidious to credit rumours which have circulated about intemperance on the part of General Gordon, but suffice it to quote a reliable source in the camp which reports that the General's seclusion and discomfiture on that evening were amply solaced by medicinal stocks of brandy.'

In London, where there was universal rejoicing at the rescue of the hero of Khartoum, Pearse's first sentence was printed exactly as he telegraphed it. The editor's pencil deleted all the rest of the paragraph.

At Korti, grown into a small town of cantonments as a forwarding base for the Bayuda expedition, Wolseley rode out to a ridge of high ground from which he could look for the coming of the convoy that would bring his friend Gordon. The last occasion he had held a vigil on the desolate escarpment had been on the penultimate afternoon of the old year when he had watched the departure of the Camel Corps until it was no more than a shimmering haze of dust on the desert horizon: barely more than six weeks gone, and yet it was a hundred years and a hundred uncertainties ago. His strategies had been vindicated and Gordon, the object of them, was coming home. Wolseley, however, was conscious of an ambivalence in his feelings. His joy at the prospect of greeting his dear friend was tempered by the warning signals he had received from his commanders in the field. To put it bluntly, they were suggesting that Gordon was 'off his head' with reproach and recrimination.

Wolseley wrote afterwards to his wife, Louisa: 'Gordon is as fit as any man can hope to be who has undergone the trials that he has. How white his hair is — though he tells me that *I* am greyed in the process! He is saved, that is the main thing, and with him

England's honour.

'I fear he is set to kick up a pretty hullabaloo. He blames Gladstone — and for that he has my every blessing — for the spineless vacillation that has brought about the abandonment of the Egyptian garrisons; a stain on England, Gordon says (I would go further and say that the old crocodile has carefully planned our country's disgrace).

'I set little store by a hysterical letter received from Sir Charles Wilson, which is uncomplimentary to Gordon and doubtless coloured by his own injury (they have had to amputate his leg) and his exposure to fire. I never had much faith in him, as you know, but all up, he has done an excellent job of work in getting Gordon out — though I warrant Beresford had to spur him. As for his complaints, they can wait till I see him.

'But there are some alarming inconsistencies in Gordon's attitudes that must be put down to the ordeal he has suffered these past 12 months. He is angry, of course, at being compelled to come down to Korti. He also feels that we have dallied on the Nile, should have gone by Suakim and Berber, etc, etc. It is all I can do to restrain him from calling for an enquiry of some sort. He cannot know what troubles I have had with those laggardly fellows in Cairo, Stephenson, Wood and the rest of the Cairo sluggards (I have had to bring Wood up here where I can keep an eye on him).

'Well, Gordon has gone down to Cairo. He swears that he will never set foot in England again; be that as it may. I can keep those drones, the newspaper correspondents, away from him while he is on the Nile and under my protection. But I fear he is proposing to talk to Mobberly Bell who represents *The Times* in Cairo and even of sending for that Stead fellow.

'In the meantime, as you no doubt know, Gladstone has decided that we are to withdraw. I must concede that I cannot put up much of a case for a serious offensive until the autumn when it becomes cooler and the Nile is higher (it is nearly 100 in the shade here today), and only then if they give me two more brigades. But what a pest that contemptible man Gladstone is with his "butcher and bolt" policies!

'All that remains now is to pull out our force. The Mahdi has had sufficient lesson from us to keep away. I can rely on Buller to finish the job.'

# Chapter 25

## *Blindness at Gubat*

'The Sudan is not logical; it does not do what is expected of it, and the unexpected has a habit of happening with remarkable suddenness.' Edward Gleichen approved what he had written as a closing sentence of the nightly entry in his journal. He put his notebook in the battered green hand-valise which bore in gold leaf the family crest and scrolled monogram of the Hohenloe-Langenburgs, stuffed the bag under the camel saddle he used as a pillow, blew out the candle and went to sleep. He was not bothered by the water still dripping through the straw roof of his lean-to shelter at Gubat.

The unexpected had happened twice between dusk and midnight — as Gleichen had recorded in his journal. Out of a starlit sky had come one of those storms that the Sudan can conjure up from God knows where: a flicker of lightning, and without warning bloated drops of rain, and wind rushing down, snorting, tearing at tents and shelters and ripping them apart; a downpour leaving soldiers drenched, yet not an atom of moisture in the baked watercourses the next day, nor a millimetre of difference in the levels of the brackish wells.

And then, at the height of the brief storm while the soldiers' attention was diverted, came the sound of hoofbeats and a nerve-piercing cry of 'La ilaha il'allah' on the wind. In the lightning's flash a solitary Baggara horseman was etched silvery grey against the black desert. His horse reared and his right arm hurled a lance which soared over the startled outposts and landed quivering in the sand. He wheeled and vanished into the darkness, ahead of futile shots from the sentries.

The Mahdi's army was not accustomed to fighting at night, least of all the Baggara horsemen. The night visitor's appearance was taken for what it was — a solitary gesture in the name of his god by

213

an over-zealous warrior. It caused a good deal of comment in the British camp, however, because this was a time of tedium at Gubat and the other Bayuda forts. Of recent there had been little sign of the enemy.

The convoys from Jakdul had sighted dervishes in small parties on the slopes of distant hills, too far away to be fired on, too few in number to worry about. The pickets at Abu Klea found evidence of Arabs coming down in the night and carrying their dead from the battlefield; it was not a practice the British commander felt disposed to interfere with. Around Gubat the sole operational preoccupation was with the fortified village of Metemmeh, close by on the river. Action extended to no more than a continuing reconnaissance by the 19th Hussars and an occasional sally by the Royal Artillery's screw guns.

The camp known as Gubat was a triangle of defence works. One corner of the triangle rested on the river, a pestilential spot, swampy and mosquito-ridden and loathed by the infantry who manned it. Here a small fort of earth was built and a rough-and-ready barricade was made by piling debris between a group of ruined huts. Separated from the river outpost and higher up a sloping gravel terrace was a second angle of the triangle, Gubat itself, truly one of Churchill's 'squalid villages', the Camel Corps' base. Huts of primitive cement were loopholed, their conical or flat roofs of straw and durra stalk removed. Linked by debris, they made a semi-circular breastwork some eight to ten feet high. By the time of Buller's arrival on February 10 this parapet was being buttressed on the outside by slopes of packed gravel as protection from artillery. Buller expressed his doubts about the buttresses — the Mahdi had precious little artillery, but plenty of men who could run up slopes — but he let the work continue. Within the breastworks was built a three-cornered redoubt, a fort of rubble, ammunition and biscuit boxes, and sandbags. Around the whole encampment, some way out, the engineers laced fresh supplies of barbed wire through a thorn-bush zeriba built by Wilson's men on the night of their arrival.

The third corner of the triangle was the zeriba a few hundred yards upstream where Gordon's 'hens', the Egyptians and hangers-on, had been placed in isolation by Beresford 'so that in the event of a force advancing from Khartoum, and the consequent revolt of the 'hens', we should not be placed between two fires'. The officers of this 'garrison' were Egyptians, Turks,

Cypriots, Greeks and half-breed bashi-bazouks — the Egyptians and Turks 'slippery', the others 'the scum of Europe', noted Gleichen. They lived, bickering and fighting, in a shanty town of makeshift huts which they now shared with a large influx of Sudanese blacks from the steamers. The blacks were generally a cheerful crowd, many of them dressed in a motley assortment of clothes stolen from the British lines — Camel Corps breeches, a scarlet tunic or two, even a few sun helmets and blue veils. 'They amuse me, but I have a feeling they would be just as happy fighting and thieving in the Mahdi's army as in ours,' Gleichen observed.

Buller did not like what he found at Gubat. He arrived itching for a fight, but quickly had to concede in a message to Wolseley: 'The force is in no state to undertake offensive operations on any considerable scale at the present time'. He had under his command about 2,000 British troops, but they were spread over 40-odd miles of desert, with a garrison holding the wells at Abu Klea, a small outpost at Abu Kru a few miles from the river, the main force at Gubat, and detachments on despatch and escort duties between these points. Eighty miles off, and almost half way to Korti were the vital rock pools of Jakdul, considered 'safe' territory and the responsibility of Evelyn Wood whom Wolseley had sent forward with a half-battalion of the West Kents.

The original flying column was in an appalling condition. Many were sick; dysentery, heatstroke and sheer physical exhaustion had debilitated them and typhoid had broken out at Gubat. More than 200 wounded and seriously ill were in the hospitals. There was hardly a recognisable uniform in the force, nor a pair of serviceable boots. Even some of the newly arrived Royal Irish marched the last miles with strips of rifle-bucket leather tied to their feet. Stores and ammunition were short. Transport had broken down owing to the disastrous under-estimation of the number of camels that would be required. There were barely 800 left and these were worn out; there was practically no fodder for them. The camels of the Lights, who were soon to arrive, had fared no better, thanks partly to the carelessness of the commander, the Duke of Cambridge's nominee, Colonel Stanley Clarke; many had been lost, others ruined by ill use. The ponies of the 19th Hussars, Buller's only scouts, had been worked into emaciated wrecks. Of the remaining steamers, the *Tewfikieh* could be used only for ferrying, and the *Safieh*, its damaged boiler threatening to blow at any moment, might be 'good for a short raid, nothing more', in Beresford's opinion.

The decisions were being made for Buller 3,000 miles away in London. Dearly as Wolseley would have relished going on to crush the rebellion and achieving another Tel-el-Kebir to crown his career in the field, given sufficient men and arms, he had telegraphed to Hartington his views on an autumn campaign. He was not surprised, therefore, to receive orders to retrieve the desert column and retire the river force — which on February 11 defeated 2,000 Arabs at Kirbekan and lost its commander, General Earle, to a dervish bullet.

Gladstone could see his way out of the Sudan. With the release of Gordon the object of the expedition had been accomplished. Britain was in a fever of celebration. No hisses now for Gladstone. When the Grand Old Man attended a Mansion House lunch in the City of London, a crowd of delirious onlookers in the street cheered him to the skies, and only the restraint of police prevented them from carrying him shoulder-high from his carriage to the doorway. To press on to Khartoum now would bring a nasty echo of his words of last May — 'a war of conquest against a people struggling, and rightly struggling, to be free'. Britain must get out of the collapsing house that was the Sudan and slam the door shut at Wady Halfa.

Buller doubted whether he could retire his whole force in one go. He just did not have enough camels — and, despite the alarm signals which had been passed down the line since the Camel Corps started out from Korti at the end of the old year, purchasing had not been recommenced on any significant scale. 'As for the few camels that remain "alive",' Buller wrote to Wolseley, 'there is not one animal which would stay on its feet if a man leaned against it.' He would have to send half the column to Abu Klea with the sick and wounded, then the camels would return under escort to carry the supplies, guns and ammunition needed by the second contingent. As for the fighting men, they would have to walk: no camels could be spared for riding. And so, shuttling to and fro between Gubat and Abu Klea, Abu Klea and Jakdul, Jakdul and Korti, the weary soldiers of the desert column would once again, it seemed, reap the harvest of the high command's misjudgements, internal jealousies, personal vendettas and bad management.

A tremor of apprehension raced through Wolseley's mind when

he learned Buller was planning to split his force. Buller, too, saw the dangers, but there was no other option open to him.

Arrangements for the departure began with the dumping of food in the river. The guns were taken off the steamers. Then the ships themselves were made unserviceable (in recent days neither the *Safieh* nor the *Tewfikieh* had been able to pass a large sandbank which had been revealed by the rapidly falling Nile). Beresford was near to tears as he watched his precious stocks of lubricating oil, brought all the way up the cataracts and through the desert, poured on to the sand.

A new urgency in the preparations for withdrawal was detected by the men. Buller was uneasy. Big, bluff and brave, he was a man of action who operated on his soldier's instincts. He had little understanding of the use of military intelligence and less liking for intelligence officers. When intelligence presented him with unpalatable information he resented it, preferred to brush it aside. It made him irritable. The messengers were blamed for the bad tidings they carried. Paradoxically, the man of action became irresolute. And so Buller failed to heed signals that should have told him all was not as quiet as it seemed out in the Bayuda, and north and south on the banks of the Nile.

On the way through to Gubat, Clarke's Light Camel Regiment experienced a few minor skirmishes. On one occasion, half a dozen Dongolawi surrendered without a fight and apparently without attempting flight. They told their captors there were no more than a few hundred Ansar in the area. Their information seemed to some officers in the column suspiciously gratuitous; Clarke declared that the Arabs were probably speaking the truth and that the main Mahdiist force was far away to the south, enjoying the spoils of Khartoum.

Kababish 'friendlies', copper-faced camelmen with thick mops of black hair, came in with some cartridges they had found on the scene of a brief fracas with a group of Ansar. The cartridges bore the Khartoum arsenal mark. The Kababish, who acted as guides and ran despatches for the British, reported that harassment by bands of Ansar had increased of late on the desolate tracts between Abu Klea and Jakdul.

To Major Kitchener, the eccentric roving intelligence officer, the most eloquent signs were those which did not exist. He had arrived from a mission in the northern Bayuda where he had been communing with the Shagiyeh tribes on the route of Earle's boatborne expedition. Three pieces of evidence retailed to him aroused his concern: Metemmeh, aside from its non-stop barrage of drumming, had been unusually quiet in recent days, with fewer Arabs seen on the walls and no discharges of canister shot from its Krupps, which were customary when the hussars made their regular reconnaissances; the to-and-fro movement of Arabs on the far bank of the Nile, a common occurrence since the British arrived, had virtually ceased; and for more than a week, no information had come down the left bank of the Nile, which was unusual for there had never before been any shortage of spies, no matter whether they peddled information of value or total fiction.

Kitchener contended that the lack of activity and information pointed to concealment. He counselled holding the force together in the Gubat forts while he led a scouting party up the left bank in the direction of Wad Habeshi and while another probed round the back of Metemmeh. Buller, who disliked Kitchener's irregular way of soldiering, chose to believe that no news was good news. He was disquieted by the nagging arguments of the intelligence men, but nevertheless hastened the arrangements to send his force, fragmented, across the desert.

Colonel Reginald Talbot of the Life Guards, commander of the Heavies, Beresford's cousin, was given the task of taking the convoy of wounded and sick to Abu Klea from where he would send back the camels to Buller. The Lights made up the main part of the escort, about 350 of them compared with the 135 taken from the Heavies, but Buller knew he needed in command a man more experienced than the Lights' Stanley Clarke. Realising too, that, if it came to action, the column would have to fight in square, Buller added to the cavalry men a 'stiffening' of 200 Royal Irish. 'It does not pay to pick a cavalry man to do infantry work,' Buller had said after Abu Klea.

Kitchener's suspicions about there being 'something up' in the desert persuaded Buller to strengthen the column with two screw-guns of the Royal Artillery and with two of Beresford's four Gardners manned by bluejackets under Lieutenant van Koughnet. Walter Ingram, still commissioned in the naval brigade, accompanied the Gardners with the increasingly attractive prospect in his mind of being demobilised at Korti, where he proposed to embark on the Nile as quickly as possible and return to his managerial desk at the *Illustrated London News*.

Kitchener, leading a few picked men of Khasm el Mus's

Shagiyeh, rode out with the column hoping to bring back some prisoners for questioning. The wounded and sick were carried in litters and cacolets, or camel-chairs, balanced in pairs on the humps of the camels. Among them was Sir Charles Wilson, still seriously ill from the amputation of his leg after septicaemia had set in. It was a gruelling journey for the casualties, perched high on the swaying beasts which would falter at every second step, collapse on their haunches and have to be beaten to their feet by the Egyptian and Adeni drivers. The men had also to suffer the stench of the camels' putrefying sores and the equally nauseous reek of carbolic used to treat them.

Screened ahead and on the flanks by a troop of 'The Dumpies' (the 19th Hussars' founding recruits in India had been short in stature) and led by 'Paddy's Blackguards', the Royal Irish, the column moved out before the first sun of morning on Friday, February 13. Those left beind at Gubat watched it until it was no more than a bunched, dark caterpillar, rising as it breasted a low ridge then disappearing into one of the many nullahs that seamed the huge gravel plain and reappearing, smaller and more distant.

Friday the thirteenth. Buller was not unduly superstitious, neither did he hold with the optimists who said the Arabs would never attack on the Moslem holy day: the Mahdi had shown no evidence of such scruples in the past. Nevertheless, he would be glad when this day was over. If all went well, Talbot would arrive at Abu Klea that night and the news would quickly reach Gubat by messenger. In the meantime Buller, contracted his defences around the village now that his force had been cut effectively by half. Beresford put a Gardner in a sandbagged emplacement facing downriver towards Metemmeh, and had the other hauled by Sudanese on to a southern-facing parapet where the cement hut walls had crumbled into a mound which provided a firing platform. Here the gun had an elevated field of fire covering the wire and thorn zeriba and the tussocked flat lands beyond. On the whole, however, the garrison was occupied with thoughts and tasks of departure rather than defence.

The noise was heard in the evening when sometimes a faint suggestion of a northern breeze brings minimal relief to the stifling air of the river: reverberations like the sudden breaking of a desert storm, far off. But the thunder came in single eruptions spaced at irregular intervals. To Buller and every other experienced soldier the 'storm' sounded like seven-pounders firing shrapnel.

# Chapter 26

# *Broken square*

Talbot's column, struggling up a long, wide and sloping defile between two ranges of cindery hills, sighted the Ansar flags as a shimmer of colour and movement suddenly appearing atop a rise two miles ahead and to the left. Through their telescopes, officers could count the flags: five, ten, 15, 20 . . . a rough tally made it about 40 flags. It told Talbot that there must be about 4,000 to 5,000 Arabs. He ordered the column to form a square.

The Camel Corps had perfected an efficient drill for this operation. On the command, 'Close order!', the ranks of a column riding in companies squeeze their formation into a closely packed mass, a move which is completed after the order, 'Hard all!' When the column is well jammed up, the men dismount 'amidst a diabolical bellowing and grunting from their steeds, and double-knee-lash them with the head-rope', as Gleichen put it; that is, the kneeling camels are hobbled by having their front legs tied to their necks. The men then form square in companies around the central core of camels. It is an easily executed operation under ideal circumstances, but Talbot's need was for a *moving* square to enable him to take up a more advantageous position on higher ground about 1,200 yards ahead to the right. Furthermore, most of his troops were on foot and his camel contingent, carrying wounded and stores, was in bunches within the column and trailing an extrusion of disordered knots behind the force. The column had made exceptionally good time despite the collapse of many of the camels. When the animals dropped down, loads had to be transferred to other, already overladen animals. Time after time, groups of camels bunched out through the lines. In searing heat, the Egyptian handlers and British soldiers, their clothes and skins torn by thorn bushes, struggled to push them back in the 'sack'.

Now, however, the mass of men and animals moved at tortoise pace in a miasma of dust towards Talbot's chosen fighting ground, encased in a square of bayonets.

Kitchener was concerned about the obvious show of the Arabs' strength over to the left. They were quite literally flagging their position. On a hunch, he rode with some of his Shagiyeh in front of the column towards the *right* where probing hussars were picking their way through the mimosa scrub. A scatter of shots and a sudden recoiling movement of the scouts 1,000 yards ahead told him his suspicions had been right. A wave of Arabs, followed by another, rose from the lip of a nullah and raced at the wheeling hussars. Out of the ground hundreds appeared, not in ragged masses, but in a semblance of well-ordered lines, each raya led by its emir. The very ground on which Talbot had chosen to make his fight was alive with them, but fortunately the scouting hussars had sprung the trap before the column approached too close. Thus Talbot was forced to halt his square on the bare, lower slopes of the valley side.

'It was a bad place to stand and fight, and we all understood it', Ingram wrote afterwards. 'It would have been impossible to about-turn the camel herd and seek a better place on the valley floor, with a horde of dervishes rushing down on our bayonets from the right and a second force of unknown strength over to our left not two miles away. We were pinned to that desolate slope of scrub like a fly on a spider-web. As the command "Volley firing by sections!" was given to the Royal Irish on the front face of the square and their bullets cut down the forward attacking waves of Arabs, a new hazard became apparent on our right. A vast number of blacks, many of them in cover but some standing in full invitation to our marksmen, poured down a heavy fire on our ranks.'

Abu Anga's jehadia had staked out an ambush position at a place they knew the English soldiers would pass on the route which the supply convoys had taken without variation for the past three weeks, watched and paced every time by bands of Ansar in the black hills. From their rifle pits, dug in the night, the jehadia loosed off a thousand Remingtons at the British square.

Their fire was high. It did little damage to the Royal Irish and the Heavies whose forward ranks on the front and right of the square knelt behind saddles and boxes; but dropping shots and a few better placed bullets began to take toll of those inside the square. Colonel Clarke of the Lights, perched on an ammunition box, had his telescope knocked out of his hands by a shot. The same bullet hit Captain Holland of the 15th Hussars, standing by his side, and took half of his face away. Wounded men, still strapped on stretchers and perilously exposed on the tops of camels which had not been knee-lashed by their panicking drivers, screamed to be let down as bullets found their mark with dull thumps in the hides of animals and, sometimes, in men. The bellowing camels made a terrible din. Several lay dead or dying amid pools of blood, in uncannily uniform poses, heads writhed back to humps, a sight which had become familiar to British soldiers in the Sudan.

Talbot realised he would have to do something about the riflemen before they got the proper range. The answer lay in his screw-guns. They went off with a heavy thud, then an oscillating whistle followed by a sharp crack as the shrapnel shells exploded in a firework display of silvery grey trajectories. Their damage to dug-in riflemen was more psychological than physical, but they dispersed the standing jehadia and lessened the fire of those in the pits. At the front right corner of the square a Gardner had started its rhythmic pounding. The Arabs were coming again.

Leaving about 40 of their number dead and wounded on the ground, the initial waves of Ansar had retreated, not in disorder, but with a sullen inertia. Occasionally one would turn and defiantly shout the greatness of Allah at the soldiers. A marksman could easily have picked him off, but the order to cease firing had been given. Paddy's Blackguards replied, broadly in kind.

The new attack came as it had done before, from out of the ground, but this time the Arabs were using concealing folds closer to the square. The tactic emphasised even more the vulnerability of the column's position. A Gardner now fired from each corner of the front face, supported by disciplined blasts of volley fire from the Martini-Henrys. Then, with a stutter, the right Gardner jammed, as it had done at Abu Klea. Many of the infantry were having trouble from their cartridges sticking in the hot breeches. Officers behind the front rank laboured frantically to unjam the rifles, and hand fresh weapons to the men. A dense cloud of smoke floated obstinately a yard above the ground, blocking the attackers from the view of the defenders.

An emir on a camel hurtled out of the smoke and bore down on the Royal Irish, rider and mount apparently impervious to bullets. The shock of impact hurled a section of infantrymen back ten yards into their colleagues of the reserve line, and the camel was impaled on half a dozen bayonets. The soldiers cursed and struggled to retrieve their bayonets, and when they succeeded they found them bent and twisted as many another British bayonet had been in the Bayuda. The Arab was pitched over the camel's head into a group of reeling men. He was shot, bayoneted and clubbed with rifle butts, but still he fought. The frenzy of his resistance cleared a space around him. He sat on the ground now, a blood-stained heap, his spear broken. He scrabbled around until he found a stone, and as he raised his arm to throw it, a bluejacket killed him with a shot between the eyes.

The attack was beaten off by the simple expedient of meeting the oncoming waves with devastating volleys of rifle fire at 30 yards. But every one in the column sensed that the Arabs were holding back their main strength; that they were testing the square — and giving the Gardners ample time to jam so that they were no more than a wheeled encumbrance at each corner of the front. The fighting left piles of dead and wounded in the tussock grass, from which, now and then, a warrior would rise and come charging to his death on the bayonets. And when the Arabs had retired to regroup out of sight in the depressions of the hillside, the jehadia started again their harassing fire.

Meanwhile, the force which had shown its flags two miles away across the far side of the sloping defile was now approaching within range of the column's screw-guns. The floor of the defile was not flat, however; rather an undulating expanse of gravel and grass seamed by nullahs which gave the Arabs cover. These arid slopes, as viewed from afar by the British, flowered strangely with white thistle balls which were the explosions of the seven-pounders' shrapnel shells. Somewhere on the plain, an Arab gun was firing. The British recognised it as a four-pound howitzer. A few rounds of canister came whooshing through the air to land harmlessly in the bush. One random shot, however, fell among the camels, harming neither man nor beast, but causing some loosely-tied animals to break free and career wildly about the wounded until rifle shots put a stop to their rampage.

Talbot was not unduly worried. He had more than 700 first-line troops and, although he could have wished for better ground to fight on, the success of disciplined fire against the first two attacks had encouraged him to believe he could withstand the main onslaught when it came. On experience, the Mahdiists' attacks tended to run out of steam and their emirs seemed to bow both to fate and to discretion after a bloody bout of fighting in which honour and the demands of jehad were satisfied. Moreover, night was coming on and the Arabs were not great fighters in the dark. If he could hold them off here and exact heavy punishment — there were already about 300 Arab dead and wounded lying in the bush — he planned to press on in square up the defile and over the pass, which would put him in sight of the fort at Abu Klea. Once at the wells, if the enemy was still around, he could wait in safety until the main force came up from Gubat, Buller's column having to make do with whatever camels it could muster.

The garrison at Abu Klea must have heard the gunfire. They would be prepared. Buller must be informed that the column had met Arabs, and Talbot despatched a hussar with a brief message for him shortly after the first attack. He was not asking for assistance. The message gave the column's position and bare details of the fight, adding: 'Captain Holland, 15th Hussars, and six other ranks killed, 15 o.r.s wounded. Confident can reach Abu Klea. Will post you on progress.'

The ridges on the plain were casting deep shadows in the evening sun which made it difficult for the British to follow the progress of the Arabs advancing from hollow to hollow on the left, or western, flank of the square. Thick mimosa scrub lay in grey-green swathes, crowning the edges of the ravines and filling the slopes with enough cover to hide an army. The glasses of Talbot's officers swept the floor of the defile, from left to right and back again, and discovered enough evidence in the setting sun's shadows to suggest that several thousand Arabs were swarming forward. If they needed confirmation, it came every time a shrapnel shell exploded, flushing out a scurry of leaping white figures at less than three-quarters of a mile range.

From their rifle pits higher up the eastern slope, the blacks were firing only desultory shots which did little harm. They were, in fact, faring worse than the British, for Kitchener had organised a section of sharpshooters on the right face of the square and they began scoring hits. Ingram, a dedicated big-game hunter and a good shot, joined the marksmen and believed he made two kills.

'Cease fire! Cease fire!' The command echoed around the square. The sharpshooters lowered their rifles. The two guns of the Royal Artillery were stilled. In the comparative silence of the complaining camels, the irregular cracks from the blacks' Remingtons and the groans of the Ansar wounded in front, the column strained to listen to the sound of distant rifle fire. It came from the direction of Abu Klea, about eight miles away beyond the pass at the head of the defile. There could be no doubt: the fort at Abu Klea — where about 150 men of the Mounted Infantry guarded the wells and two score of wounded — was under heavy attack.

The pause was brief. It was broken by a sudden and concentrated burst of firing from the right where hundreds of blacks emerged and, open to the British rifle sights, ran down the hill, stopping occasionally to shoot and load or loosing off rounds wildly as they moved. Most of their fire was wide, high and ineffective. Dozens went down as the Heavies poured volleys into them. But the blacks' crazed charge was only part of a huge eruption of Ansar, from the folds of the hillside in front, from behind the breast-high mimosa of the valley floor on the left, an immense crescent-shaped swathe with Arabs 12-deep in the centre, a mass of Baggara horse and camel warriors on the lower flank, and the jehadia, now followed by onrushing spearmen bunched more thickly than anywhere, on the extreme eastern end of the pincer. Above the Mahdiist crescent flew the rayas of all three divisions, the black, the green and the red, swaying and jerking as the flagbearers ran over the uneven ground; and emirs' flags of white, blue and yellow led the way.

Two shrapnel shells at point-blank range, and massed rifle fire from the 3rd and the 11th Hussars of the Lights tore a devastating hole in the leading ranks of the Baggara cavalry who were charging towards the left rear corner of the square. Riders who were following crashed headlong into a tangle of stricken animals and dying men. Terrified camels, stung by wounds, turned and galloped riderless through oncoming lines of Baggara, knocking warriors from their mounts and sometimes colliding head-on with terrible shocks. No Baggara reached within 150 yards of the square. The dead and wounded men lay in a heap amid a mass of struggling animals. The rest wheeled and rode back to regroup.

On the front face of the square the Royal Irish turned the desolate waste of tussock grass before them into a killing ground. Both Gardners were out of action and desperate attempts were being made by the armourers to clear the jammed breeches. As the rifles heated, they too were jamming in increasing numbers. But several waves of Arabs were beaten off and the slaughter left mounds of ragged white shapes 30 yards in front of the Irish line.

Some warriors, leaping over their comrades' bodies and running at breakneck speed, reached the bayonets of the soldiers. There were short, frenzied struggles in which British and Sudanese were so closely packed there was hardly room to hack or thrust. Fists and steel, gouging finger-nails and ripping knives, rifle butt and spear haft: everything and anything was used in a murderous brawl between Dubliner and Jaalin, Liverpudlian and Shukriyeh.

Many a man of Paddy's Blackguards cursed the bloody bastards who sent him to fight with guns that wouldn't fire and bayonets that twisted like tin, when, for a moment, the niggers had skedaddled and his wounded mates had been dragged to the surgeons who would try to staunch their gaping arteries with cotton swabs and their screams with doses of laudanum, and he stood waiting for them to come again, holding in his hands a broad-bladed spear taken from the dead dervish at his feet.

'Close up! Close up! They're coming again!' Time after time the shout went up. The front face was taking the brunt of the attack and holding like a rock. If the square could keep up this killing, Talbot judged, the Arabs would call it a day. But disaster was shaping elsewhere in a series of swift happenings.

A howitzer shell came swishing in from the plain and landed in the camel lines where it blew up a stack of ammunition boxes in a spectacular cacophony of exploding cartridges. Camels broke or were blown free from their hobblings and stampeded to the rear of the square, driving ahead of them, and accompanied by, a horde of frightened Egyptian handlers. The mass of racing animals and men, spurred on by flying bullets from the exploding boxes, punched a hole in Wyndham's dismounted 21st Hussars — part of the Lights — who were holding a section of the rear face near the right-hand corner of the square. About 30 of the hussars were driven out into the bush as the camels thundered over and beyond them.

Colonel Clarke, seeing some of his men thus dangerously exposed, ordered more of the Lights to advance from their positions in the centre of the rear face to give cover to the scattered men of the 21st. His order was hotly disputed by an infantry Major standing close by who realised the possible consequences. The lordly Clarke shut him up. Hussars' lives were at stake.

The Major was right. The integrity of a square must be maintained at all costs. The gap created by the expulsion of the 21st should have been filled immediately, the only help offered to them being covering fire. But Clarke's intention had already been pre-empted by an instinctive move by the Lights — hussars all — to go to the assistance of their comrades. A cavalryman's training teaches him never to be still. The static infantry disciplines of a square formation are alien to him. As the Lights on the rear face wheeled outwards, with one end of their line pivoted on the square's lower corner where the Baggara attack had come, the gap widened at the other rear corner. They had violated the basic principle of the square formation — that ranks must never be broken on any account.

'It does not pay to pick a cavalry man to do infantry work.' Against Osman Digna at Tamai it was the infantry who demonstrated how a square can be imperilled when the Black Watch, obeying a rash order from Graham, charged and lifted the lid off the box. Now, Clarke's dismounted cavalry, not comprehending their infantry role, were taking the bottom off the box.

Down the slope tumbled a white avalanche of Ansar: the very tip of the crescent-shaped attack had become the instrument of execution, the killing spearhead. The jehadia, who had been in the forefront, loosed of a few last rounds and threw themselves to the ground, allowing wave after wave of warriors with spears, swords and banners to run over them in a headlong rush towards the corner of the sundered square.

Frantic shouts of 'Close up!' went unheeded as every man fought his personal battle to survive in the mêlée at the corner of the square. A battering ram of Ansar bodies plunged deep into the square. The second ranks of the Heavy Regiment turned and fired inwards at a seething jumble of Arabs, Egyptians and camels; they stood back to back with the outside ranks who fought with bayonets and clubed rifles against an onslaught which was now enveloping the whole of the square's right side. The Lights, who had been extended in an arc, rallied and charged in an attempt to pinch off the head of the Arabs' thrust. But for every man they bayoneted ten more hurled themselves through the gap and into the square. Over all lay a pall of swirling smoke which shut out the last light of the setting sun. As wreaths of it curled and momentarily lifted, Clarke saw the flower of his light cavalry fighting desperately and vainly in knots of half a dozen men, back to back, against encircling swarms of Arabs. Then he and his staff, forced back against a screw-gun whose crew lay dead around it, made their own last stand. Clarke slumped against a pile of shell boxes with a lance in his thigh. He pointed his Smith and Wesson at a dark face and fired; simultaneously the Jaalin warrior jabbed upwards with a short spear, impaling Colonel Clarke to the ammunition boxes behind him. Another Jaalin, naked to the waist, wrenched off Clarke's scabbarded sword, a handsome silver-hilted piece presented to him by the Prince of Wales, and waved it triumphantly in the air.

The jehadia followed on the heels of the Arabs with murderous glee and embarked on an orgy of killing where wounded soldiers had been left aside in the breakthrough. They slung their Remingtons over their shoulders and snatched up the abandoned Martini-Henrys of the dead and dying British, and they followed the Ansar through to the centre of the square where the butchery of the stretcher-borne wounded began. Surgeon Connolly of the Lights poured a fusillade of buckshot from his double-barrelled shotgun before going down, speared through the chest. Sir Charles Wilson died firing his pistol from the stretcher in which he had been carried from Gubat. Colonel Talbot, his staff and a half-company of Royal Irish fought from behind a hastily erected redoubt of commissary boxes. Their barricade of tinned bully beef, Huntley and Palmer's biscuits, and Lipton's tea was overwhelmed by suicide waves of Jaalin, and the black flag of the Khalifa, the 'Raya ez Zarga', was raised over the British commander's body.

The Royal Irish on the front face and the Lights to their left were hit by fresh waves of attackers coming from the outside, and soon faced the threat presented by the Arabs *inside* the square. In fact, it was a square no longer, but merely isolated groups or double lines of soldiers, fighting back to back. Where charging Ansar could not crush these troublesome knots of English, the jehadia were summoned to deluge them with concentrated fire. By dusk the last British rifle had been silenced.

Before the final onslaught, Ingram had been part of Kitchener's picked group of marksmen firing at the jehadia. In the disordered fighting which followed the breakthrough, Kitchener, Ingram, a dozen infantrymen and bluejackets, together with a handful of Shagiyeh, were separated from the main body by the to-and-fro sway of the battle on the right of the square. Arabs, charging through the Heavies and wheeling to attack from inside the square, forced the small party to climb higher up the slopes. A few skirmishes marked their uphill progress, but on the whole the

Arabs who came near were intent on going down to the big kill.

When night fell these few survivors were two miles away from and above the place of battle, in a thicket of thorn close to the base of the dark volcanic crags which rim the valley on both sides. They looked down on the scavengers of the Mahdi's army, dancing to the beat of drums, a scene of swirling movement in the light of bonfires which encircled the debris of the square and its 900 British dead. How many Ansar had died? Three thousand? But three times that number and their battle flags were already far off down the valley, with their victorious commander Abu Anga. Through the night they would march to the Nile to keep appointment with Khalifa Abdallahi and Emir el Nejumi, whose host had come upon the English at Gubat as stealthily as theirs had in the valley of the broken square.

# Chapter 27

# *Buller's last battle*

Buller had a relief force organised before midnight. It consisted of 400 men of the Mounted Infantry Camel Regiment and the Royal Irish. Preparations had begun before the arrival of Talbot's messenger who came to tell them what they already knew: the column was under heavy attack. Talbot's trooper had literally ridden his pony to death and walked the last few miles before stumbling on an outpost picket of the Scots Guards. He was twice fired on during his ride to Gubat and lost time making detours to avoid Arabs criss-crossing the track in the wake of the column. The desert, he reported, was 'alive' with dervish. Nevertheless, he was able to bring the news that Talbot was confident about holding off the attacking Arabs, had suffered only light casualties up to the time the messenger was despatched, and was inflicting so much damage on the enemy that soon the battle would be resolved by the Arabs pulling back and the column pressing on to Abu Klea. Neither the messenger nor Buller knew, of course, that the British at the wells were also under attack.

Lieutenant Gleichen had little time to write his journal on that night of February 13/14. A few terse, scribbled notes — the closing paragraph of his desert record — reflected the uncertainties and doubts which prevailed among the British at Gubat: 'Major Barrow to take out the Mounted and the Irish before daylight. They have practically the last of our camels, and a Gardner. They are all infantry — a blessing — know how to work a square. But is Buller right splitting like this? Best go in one force — but Buller thinks we could not move fast enough. Rest follow in morning — 600 of us. Barrow moves last hours before light — no sense blundering about desert in dark — Talbot's man says it's full of niggers — Whatever way up, am sure we shall have to fight. We are in a scrape to be sure — Hope Mahdi doesn't chop us up piecemeal. Finished last of Tarragona from hospital stores.'

Buller gave orders for the outposts — four-man groups of infantry and Royal Marines — to be drawn in more tightly and increased in frequency. The relief column, in essence a reconnaissance in strength, would make a forced march in the morning, so
its men were allowed to take some sleep. The remainder of the garrison was on two-hour watches. Buller was awake all night, visit-
ing the river fort, pacing the ramparts of Gubat village, inspecting
the zeriba. The fact that there had been silence from the desert
since nightfall did not alarm him. Nobody expected the Mahdi to
fight at night. Talbot was probably safely entrenched at Abu Klea
by now, and he could be relied upon to get another runner
through to Gubat before the early hours of the morning. If not,
the column would go on its way. If the Arabs were still infesting
the road between the two British posts, the sight of Barrow's
bayonets would frighten them off at first light. And if they wanted
more trouble, well, as Buller had written to his wife before he
crossed the Bayuda, 'There is nothing in this world that so stirs
me up as a fight'.

Gordon's 'hens' were a problem. Their camp upstream, beyond
the army's wire and thorn perimeter, was practically autonomous,
and Buller preferred to leave it like that. When the main force
marched, later on the morrow, those of the 'hens' who wished to
accompany it would be allowed to do so. Some of the Sudanese,
especially those with families in Khartoum, would opt to stay and
wait for the Mahdi's troops; they would probably not be harmed,
but immediately be conscripted into the jehadia. The Egyptians
and the remainder of the cosmopolitan population of the camp
could be taken along as baggage carriers, as the last few camels
would have departed with Barrow. There was no sense in moving
the 'hens' into Gubat until the main force was ready to leave,
however: Buller regarded them as an immense liability, prone to
panic at the first shot. In the case of sudden attack, he did not want
200 'hens' running in circles behind the defenders' backs. For the
time being, they could take their chance in the quarantine of their
own zeriba. The sentries who faced the Egyptians' camp were told
to be specially watchful and to turn back anyone attempting an
unauthorised entry into the Gubat forts.

The shanty town was never quiet at night. Marissa, offloaded in
prodigious quantities from the steamer fleet, and supplemented by
camp brewers, was in ample supply. Its consumption fuelled

much of the endless brawling and there were frequent internecine battles which resulted in guns being used. If left to their own devices, Beresford had cynically remarked to Ingram, the blacks would 'solve the problem of the Egyptians for us'. On this night, the sentries looking across to the camp of the 'hens' reported that things were normal: from midnight to three am there were sporadic outbursts of shouting and a few shots; a couple of straw lean-tos went up in flames — a permanent hazard was the gale of sparks from dozens of cooking fires; and around three there was a ragged fusillade of rifle fire. None of it would warrant going into a guard Corporal's report.

After the moon had gone down, Barrow's column marched out of Gubat. It would be straight going for the half-hour of remaining darkness, over the uncluttered gravel terrace which the Mounted Infantry had got to know well during the operations of the last three weeks. After that, a pearly half light would see them well into the desert scrub. Buller was confident that the column was in good hands under the command of Major C.T. Barrow. He was from the Scottish Rifles, a sound infantry officer who knew what fighting in square was all about, and who had acquitted himself well in the Bayuda. It was regrettable that the Mounted's commander, the Honourable G.H. Gough, had been wounded and thus was not able to lead the column; but Gough was, after all, a cavalryman — 14th Hussars — and this was, as Buller recognised, a job for the foot soldiers, even if few of them possessed a pair of boots worthy of the name.

The Rifle Brigade, King's Royal Rifle Corps, South Staffordshires, Essex, Gordon Highlanders... like the other camel regiments, the Mounted Infantry were a mixture of units; half their effective number were defending Abu Klea and its wells. With the Royal Irish, they formed 400 of the fittest men under Buller's command, and were not hampered by a 'soft' core of wounded on litters. The few camels they had were to carry their stores, ammunition, and Sub-Lieutenant Colin Keppel's Gardner gun. Buller was sure that if Talbot needed relief, they would provide it — and pave the way for the passage later in the day of the remainder of the force.

They were not two miles from the fort, marching almost due west to avoid any contact with roving Ansar from Metemmeh, when the scouts met a barrage of rifle fire from what turned out to be a low rise: in the darkness the British could see only the muzzle flashes. Barrow's men were targeted clearly against the lightening eastern horizon, but most of the shots were wide and high. This was no wandering band of Arabs, however. The shots came in volleys, ragged but disciplined nonetheless. Whoever fired was trained in the ways of the rifle. Furthermore, the sound of the shooting was not that made normally by troops equipped with Remingtons. A few dropping bullets, almost spent, reached the column. Barrow and his colleagues inspected them and recognised them as those from the Boxer brass cartridges: the shots were coming from Martini-Henrys. Could they be Talbot's men out there? A bugler from the South Staffordshires blew an identifying call. The only response was a quickening of fire. It was obvious that the shots were coming from the Mahdi's jehadia. And with this realisation, the column knew with sickening certainty that the enemy was using rifles they could have acquired only from the British, from Talbot's column.

Barrow's four hundred fused into a tightly packed square, double lines of 50 men each on each of the four sides, the front ranks standing ready to fire, after which they would kneel and load while the second rank fired over their heads. Within minutes of bunching in square, and while the Gardner was still being assembled at a corner, the terrible ballet began: front rank fire, kneel, load; second rank fire, load; front rank fire . . . and so on, a relentless, mechanical routine which produced a curtain of bullets from single-shot breech-loaders as lethal as a bank of machine-guns.

From out of the darkness, the two prongs of the Mahdiist crescent had appeared, bearing down simultaneously on two corners of the square. The rush had caught the infantry scouts out in the open, men of the South Staffordshires. At Abu Klea on January 17, the square had been forced to withhold fire because its scouts were in the way. 'Lie down! Lie down!' bellowed a Sergeant in the front rank of Barrow's square. The dozen exposed Staffordshires flung themselves to the ground. The volleys of their comrades scythed over them, and the Ansar's first rush evaporated, leaving scores of dead and wounded in heaps. The scouts sprang up and sprinted for the safety of the square. In the lull before the next attack the men of the column could hear, behind them from the direction of Gubat, and uproar of shot and shell. The garrison was fighting for its life.

In Gubat they heard the rifle fire from the hinterland and the bugler sounded 'To arms' just before the first shell exploded beyond the zeriba. More shells came over, heralded by a thud and a hiss. Most exploded harmlessly, wide of the forts, but one wounded some Grenadier Guards manning the south-facing parapet. Buller's first reaction had been to think of the Arab artillery hidden behind the walls of Metemmeh, but he quickly realised that the shellfire was coming from the south — from beyond the shanty town of the Egyptians and Sudanese: four-pounders normally used by the Egyptian army. A firework display of rockets, with their familiar hissing splutter, pinpointed the source of the shelling more precisely. The fire was coming from *inside* the camp of the 'hens'.

A thin line of soldiers manned the zeriba perimeter on this side of Gubat. They now saw coming towards them a ragged, dense mass of figures, gesticulating wildly, looking behind them as they ran, recognisable at 200 yards as terrified Egyptians and bashi-bazouks. The troops held their fire. The frightened herd had almost reached the zeriba when the British realised, too late, that it was being driven like cattle by the spears of the Ansar, who were in vast numbers behind the human screen. Bugle notes recalled the zeriba pickets to the safety of the breastworks. Most were able to cover the distance in time, but, here and there, scattered Guards were overwhelmed by Arabs who burst through the Egyptians, leaped or climbed the zeriba and hacked with their short stabbing spears. Pushed from behind, the Egyptians were impaled on the wire and thorn in a screaming, struggling mass, and used as a carpet over which the Ansar climbed in huge numbers.

While the British had busied themselves with the preparations for the column's departure, el Nejumi's Jaalin and a corps of jehadia had stealthily taken the 'hens' in the early hours. Gordon's Sudanese, the best mettle in the camp, had bowed to expedience when an infiltrating advance party of their fellow men in the jehadia persuaded them of the realism of joining the Mahdi. There had been one brief, ruthlessly crushed outburst of opposition from some Shagiyeh — the shooting heard at three o'clock — but for the most part the non-Sudanese 'hens' had been too frightened to resist.

Abd el Hamid, the renegade steamer captain placed in the 'pro-tective' custody of the murderous Nur Angara, had briefed his new masters well: the Egyptians' camp was the soft underbelly of the British at Gubat. Once the camp was secured, four mountain guns and some rockets were moved in and the pressed artillery-men from Khartoum were given the task of firing the first shots. Having sealed off all the camel routes into Gubat from the south, Abdallahi and el Nejumi had struck their greatest luck in the swift fall of the Nile, which had hemmed in Beresford's *Safieh*. Without the steamer, Buller had been robbed of his eyes on the river and the Ansar army was able to mass between Wad Habeshi and Gubat, poising itself for the onslaught after a forced march under cover of darkness during the night of the 13th-14th. The guns had been Abdallahi's idea. Their intervention was more diversionary than harmful — except for one shrapnel round which burst over Beresford's Gardner on the southern parapet, wounding most of his naval crew. Gleichen, who was nearby, engaged on the officers' inevitable duties — unjamming his men's rifles — went to help Beresford handle the gun.

Barrow's square, moving slowly back towards Gubat, a hundred yards at a time, halting to beat off another attack, then crawling another hundred yards, was almost surrounded. Abu Anga's army, its fighting fury and zeal unslackened by the previous evening's battle and a gruelling 30-mile march, had been joined by several thousand Ansar who appeared from behind Metemmeh — the tribes from Berber, rallied by the Mahdi's emissaries. Supported by 'suicide' forays of rifle squads from the jehadia which wreaked much damage on the British before being mown down by the fire of the square, the joint force delivered a series of hammer blows in one massed attack after another. Barrow abandoned the Gardner gun; had it not jammed it would have run out of ammunition after two more magazines. He abandoned, too, the baggage camels in the hope that a break in the swirling masses of Arabs around the square might open the opportunity of a last, desperate fighting dash to the fort. But the hope died when el Nejumi's attack from the south linked up with Arabs from Metemmeh, sealing Gubat from sight behind a massive, moving wall of flag-waving tribesmen. And in Gubat the garrison was in no less peril then that faced by the smoke-wreathed knot of survivors standing back to back on the gravel plain.

Beresford methodically cranked the Gardner. Slowly. Slowly. The temptation was to crank faster but haste would only jam the damned thing. The storm of bullets from its five barrels slammed into a wave of Arabs who were scrambling through the wire and thorn-bush barrier 100 yards out. It held them there, pinned them on the spiky mimosa and wire barbs, a ghastly frieze of limp or writhing bodies in white loin-cloths and jibbehs, like a line of washing. Some of the dead were headless. More Ansar came running, using their own dead and wounded to cushion the barbs.

First there was one spearman inside the zeriba, then there were a score, and a hundred. Gleichen rammed home the magazines one after another. Beresford was part of his Gardner, a machine cranking, traversing, pausing momentarily for the blue haze of machine-gun smoke to lift, and starting again, from left to right and back again. Arabs were piled on the inside of the zeriba in a confusion of servered limbs, bloodstained jibbehs, muskets, spears and banner staves. Smoke rose from some of the heaps where clothes had caught fire from the discharge of antiquated rifles.

But now more and more were reaching the inner ground beneath the angle of fire of the Gardner high on the parapet. Beresford realised he could not depress the gun far enough to reach them. As though they, too, realised it in the same moment, the Arabs gave a great roar and ran on and over one another in a scramble to breast the earthwork buttresses. What should have been defensive works became a causeway into the fort for those outside. On either side of Gleichen and Beresford, the Guards gripped the searing barrels of their jammed rifles and clubbed heads and parried spear thrusts. When rifle stocks broke they hurled lumps of cement and ammunition boxes, grabbed lances and swords from dead and dying Arabs, and hacked with pick-axes and shovels.

The Gardner was silent, inevitably jammed. Yards below and racing up the slope was a fresh mass of densely packed Arabs, another thicket of black and coloured battle flags in its van. Beresford gestured to Gleichen. They lifted the trail and levered the wheeled gun over the rim of the slope, where it careered, somersaulting and skewing, headlong into the phalanx of emirs and flag bearers.

Where one flag fell there were three more to take its place, and 100 more Ansar behind each flag. Charlie Beresford's last gamble won him a few moments' breathing space, time enough to order the thinned lines of Guards on the parapet to retreat to the inner redoubt. Then he and Gleichen were downed beneath an onslaught of Jaalin. Rank after rank, the Ansar's front line troops poured over the lip of the parapet and descended on the scattered bunches of British soldiers trying to reach the central redoubt.

Behind the assault waves came those who were not so brave, the Mahdi's second corps of executioners and spoilers. They speared the wounded, ripped uniforms from the dead, gathered up Martini-Henrys and pistols, bandoliers and swords, and at the place on the parapet where the Gardner gun had fired they hacked and spat at what had been Lord Charles Beresford and Count Gleichen.

The fort by the river, held by some Sussex and Marines, was taken by weight of numbers. The Khalifa Abdallahi, no great soldier himself, was willing to pay a massive price in Ansar lives to be hailed as the architect of victory at Gubat. He had sent the Ansar into battle with a ringing quotation from the Koran as his 'order of the day': 'Are not the favourites of God those on whom no fear shall come, nor shall they be put to grief'. Ansar bodies choked the embrasures of the little fort before resistance ceased. Gascoigne and Trafford and others who had brought Gordon from Khartoum — men of the Sussex — died there. A handful of Marines ended their fight in the shallows of the Nile at a place where Arab horsemen had swarmed over the newly uncovered sandbanks. Their graves and those of their adversaries, the Baggara, were amid strands of luxuriant alfalfa-type weed where the river streamed sparkling green in the morning sun.

Abdallahi, at the express wishes of the Mahdi, had ordered that prisoners be taken so that the enslaved and shackled English might be shown to the people. So savage was the final fight at the inner redoubt, however, that few British remained alive, and most of these were wounded who would not survive the march to Omdurman. El Nejumi personally gave quarter to a handful of soldiers who, ammunition exhausted, rifles broken and bayonets bent like fish-hooks, had nothing left to fight with. His men of the Red Flag saluted their captives with raised banners and a fusillade of rifle shots in the air.

Sir Redvers Buller died in the redoubt from a jehadia bullet just as the remaining few of his regimental comrades of the King's Royal Rifle Corps were overwhelmed a mile away with the survivors of the square. Stuart-Wortley, the last of the witnesses of Gordon's rescue, was killed in a mêlée of hand-to-hand fighting within the fort. The scavengers poured in, decapitating, and amputating limbs from those bodies they recognised as officers'.

The sun was full up when Khalifa Abdallahi rode through the exultant legions and into the centre of the forts. The pristine jibbehs of his lordly Baggara bodyguard, with their neat and symmetrical black and red patches, were in stark contrast to the blood-smeared, powder-burned rags of the fighting Ansar. Abdallahi dismounted and embraced the hammers of the English: Abu Anga, the breaker of English squares who had come from triumph in the desert to victory on the Nile; el Nejumi, victor of Khartoum and conqueror of Gubat.

The Khalifa, limping from an old bullet wound received at El Obeid, toured the site of victory. With benedictory gestures he acknowledged the Ansar's salutes, in which the Baggara were noticeably more enthusiastic than the riverine Jaalin and Dongolawi. He was 39 years of age, of middle height, broad-shouldered. He had the light brown complexion of his tribe, deeply pitted by smallpox marks. Black hair framed his cheeks with a thin fringe and grew more thickly under his chin. When he smiled he showed glittering white teeth, but there was neither humour nor warmth in his smile or his eyes. His enemies — and there were many in the 'Ashraf', or family of the Mahdi — called him cruel and ignorant, the one because of his frequent black and murderous moods, the other because of his near-illiteracy. The 'Caliph of the Guided One' would succeed in a little over four months to an Islamic empire, ruling it as a merciless despot with temporal power where Mohammed Ahmed the Mahdi had led by spiritual influence, and turning it from a religious state into a military dictatorship. He now stood amid the warlike and domestic detritus of an army sent by one of the most powerful nations on earth to defeat and annihilation.

Custodians of the Mahdiist treasury, the beit-el-mal, rigorously supervised the collection of arms, ammunition and riches: an over-enthusiastic charge of gunpowder blew asunder an iron safe in an explosion which showered a crowd of delighted Jaalin with gold sovereigns, every one of which was retrieved and placed in the official bags. Among the miscellanea of a defeated army, however, there was a free-for-all scramble.

Jehadia stuffed their red-leather bandoliers with tins of sardines; they tasted Elliman's Embrocation and Scrubb's Cloudy Ammonia, and tossed them away in disgust; bottles of champagne and casks of beer were smashed with axes; the Navy's stocks of oakum were prodded, sniffed and left aside in bafflement. Flour, jam and canned Leibig's soup were eagerly sampled and hoarded, tins of beef cleaved open with a blow of an Ansar sword, coffee mills, bellows and shaving mirrors coveted as trophies. Many of the British corpses were stripped of their tattered uniforms. Here and there Ansar squatted by the dead and cut up red serge and blue flannel to use as patches on their jibbehs. And, as always where many soldiers have died together on the field, there was paper in profusion — letters, diaries, portraits of loved ones, commissary lists, orders of the day, sheaves of forms representing personal memorabilia and the bureaucracy of battle.

A tall Baggara laid down his lance and bundle of stabbing spears and took a rifle from the hands of a dead soldier. The breech was hopelessly jammed by a cartridge. The bayonet was a warped stump. He wrenched off the soldier's boots. They disintegrated in his hands. The warrior shrugged and cast the possessions back to the dead.

A Dinka tribesman of the jehadia, overburdened with cases of surgeon's instruments, splints, bandages and other medical paraphenalia, picked up a green leather bag, looked inside and flung it down when he discovered it contained nothing but paper. Following him, a Jaalin emir retrieved the case; he gazed uncomprehending at the monogram of Edward Gleichen's noble family and, attracted by the gold embossing, thrust the case with its contents into the goatskin bag under his arm.

Before the human scavengers had finished, before the vast flocks of vultures descended on the river plain and in the valley of the broken square, the news spread north and south on the Nile, and across the Bayuda. In Khartoum and Omdurman there would be great rejoicing. In Britain, after this ghastly, unscripted grand finale, there would be no more jokes about the 'Nile circus'.

# Chapter 28

# *Telegrams to London*

Britain was in a fever of festivity. *Punch* published a cartoon showing Wolseley's lion cubs of the desert column carrying home, shoulder high, 'the Lion of Khartoum'. Newspaper offices in London and provincial towns pinned up the latest telegrams in their windows — Gordon had arrived safely at Gubat . . . Gordon had reached Korti . . . Gordon was on his way down the Nile to Cairo. The *Daily Telegraph* reported: 'Men, youths, and even ladies, stood at the street corners and on the pavements, reading and discussing the news. It is many a long day since the clubs of the West End have been so well filled before noon.' Children throughout the land were given a day's holiday from school. At the Royal Academy the life school was interrupted while the latest news was read to the students. The potters of Staffordshire put into effect their long prepared plans for an avalanche of decorative china commemorating the relief of Gordon. Pictures of Wolseley and Wilson — and even Gladstone — were linked with Gordon's in window displays of shops and homes. The indefatigable Baroness Burdett-Coutts, who had steered the Gordon Rescue Fund, was the centre of a hysterical tizzy of social activity, making preparations for a grand celebration ball.

Earl Cardigan, a leader of the Patriotic Association and joint organiser of the ball arrangements, suggested in a letter to *The Times* that the venue should be St James's Palace. When, however, the cabinet minister, Sir Charles Dilke, was approached on account of his intimacy with the Prince of Wales to pursue the possibility of royal patronage for the event, his reaction was cool: 'General Gordon has a number of pertinent questions to answer', he replied. The Duke of Cambridge, similarly approached, was equally wary: he could foresee much credit being reflected on to Wolseley and the thought gave him no pleaure at all. Captain

Brocklehurst, tested on the delicate question of whether his friend, Gordon, would attend as guest of honour, opined that the happening was about as likely as an appearance by the Mahdi. Such cavilling murmurs were rare, however. The prospects of a knighthood, even a peerage, for Gordon were bandied about. In the climate of national rejoicing, even the most strident right-wing opponents of Gladstone were muted in their criticism of his decision to 'bolt' from the Sudan now the 'butchering' was over.

On Wednesday, February 18, Moberley Bell's despatch from Aswan in Upper Egypt was published in *The Times*. From the newspaper's early editions the news was pirated by every morning paper in London, and quoted later in the day by evening editions throughout the country. Gordon had summoned the *Times* correspondent from Cairo to meet him on the river and had retailed to him a number of grave charges. Gordon was resigning his commission, accusing the government and military of serious dereliction of duty in the Sudan, impeaching Sir Charles Wilson for exceeding orders and refusing to fight the Mahdi in Khartoum, and claiming that he, Gordon, had been taken away from the city by force, illegally and against his wishes. Furthermore, while the public was in a ferment of admiration for the glorious exploits of his rescuers, here was Gordon talking about 'twaddle'.

The interview mystified and disquieted millions of readers and threw at least one eminent subscriber to *The Times* into a paroxysm of fury over his breakfast: at 10 St James's Square, the Prime Minister's residence, the correspondent's telegraphed message produced in William Ewart Gladstone a reaction similar to that which consumed him when he read the 'burn Berber' report at Brechin Castle. He summoned an immediate emergency meeting of ministers in the cabinet office.

It little helped Gladstone's temper to receive a telegram on the same morning from Queen Victoria: 'It is a matter of no surprise to the Queen that General Gordon, a hero of heroes, should voice such grievances against Mr Gladstone's government, even if his manner of doing so is rather unorthodox. Truly the chickens of indolence and irresolution are coming home to roost. The Queen trusts that Mr Gladstone and Lord Hartington will pay attention to General Gordon's experienced judgement and that the government will immediately reconsider the decision to scuttle out after killing some thousands.'

Gladstone was in no mood for niceties in reply. His answering telegram contained these words: 'Gordon is indeed a hero of heroes. It was unfortunate that he should claim the hero's privilege by turning upside down and inside out every idea and intention with which he left England and for which he had obtained our approval.' Within two days he would use exactly the same phrase in the House of Commons.

Parliament was in recess. It would reassemble on the following day. At the opening, Lords and Commons would hear of the government's intentions towards policy and legislation in the coming session. Gladstone's obsession, the Franchise Bill, was neatly tucked away, having been passed in the Lords during the last session, and the second reading of the Redistribution Bill had been successfully negotiated through the Commons before the adjournment on December 6. The plucking of Gordon from Khartoum was considered by Gladstone, in his cynical heart of hearts, as an irrelevancy in the Sudan question as a whole; he would have agreed with John Morley's views on Gordon's fate, delivered the previous April: 'If his death had happened two months ago, it would have turned out the Ministry. Now people are tired of Gordon, and, though there would be a row, it would blow over.' Nevertheless, Gordon's rescue had happened fortuitously for Gladstone in terms of his government's public relations: he was personally basking in the reflected glory of universal approval; and the government, freed of obligation to respond to public sentiments of revenge, could now see its way clearly to withdrawal from entanglement in the Sudan. Thus, withdrawal would be one of the aims of government policy to be announced formally on the following morning — a course acceptable on the whole to the public at large which was diverted by patriotic fervour over Gordon's deliverance.

Into this felicitous and neatly packaged scenario of the Prime Minister's there had suddenly intruded the spectre of Gordon, back from the dead, epitomising in his *Times* outburst everything Gladstone had come to expect from him: unrest, disturbance and irrationality. At the ministers' meeting, Dilke strongly advocated placing Gordon under arrest for having made indiscreet statements as a serving officer; Gladstone gloomily predicted the result would be to bring down on the government's head a torrent of adverse public opinion if the nation's hero were treated in this way. The Lord Chancellor, Lord Selborne, who had threatened to resign in 1884 if a relief expedition was not forthcoming, felt that things should be allowed to blow over: it was well known that the intentions proposed by Gordon one day had a habit of evaporating into nothing on the following day; a suitable honour and a suitable appointment would assuage any ruffled feelings Gordon might have in the wake of his trying ordeal.

Gladstone had to admit that there was not a great choice of options open to the ministers. There was a final consensus to instruct Baring to attempt to detain Gordon in Cairo for the time being in order to allow General Graham to use his pacifying influences on his old friend and comrade of the Engineers. Such a 'cooling down' period would be useful until the completion of a full and detailed report by Wolseley who, up to that time, had been afforded no opportunity to talk to another principal in the affair, Sir Charles Wilson.

The suggestion to employ Graham's ministrations came from Lord Hartington, who had matters of more pressing and potentially more serious import to discuss than the disaffection of General Gordon. In the early hours of the morning the War Office had received an alarming message, telegraphed from General Stephenson in Cairo. It quoted native reports, reaching Wolseley's advanced headquarters at Korti, of heavy fighting involving the British column in the Bayuda desert. The reports were unconfirmed, but they spoke of large concentrations of the enemy. Korti was in a state of alert and Wolseley had sent the remainder of the West Kents to reinforce the 300 of the half-battalion at Jakdul under Sir Evelyn Wood. The ministers agreed that no public announcement should be made until some confirmation of the desert reports was received. In the meantime, the telegraph line from Wolseley in Korti to Stephenson in Cairo was being reserved for priority traffic.

On the following morning of Thursday, February 19, special late editions of the morning newspapers quoted Cairo rumours of a possible disaster in the desert. There were few details. One report said Gubat had fallen. Another spoke of heavy British losses. Yet another said that General Buller's column had beaten back overwhelmingly superior numbers of Arabs and fought its way to Jakdul.

*The Times*, which carried a report prominently on the main news page, was embarrassingly encumbered with a second despatch based on Moberley Bell's interview with Gordon, in which the latter criticised not only Gladstone's policies and the high command's strategies in choosing the longer river route in preference to the Suakim-Berber road, but cast aspersions on the Army's effort and resolution. Bell quoted from the Khartoum Journals (many passages of which Gordon was able to remember by heart): '. . . if you wanted to find Her Majesty's forces you would have to go to Shepheard's Hotel in Cairo'. During the succeeding days of public anguish it was a phrase that was to rebound bitterly on Gordon and his supporters as realisation of the enormity of the military disaster set in. *The Times'* own embarrassment was further compounded on that Thursday morning by a leading article, supporting some of Gordon's allegations. To describe Gladstone as 'The Grand Old Mystifier' was pursuit of fair game. But to go on record with the statement that 'Messrs Gladstone & Co. negotiated with Messrs Cook, the tourists' providers, for a cheap third-class return ticket for Lord Wolseley and the Camel Corps to Khartoum and back' was inopportune on a day when the gnawing uncertainties of the morning became numbing reality by the evening.

To a Parliament which had been formally apprised of the government's proposals for withdrawal from the Sudan, Gladstone delivered a brief and sombre statement which prepared the country for the worst. Grievous losses . . . enemy in overwhelming strength . . . gallant resistance . . . a nation's sorrow . . . situation under control: the stereotyped phrases could not hide, nor were they designed to hide, the awful truth that Britain had lost an army in the Bayuda wastes. Gladstone allowed himself one sentence of reproof aimed at the source of his Wednesday morning irritation: 'It is consumately to be wished that, in this hour of the nation's grief, certain notes of petulance and personal interest may now be stilled'.

The details of the massacre gradually filtered out to the people through the fog of military reticence and the barrier of remoteness. Buller and his garrison had met with annihilation — so much was known immediately. But it took months for the full picture of what happened at Gubat to be pieced together by men like Kitchener, a survivor of the fight in the valley, and Wingate. They learned the facts, in the way of desert intelligence men, by talking to the tribes, by probing forward into Mahdiist territory from the fringes of the ebbing frontier of Anglo-Egyptian power and taking prisoners, by bribery and more forcible methods of persuasion.

Walter Ingram, who escaped from the Bayuda with Kitchener's little group, was able to send his newspaper, the *Illustrated London News*, an eye-witness account of the end of Talbot's column. In the night after the battle, the band of survivors skirted the wells of Abu Klea which were patently in Mahdiist hands. On the following day they fell in with a group of friendly Kababish who gave them water and guided them to Jakdul. With the Kababish was a survivor of the attack on Abu Klea, Private Michael Sealey of the Somerset Light Infantry, from Shepton Mallet. Ingram included in his despatch a description of the fight at the wells, based on Sealey's account:

'The Arabs came in overwhelming numbers and fired the zeriba which was perilously close to the hospital tents and huts. Some of the wounded were burned to death as they lay helpless in their litters. The Mounted Infantry put up a valiant resistance but were overcome in the space of 20 minutes. The Arabs were seen to slaughter most of the wounded, and it is feared that General Stewart must have been among those killed. Sealey is a cook — and to his calling he owes his life. He was beyond the zeriba foraging for kindling when the sudden attack came. Prevented from rejoining his comrades, he lay in a place of concealment from which he had a clear view of all which went on. He thinks the Mahdiists took some English soldiers away alive.'

At Jakdul, the most abundantly supplied watering place in the Bayuda, where a necklace of ice-green pools is strung up the face of a perpendicular wall of black rock, General Wood's 300 West Kents dug in to await the help that was on its way from Korti and anything which might come at them from the desert. There was sporadic firing and some half hearted dashes at the outposts by Baggara horsemen, but otherwise, the British at Jakdul were left alone. The Khalifa's army was sated with victory. Two days after Gubat, the main part of the host passed through Wad Habeshi on its way to Omdurman with 50 British prisoners. The Berber tribes went north to join those who were harrying the retreating British river column. Here, where the Nile makes its wide 'question-mark' bend round a massive obstruction of rock, the Shagiyeh, part of the Bisharin and even some of the Kababish had gone over to the 'rising sun' of the Mahdi.

The Ansar attacked the British where the river runs through the Monassir desert — 'Throughout the whole length of the Nile there is no more miserable wilderness', wrote Churchill. Past the site of the previous week's battle at Kirbekan, past the bullet-holed wreck of Donald Stewart's *Abbas,* the Gordons, Black Watch, Staffords and Duke of Cornwall's struggled to manoeuvre their boats down the rapids; the glare and spray veiled their vision and swarms of blood-sucking flies feasted on their bodies. Their path was choked by polished boulders, their route lined by knobbly masses of porphyry, gneiss and basalt. Most of the boat-handling voyageurs had gone home, and Brackenbury could not use his hussars as vedettes because of the rough ground on either side of the gorges. There was not a pitched battle, but a series of scattered ambushes in which the Ansar waited for a boat-load of Gordons or Staffords to become separated, or wrecked on a sandbar or rock. Three thousand bashi-bazouks, employed by the Mudir of Dongola to control the tribes on the river route, went over to the Ansar; at Dongola the Mudir was arrested and sent down to Cairo under escort. Miraculously, Brakenbury extricated the bulk of his column. The rearguard of Highlanders arrived at Korti early in March. Behind them, the cataracts kept 300 British dead.

Wolseley, once called 'the luckiest man in the army', supervised the unenviable task of withdrawing what remained of the expeditionary force to Wady Halfa near the Egyptian frontier. Thousands of people fled north from Dongola. On a tide of religious fervour, more prizes fell to the Mahdi. Osman Digna, hugely reinforced by converts to Mahdiism, took Suakim under the nose of a British naval squadron while London wavered about sending another expedition; his prestige mounted further when his troops defeated a force of native levies defending Italian territory on the Red Sea coast. Senussi, the leader of the Tripoli Arabs, who had earlier been offered and had refused the fourth Khalifate of the Mahdi, now announced his intention of embracing the leader of the Sudanese movement in a pan-Islamic union. The news sent shivers of apprehension through French North Africa, which could be the next seat of religious upheaval. Britain's troubles in the Sudan had been watched by the Italians with sympathy, and by the French with cynical satisfaction: now both had cause for alarm.

In London, where national rejoicing had turned to grief and anger, Gladstone's government was fighting for its life, and the worshippers of Gordon experienced the first bitter taste of disillusion.

# Chapter 29

# *Retribution*

'This appalling defeat of British arms, this national tragedy, must be laid at the door of a government which was guilty of culpable delay in the despatch of the expedition in the first place, and having sent too little too late, allowed its maladies of vacillation and confusion to infect those who constructed a strategy of disaster.' Sir Michael Hicks Beach, a leading opposition speaker in the parliamentary censure debate which followed hard on the announcement of the Bayuda débâcle, waited for the roar of Conservative approbation to die . . . 'Does this House release that Her Majesty's government has forfeited the lives of more British officers than died in the Battle of Waterloo?' From the Liberal benches swelled a different noise, a deep-throated coughing which might be taken for the beginnings of a Zulu battle cry, but which students of parliamentary debate would recognise immediately as a signal of derision. 'Hypocrite!' 'Cant!' 'Remember Isandhlwana!'

Remember indeed. Almost exactly six years earlier Hicks Beach, as colonial secretary, had himself fended off similar allegations after the Zulus destroyed a British column at the hill called Isandhlwana. There were nerly 1,000 British dead, 52 of them officers. The toll in the Bayuda was even more fearful — some 2,700 British soldiers and sailors, including those killed in the earlier Abu Klea fighting and on the river. Of these, more than 130 were officers; at Waterloo, 48 officers died.

Horrific as the statistics were in themselves, the calamity was heightened for the general people and MPs because of the public identities of many of the victims and the multiplicity of regiments involved. There were names of long-standing renown — Generals Buller, Earle and Stewart, Colonel Burnaby, Lord Charles Beresford; and others whose brief fame had been born in the expedition — Sir Charles Wilson, Gascoigne, Trafford and Stuart-Wortley. The Household Cavalry, eight regiments, of dragoons and lancers, nine of hussars, three foot guards regiments, 14 infantry and rifle regiments, the artillery, engineers, navy and marines all lost detachments. The press's jokes about a 'salad dressing' and Cambridge's jibe about the 'Nile circus' came home with a vengeance. 'The finest troops in the world', Wolseley had called his Camel Corps. Recruitment for the corps of the finest in so many regiments ensured that, when the column was destroyed, the tragedy bit deeply into homes and messes from Cornwall to Aberdeen and from East Kent to County Mayo. Among the officers the deaths of a constellation of titled figures and many scions of great houses engendered in influential circles a hunger for retribution.

Isandhlwana was, after all, but a short time ago. It could never happen again, they said. Never again would a British army let itself be attacked while in loose formation. But Wolseley's troops had been smashed in square and in prepared positions, and with them the bulwark of Victorian self esteem and complacency had given way. 'What is the price', the Liberal Sir Wilfred Lawson asked in the Common, 'we were prepared to pay for one man? One thousand British lives, two, three? Not to mention the countless thousands of lives of a people struggling for their freedom?'

The Conservatives sensed their opportunity: Gladstone's square was cracking at the corners. A flurry of activity was set in motion — protest meetings and rallies. Lord Salisbury gave notice of a censure motion and, with the Radicals moving ever further away from Gladstone's camp, the Conservatives could scent victory. Once in power, they would have fewer opportunities for criticism. With the whole country dismayed by the bloody fruits of Liberal policies, every opening must be exploited to undermine confidence in the Liberals among the electorate at large.

A vast and rowdy crowd jammed Princes Hall in Piccadilly, London, and overflowed on to the pavement and road. Around the hall's interior, completely encircling it, two long banners recalled the government's prevarication during the Gordon crisis of the previous year. From Gladstone on May 19: 'Whatever measures the Government take will be in the direction of making effective arrangements with regard to bringing all the difficulties to an end'. And a classic piece of Hartingtonese, delivered on September 17: 'In arriving at this decision, Her Majesty's Government desire to remind you that no decision has been arrived at'. Placards held by the crowd transposed the initial letters of Gladstone's 'Grand Old Man' sobriquet to read, 'MOG — Murderer of Gubat'. The Duke of Portland, a pillar of the Patriotic Association, chaired the meeting, but the most rapturous applause was reserved for Lord Randolph Churchill who thundered: 'The followers of Mr Gladstone have so wallowed in a stifling morass of the most degraded and servile worship of the Prime Minister that they have sunk below the level of slaves. They are become puppets, the objects of derision and contempt, they have lost all claim to the title of Englishmen, I think they have lost all claim to the title of rational human beings.' Sir Robert Peel called for action in the Sudan, reinforcement of the army on the Nile, a powerful expedition to Suakim supported by troops from India, a joint push in conjunction with the Italians acting from Massowa on the Red Sea coast: 'Where there is a dangerous infection, and the Mahdi represents nothing more than that, the spores of foreign intervention will multiply. Must we wait until the Tricolour flies in Khartoum?'

Rumours of French influence on and help for the Mahdi abounded in the press: it was said that a Frenchman had taught the Mahdiists how to attack a British square, how to construct fortifications. As early as December 1884 the *New York Times* had reported the presence of a French spy in the camp at El Obeid (Slatin recorded how he met a French adventurer called Olivier Pain in the Mahdi's community who wanted to fight the British, but he appears to have been no more than a solitary eccentric; he became ill and died shortly after his arrival). In Paris, *Nouvelle Revue* gloated that 'the secret role of the English in the Sudan' had been unmasked and had met with failure, the aim having been to annexe the Sudan.

Britain's grief and anger had its descent into Victorian bathos. Stanzas of flowery poetry filled the columns of the newspapers and the weekly reviews. Some of it was little less remarkable than the immortal lines of one William McGonagall, a Dundee handloom weaver whose poetic talents were unsung and unrecognised for nigh on a century. His epic fell uneasily between desire to celebrate Gordon's release. . .

*'Let patriots hail the great news from Khartoum,*
*Where Gordon was plucked from a terrible doom,*
*Bringing joy to all classes where hope was forlorn,*
*Not omitting our Sovereign at the house called Osborne.'*

and mourning for the British dead . . .

*'But now England's flower has paid the full price,*
*And for the great Gordon, this will not suffice;*
*He'll flail those in politics who could have done more,*
*While neath alien sun brave men gave of their gore.'*

There were other bizarre, even lunatic, fringes of reaction. A group of retired officers — bolstered by the moral support of some who should have known better, such as Lord Napier of Magdala and Earl Cardigan — revived Burnaby's idea of a freelance expeditionary force composed of 2,000 sportsmen and officers on the inactive list. It was to be called, in fact, the Buller-Burnaby Memorial Expedition, and its aim was, if not to dislodge the Mahdi, to dislodge the government from its avowed intention of withdrawing from the Sudan. In Chicago, a similar scheme was being hatched with different motives. A Fenian organisation announced that it was recruiting 1,500 men in the mid-west and the deep south, to be led by a Confederate Civil War hero, General Fitzhugh Lee; they would take either Alexandria or Suakim and link up with the Mahdi in a grand anti-English adventure. In Britain, fickle public opinion veered perceptibly away from Gordon when the price of his freedom was accounted in soldiers' lives. His picture was less visible in public places. Letters criticising his conduct in Khartoum — almost non-existent until now — appeared in the London papers, including even Stead's fervently pro-Gordon *Pall Mall Gazette*. By past association, the Anti Slavery Society suffered from a brick thrown through the windows of its New Bond Street offices, although that august body had long since been disenchanted with 'God's Governor-General' owing to his demands for Zebehr and his slave-owning proclamation at Berber.

On Wednesday, March 4, after three days of bitter debate in the Commons, Gladstone's government was defeated on a vote of censure. The Conservatives had rightly defined that there would be sufficient unrest among the Radicals to result in abstentions which would more than wipe out the dozen or more votes by which the old parliamentary fox had survived similar trials in the previous 12 months. Furthermore, Hartington, feeling that ultimate responsibility for military disaster lay at his door in the War Office, had mooted intentions of resignation. As was usual with him, the deed lagged behind the spoken thought, but his mis-

givings had the effect of weakening Gladstone's vital under-
pinning, provided by the Whig faction of which Hartington was
the leader. Resignation was Gladstone's only course. On the day
following the vote, Salisbury agreed to form a government, to the
irrepressible delight of Queen Victoria. William Henry Smith, the
rich W.H. Smith of the newsagents' chain, moved into
Hartington's seat as Secretary of State for War.

The British public smelled revenge in the air. Clubmen in the
West End of London wagered immense amounts of money on the
time, place, nature and scale of intervention in the Sudan. In the
bigger casino of world politics the possible moves the new government would make were appraised by the nations of Europe.
Among them, Russia, with no stake in Africa, took stock and
prepared to make a critical gamble.

# Chapter 30

# *Homecoming*

Gordon returned to Charing Cross Station in London one year and 49 days after he had left it on the 8 pm boat train. Waiting to greet him was a small group of friends, including Lord Esher, Captain Brocklehurst and the Rev Barnes, augmented by a handful of officials from the Foreign and War Offices. A knot of curious passers-by, attracted by the assembly of officials, gathered at the end of the platform, but there was not a vestige of the enthusiastic, massed welcoming party that would have met his homecoming two to three weeks earlier, before the news of the army's disasters reached London.

Ragged cheering was punctuated by a few boos. Some of Gordon's statements of recent time and of the previous year had been retailed by anti-Gordon factions in the weekly and fortnightly reviews and they had rebounded to his discredit amid the public mourning. The dead Wilson, attacked by Gordon, had assumed the mantle of a martyr. Extracts from the Khartoum Journal had begun to leak to the press: Gordon's remarks about the army dallying in Shepheard's Hotel, Cairo, had infuriated many; revealed at this time, an observation about Baring (author of a manual on battle simultation) — 'A nice way he has manoeuvred us and carried on his war game' — also had an unfortunate ring. Fickle, self-righteous, the public was exercising its prerogative as maker and breaker of idols.

Gordon's first action, on repairing to Brocklehurst's apartments, was to send for his admirer, W.T. Stead of the *Pall Mall Gazette*. In a three-hour meeting with the editor he delivered a bitter tirade against the follies and crimes of the Gladstone government. 'If I had been supported instead of being thwarted, how different might have been the result of my mision', he said. From the beginning his schemes had been negated. He was forbidden to seek a meeting with the Mahdi — 'I was refused permission to try peace, and afterwards refused permission to try war'. He poured out scorn: 'I was asked to state the cause of my intention to stay at Khartoum; I stayed at Khartoum because the Arabs shut us up and would not let us get out'. And reproach: 'Is it right that I should have been sent to Khartoum, and no attention was paid to me till communication were cut?'.

Stead was in a sensitive position. A devotee of Gordon (although the flame of his passion had lessened), he was nevertheless the editor of a newspaper which supported the Liberal cause. Gladstone had fallen: this was no time to rub salt into his wounds. The resulting article contained little of Gordon's political criticisms, but ran at length on the subject of his complaints against the military — the mistaken strategies, the delays on the Nile, the circumstances of his removal from Khartoum. Undeterred by Stead's selective editing, Gordon turned to *The Times,* and had the satisfaction of seeing his acerbic indictment of Gladstone printed in detail. The mission failed, Gordon was reported as saying, because he was refused Zebehr Pasha — who 'is fifty times the Mahdi's match', and refused troops, whether Turkish or Indian.

'The mission failed', Sir Charles Dilke, the former minister, echoed in the House of Commons, 'because General Gordon spent three months thinking up plots to smash the Mahdi — three months from his arrival in Khartoum until the date of Berber's subjugation. In that time a considerable portion of the Sudan garrisons might have been withdrawn to Berber by steamer. To argue otherwise is, to borrow General Gordon's favourite word, "twaddle". He was not sent to Khartoum with orders to secure the retreat of every man, woman and child who wished to leave the Sudan, but to do the best he could to carry out the evacuation. The House will judge him on the results. And the House must ask this question: why, on September 8, when General Gordon sent Colonel Stewart down the river in the *Abbas,* did he send away on the steamer the official cyphers, without which he could not read any coded messages despatched to him? The answer must be that he wished to place himself beyond advice, beyond control, beyond reason.'

They were hard words, coming from a former member of the cabinet which had chosen Gorden, but Dilke was convinced that the memorandum of proposals drawn up by Gordon on his journey out to Egypt had been deliberately framed on peaceful lines to deceive ministers as to his true intentions. He now perceived Gordon's alleged duplicity as the cause of the desert disaster and the source of the government's misfortunes.

While Dilke and other enemies fumed, and friends rallied to Gordon's support on public platforms and in newspaper columns, a time bomb was ticking away under the already tottering idol. Walter Ingram, resting at Luxor and indulging in his passion for Egyptology after his escape from the desert massacre, had become aware of Gordon's allegations of misconduct laid against Sir Charles Wilson. He was incensed. Apparently he alone — from conversations with Gascoigne, Trafford and Stuart-Wortley aboard the *Safieh* — knew what had transpired in the palace at Khartoum. On March 5 he sent the full story to his brother, William, the proprietor of the *Illustrated London News*. William Ingram published it almost in its entirety 'in duty to those gallant officers who cannot speak for themselves'.

The most damning parts of Walter Ingram's testimony were Bordeini Bey's allegations of Gordon's absences in the last week of Khartoum's siege and the evidence of his abberational behaviour in front of the officers. Wilfrid Scawen Blunt, radical champion of the Arabs' cause who was at one stage in 1884 considered by Gladstone as a possible envoy to Khartoum, posed a question in an interview given to the Liberal *Birmingham Post:* 'Was there a simple human failing behind the Governor-General's otherwise incomprehensible seclusion? A failing tragically common among those who labour in the isolation of tropical climes?'

In the Commons, John Morley was more forthright: 'I suggest that General Gordon's dereliction of his duties in Khartoum's fateful last hours may be ascribed not only to his communing with *Isaiah,* but also to his seeking consolation from the bottle'. It was a cruel and crudely put allegation and it was met with a storm of protest from both government and opposition benches.

Blunt had heard earlier rumours about Gordon's drinking. Now, however, they were the main topic of gossip in London clubland. There, the scandal was fuelled when news leaked out from the *Daily News* office about Harry Pearse's unpublished observations on Gordon's being 'amply solaced by medicinal stocks of brandy' in the desert. Amid a profusion of pamphlets and sixpenny booklets which were published on the Sudan débâcle, one of the more scurrilous cartooned Gordon retiring from Khartoum, leaving a wake of empty bottles bobbing in the Nile, each one labelled with the name of a British regiment. Lord Randolph Churchill attacked what he saw as attempts to shift the blame entirely on to Gordon: 'He was not, perhaps, the ideal choice, his influence with the Sudanese was not as powerful as the former government believed, but this character assassination is unworthy of a civilised nation. The late lamented General Sir Redvers Buller was not celebrated for his abstinence, but no one would have the impudence to suggest he shirked his duty thereby. Let this howl of cant be stilled, and let those who voiced it look nearer home for the seat of England's woes: the self-intoxication of the honourable member for Midlothian [Gladstone].'

In letters, telegrams and official conversations, the Queen ignored the vulgarities of the wrangle over Gordon's alleged intemperance. She was, however, distressed by the wider controversy which centred on him and, inevitably, ascribed it to a Gladstonian plot to discredit the hero of Khartoum. A staunch upholder of Gordon throughout his ordeal in the Sudan, she had received him at Windsor shortly after his arrival in England. The affair tested still further her already strained dealings with her son, Edward, Prince of Wales. In the highest places personal relations were affected by a tangled web of enmities. The Duke of Cambridge disliked Wolseley intensely and blamed him for the débâcle, a view which found ready support in the Prince. The latter was, of course, an intimate of Dilke, a confirmed Gordon-denigrater. Therefore, within the Edward-Cambridge-Dilke axis, Wolseley and Gordon were perceived as the joint architects of the disasters. Victoria's regard for her son was not improved by his habit of having consistently shown social courtesy and civility to Gladstone. Thus, when the Prince appeared to espouse the anti-Gordon movement, the Queen became more than ever entrenched in her support of Gordon.

Gordon made no public riposte to the scandal-mongers. He had not sought public acclaim; it bothered him not at all when it was withdrawn. In a letter to Barnes he paraphrased *Proverbs* — 'Wine is a mocker, and I am not mocked'; and *Leviticus* — 'Let me go for a scapegoat into the wilderness'. What, he asked Barnes, would he be accused of next? 'For a remedy against many ailments, I swear by the virtue of Dover's Powders, which contain ipecacuanha and opium. I have tried laudanum for my angina — but it does not agree with me and I agree with *it* even less. Gordon, the incorrigible drug-taker!' He was deeply wounded, however, by a coolness and prevarication in King Leopold's reply when, by letter, he raised once again the question of his going to the Congo. By mid-May, Gordon had left the country quietly and was on his way to Palestine to see the Rev J.E. Hall, who had once offered him work in his mission at Jaffa.

On March 30 Russia attacked a remote outpost in Afghanistan where the River Oxus flows between the two countries. Salisbury reacted swiftly to what he perceived as a grave foreign incursion in a sphere of British interest while London's attentions were focused on the valley of the Nile. Another 'squalid village' — called Pendjeh — was thrust into the notoriety of newspaper headlines. Pendjeh became 'the victim of bloody Russian aggression', which it was, and 'the critical gateway to India', which it wasn't. 'The Government deems it necessary to hold all the military resources of the Empire, including the forces in Egypt and the Sudan, available for service wherever required', Salisbury reported to Parliament. The British public was in no mood for another military insult: Russia's move was seen partly as a direct consequence of the reverse of British arms on the Nile. The army in India received substantial reinforcements from the 130,000 home reserve, British garrisons in Malta and Cyprus — and Egypt. The Foreign Office stage-managed an invitation from Britain's ally, the Emir of Afghanistan, to a large Anglo-Indian army which positioned itself uncomfortably in the desolate mountains south of the Oxus, arguably one of the world's least penetrable 'gateways'. Britain's massive over-reaction resulted in a similar build-up of troops on the others side. The Russians withdrew from Pendjeh, leaving it somewhat more ruined than when they found it, but for four months lion and bear growled dangerously at each other. In that time an outbreak of cholera killed more British soldiers than died in Buller's column. The Pendjeh dispute finally subsided into obscurity beneath a mass of paperwork of the revived Anglo-Russian boundary commission.

The Russian diversion wiped out any hopes of Gladstone's Sudan withdrawal policy being reversed by Salisbury. An extra twopence on income tax (the second such imposition within a year) to pay for the vast cost of Britain's military posturing on the Oxus helped increase middle-class disillusionment with Salisbury's government. In 1884/85 a government had sent the army 1,400 miles up the Nile to be massacred by religious fanatics armed with swords and spears; in 1885 another government had sent the army, at even greater expense, half way across the world to stand idle in the face of insults from a cruel and powerful aggressor. In June 1886, after a general election, Gladstone formed a new ministry. Intervention in the Sudan was a policy furthest from his mind.

When the Pendjeh crisis flared up, Wolseley was summoned back to London where he was needed at his Adjutant-General's desk; there were many, led by Cambridge, who maintained he should never have left it in the first place to join in the Gordon adventure. Now the *'unluckiest* General', Wolseley anticipated the hostile reception awaiting him. 'What a host of enemies I have. . .is there something about me that makes men bear me ill-will?', he wrote to Louisa. The *Saturday Review* savagely attacked him by comparing his achievements and experience with those of European commanders and American Civil War Generals, and describing him as a miliary leader 'of doubtful genius who had never met a worthy opponent in the field'. General Sir Lintorn Simmons, Governor of Malta, added to the public controversy when he revealed that Wolseley had in his possession a letter from Sir Charles Wilson, explaining the facts of Gordon's behaviour in the palace on the night of Khartoum's fall. Simmons knew this from a letter Wilson wrote to him while in hospital at Gubat. Wolseley, forced to reply to the charge of concealing evidence, retorted that Wilson's letter to him was a private communication, not a military despatch, therefore he had been under no obligation to reveal its contents. It was all music to the ears of Cambridge who, on his retirement as Commander-in-Chief of the Army in 1895, achieved his aim of establishing another Royal Duke, Connaught, as his successor in preference to Wolseley who had fervently hoped for the crowning appointment of his career.

Thus, the Army reforms for which Wolseley had assiduously worked, and against which Cambridge had just as perseveringly fought, were delayed in their implementation. An official inquiry, held at the Horse Guards, into the failure of arms in the desert produced an overhaul of the ordnance department's purchasing and inspection system and, as a side issue, the efficacy of the British square was seriously questioned: even the diehards recognised its limitations against hordes of fanatics, and its patent uselessness in an age of artillery. But the Army's 'cold steel' complex died hard. The failure of the Gardners actually stiffened the opposition in some quarters to machine-guns, regarded by several Generals as 'dammed carts' which got in the way of the smooth movements of massed infantry. The Sudan campaign, however, was the last in which the British Army fought in red coats.

When the Mahdi died in June 1885 there was a fresh outcry for action in the Sudan. 'No frontier force can keep the Mahdiists out of Egypt, and sooner or later they must be smashed, or they will smash you', Wolseley told the Cabinet. Britain's political and military eyes, however, were on the distant mountains of Afghanistan.

Abdallahi — henceforth known universally in the western world as the Khalifa — succeeded to the Mahdi's temporal domain. His tyrannical reign, bolstered by the savage and pampered Baggara, aroused bitter resentment within the Sudanese nation, not least among the power group of the Mahdi's family, the Ashraf. The Red Flag division under the spiritual leadership of the Mahdi's son-in-law, Mohammed Sherifa, became the rallying centre of opposition against the Black Flag, now commanded by Abdallahi's opportunist brother Yakub. El Nejumi, grown immensely in prestige following the victory over the British, emerged as the military champion of the Red Flag's cause. While epidemics of cholera ravaged the civil population of the Sudan, Ansar fought Ansar in a series of scattered engagements. On June 22 1888, coincidentally the third anniversary of the Mahdi's death, an army jointly commanded by el Nejumi and Osman Digna — for long jealous of Abdallahi's pre-eminence — defeated the Black Flag in battle at the confluence of the Nile and Atbara rivers, south of Berber. Abu Anga, the Khalifa's commander, was killed. Abdallahi retired to the Darfur fastness of his Baggara tribes. An uneasy triumvirate of Mohammed Sherifa, Osman Digna and el Nejumi reigned in Omdurman.

During the latter half of the 1880s two of the principal figures in the Sudan affair went about their business in varying degrees of obscurity. An embittered Wolseley soldiered on as Commander-in-Chief in Ireland. Gordon, determined to experience 'the joy of never seeing Great Britain again', sought God in Palestine and the Garden of Eden in the Seychelles. Successive governments in London agreed that the question of the Sudan would have to be tackled, but put off doing anything about it other than pressing ahead with the reorganisation of the Egyptian army. Their resolution might have been strengthened had France exploited the international power vacuum in the Sudan, but French resources were concentrated in North Africa where religiously based insurrections were indirectly traceable to the spread of militant Mahdiism in mid-decade.

A recurring concern in Britain was the fate of the half-hundred British prisoners taken to Omdurman after the massacres in the Bayuda. Following the Khalifa's banishment in 1888, hopes rose that the new régime would be open to negotiation over the release of the captives, of whom more than 30 were reported still alive. Attempts at conciliation through the king of Abyssinnia and the Senussi Arabs of Tripoli failed. Statesmen began to favour the idea of a direct approach at Khartoum to Osman Digna, whose commercial background made him a likely prospect to consider a ransom arrangement and whose heartland of support, the Red Sea coast, was most vulnerable to direct naval and military threat. Wilfred Scawen Blunt, who offered himself as a plenipotentiary, was unacceptable to a Conservative cabinet. On February 14 1890, the fifth anniversary of the battle of Gubat, a rally organised by the 'Free the Prisoners' movement in Hyde Park, London, attracted 100,000 people and stirred a crisis of conscience in the nation. The message was simple: if Britain could not muster an army, it should send a brave and forthright envoy to Khartoum.

A week later, Queen Victoria wrote to Lord Salisbury. 'The Queen believes that there is one man, and one man alone, who can shoulder this burden for England. You must summon General Gordon and send him to Khartoum.'

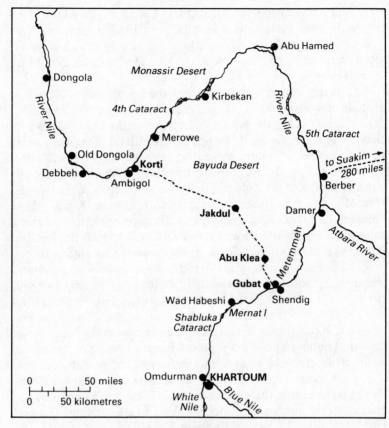

*Above: Khartoum and the question-mark of the Nile.*

*Right: Khartoum in January, 1885.*

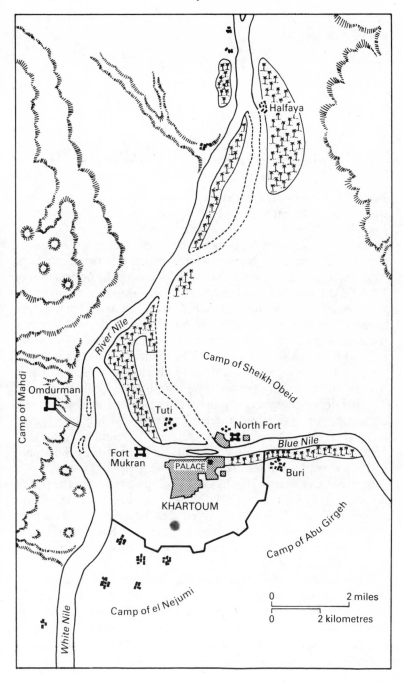

# Notes and acknowledgements

Book Two draws on real people, and on many actual events and quotations in an attempt to lend verisimilitude to an exercise in hypothesis. The reportorial talents of Lieutenant Count Gleichen, so vividly displayed in his book on the Camel Corps, are borrowed to shed light on those parts of a story which otherwise could not have been told in personal narrative following the destruction of Buller's column; the circumstances of his journal's discovery in Chapter 19 are set in an event at Shendy purloined from the campaign of reconquest in 1898. Walter Ingram, of course, was a member of the crew of the *Safieh* in which Lord Charles Beresford rescued Wilson's stranded party. The events of Wilson's real, and unsuccessful, voyage to Khartoum and back were so dramatic that history outshines any fiction. The narrative of Chapters 20 and 21, therefore, draws heavily on the true record of the journey. Similarly, Abd el Hamid's defection to the Mahdi is a fact of history; Slatin accused him of deliberately running the *Tel-el-Hoween* aground and recorded that he was honoured by the Mahdi and rewarded by the release of his womenfolk.

Bordeini Bey's testimony in Chapter 20 is taken from the text of his journal, quoted extensively by Wingate in *Mahdiism and the Egyptian Sudan*. Wingate observed that Bordeini Bey's account was 'corroborated by many others present in Khartoum during the seige', although Allen seriously questioned the merchant's reliability as a witness.

Some of the circumstances of the disasters in the desert are projected from British military mistakes which occurred at El Teb, Abu Klea and the battle of McNeill's Zeriba. General Buller's failings, which bring his career to premature end in Chapter 27, are in historical record as a primary cause of Britain's misfortunes during the early part of the Boer War.

And so to bathos. William McGonagall's pen never had cause to tackle the glorious subject of Gordon's salvation, but some of his most celebrated works encompassed El Teb, Abu Klea, Gordon's death and McNeill's Zeriba, and they remain classic examples of the genius of 'the only truly memorable bad poet in our language'. The American Irish plan to invade Egypt and link up with the Mahdi was reported in the *New York Times* in March 1885.

My grateful thanks go to: Anne, my wife, Christopher and Matthew, my sons, and Joseph Martin, who provided suggestions, research assistance and support; at Phillips, the fine art auctioneers, Chris Halton, Victoria Sanders, Caroline Lavender and Andrew Clayton-Payne who supplied illustrations and archive material; Abdullahi Gallab, Information Counsellor at the Embassy of the Democratic Republic of the Sudan in London; the National Army Museum; Stephen Dance of The Victorian Military Society; General Sir Charles Richardson, Chairman of the Gordon Boys' School; *Forbes* Magazine, New York; Remigio Gennari in Rome and Charles Plouviez in London, who made available relevant material from their libraries; John Pawsey, my agent, who started me on this expedition; and P&O Cruises, London, whose generosity helped take me to the banks of the Nile.

# Bibliography

Allen, Dr Bernard M.: *Gordon and the Sudan*, Macmillan, London, 1931.

Arthur, Captain Sir George: *The Story of the Household Cavalry*, Constable, London, 1909.

Beckett, I.F.W.: *Victoria's Wars*, Shire, Aylesbury, 1974.

Beresford, Lord Charles: The Memoirs of, Methuen, London, 1914.

Brander, Michael: *The Perfect Victorian Hero, The Life and Times of Sir Samuel Baker*, Mainstream, Edinburgh, 1982.

Burleigh, Bennet: *Khartoum Campaign 1898*, Chapman & Hall, London, 1899; *Sirdar and Khalifa*, London 1898.

Chaillé-Long, Colonel Charles: *My Life in Four Continents*, Hutchinson, London 1912.

Churchill, Winston S.: *The River War*, Eyre & Spottiswoode, London, 1899.

Compton, Piers: *The Last Days of Gordon*, Hale, London, 1974.

Delebecque, Jacques: *Gordon et le Drame de Khartoum*, Hachette, Paris, 1935.

Dixon, Norman: *On the Psychology of Military Incompetence*, Cape, London, 1976.

Elton, Lord: *General Gordon*, Collins, London, 1954.

*The Egyptian Red Book*, Blackwood, Edinburgh & London, 1885.

*The English in Egypt*, Frederick Warne, London, circa 1885-90.

Farwell, Byron: *The Great Boer War*, Lane, London, 1977.

Garrett, Richard: *General Gordon*, Barker, London, 1974.

Gleichen, Count: *With the Camel Corps up the Nile*, Chapman & Hall, 1888.

Goddard, John: *Kayaks down the Nile*, Brigham Young UP, Provo, Utah, 1979.

Gordon, Charles George: The Journals of Major-General CGG,

Kegan Paul, Trench, and Co, London, 1885.

Graham, General Sir Gerald: *Last Words with General Gordon*, article in *Fortnightly Review*, January 1887.

Greenhill Gardyne, Lieutenant-Colonel C.: *The History of the Gordon Highlanders*, Medici.

Hill, Richard: *A Biographical History of the Sudan*, Cass, London, 1951.

Holt, P.M.: *The Mahdiist State in the Sudan 1881-1898* OUP, 1958.

*Illustrated London News*, 1870-1900.

Jackson, H.C.: *Osman Digna*, Methuen, London, 1926.

Johnson, Peter: *Front Line Artists*, Cassell, London, 1978; *A Year for 'Gordoniana'*, article, *Collectors' Guide*, April 1980.

Lehmann, Joseph H.: *All Sir Garnet, A Life of Field-Marshal Lord Wolseley*, Cape, London, 1964.

Magnus, Philip: *Kitchener, Portrait of an Imperialist*, Murray, London, 1958.

Moorhead, Alan: *The White Nile*, Hamish Hamilton, London, 1960.

Nutting, Anthony: *Gordon, Martyr and Misfit*, Constable, London, 1966.

Ohrwalder, Fr Joseph: *Ten Years' Captivity in the Mahdi's Camp*, Sampson Low, Marston, London, 1892;

Ponsonby, Arthur: *Henry Ponsonby, His Life from His Letters*, Macmillan, London, 1942.

Porter, Whitworth: *History of the Corps of Royal Engineers*, Longman Green, London, 1889.

Prior, Melton: *Campaigns of a War Correspondent*, edited by S.L. Bensusan, London, 1912.

*Punch*, January 1884-December 1885.

*Regimental Nicknames and Traditions of the British Army*, Gale & Polden, London, 1916.

Ross-of-Bladensburg, Lieutenant-Colonel C.B.: *A History of the Coldstream Guards from 1815 to 1895*, Innes, London, 1896.

Royle, Charles: *The Egyptian Campaigns 1882-1885*, Hurst & Blackett, London, 1886.

Salgari, Emilio: *L'Eroe di Karthum*, Sonzogno, Italy, 1935.

Slatin, Rudolph: *Fire and Sword in the Sudan*, Arnold, London, 1903.

Stansky, Peter: *Gladstone: A Progress in Politics*, Norton, NY & London,1979.

Steevens, G.W.: *With Kitchener to Khartoum*, Blackwood, Edinburgh & London, 1898.

Strachey, Lytton: *Eminent Victorians*, Chatto & Windus, London, 1918.

*Sudanow* magazine, Khartoum: *Armageddon at Omdurman*, October 1982, and other issues.

Symons, Julian: *England's Pride: The Story of the Gordon Relief Expedition*, Hamish Hamilton, 1965.

Trench, Charles Chenevix: *Charley Gordon: An Eminent Victorian Reassessed*, Lane, London 1978.

Vetch, Colonel R.H.: *Life, Letters and Diaries of General Sir Gerald Graham*, Blackwood, Edinburgh, 1901.

Watson, Sir Charles M.: *The Life of Major-General Sir Charles Wilson*, London, 1909.

Wilkinson-Latham, Robert: *From Our Special Correspondent*, Hodder & Stoughton, London, 1979.

Wilson, Sir Charles W.: *From Korti to Khartoum*, Blackwood, Edinburgh & London, 1885

Wingate, F.R.: *Mahdiism and the Egyptian Sudan*, London, 1891.

# Index to Book One